Bidwell Park

Personal Reflections and Casual Conversations
About Chico's Crown Jewel

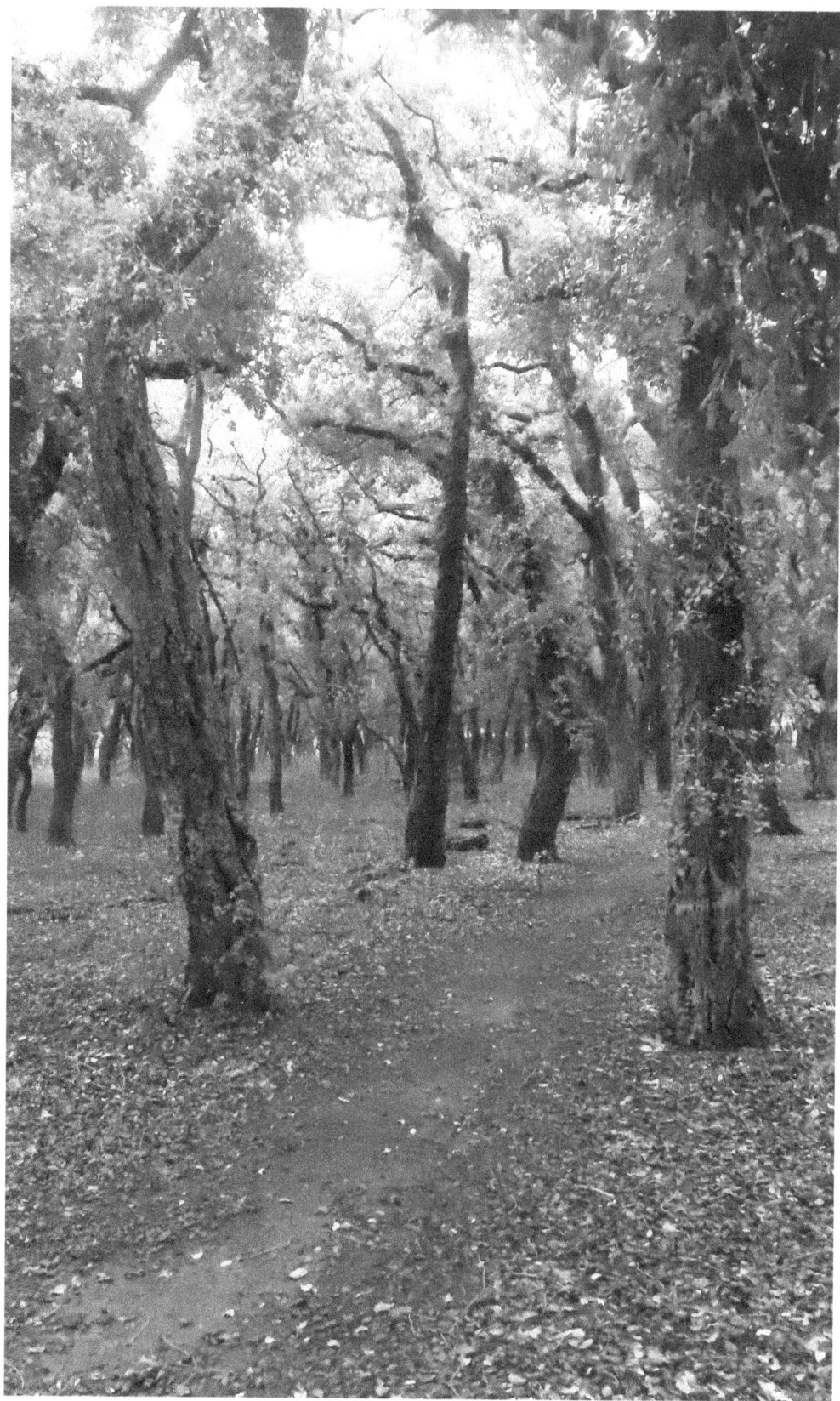

Bidwell Park

Personal Reflections and Casual Conversations
About Chico's Crown Jewel

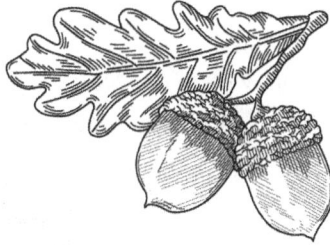

PAUL BELZ

ANCHR
CHICO, CA

This book is dedicated to Wes Dempsey, 1926-2022.
He loved, shared, explained, and
defended Bidwell Park

Heartfelt thanks to Phyllis Dempsey and sons Thomas and James Dempsey for
providing this photograph of Wes doing what he loved—hiking Bidwell Park

FRONTISPIECE: Cork Oaks, World of Trees
FRONT COVER: The Iconic Monkey Face above Horseshoe Lake
BACK COVER: Iron Canyon in Upper Park
All photos from Paul Belz unless otherwise cited.
Acorn/oak leaf clipart from pch.vector on Freepik.com

Cover design and book layout by Josie Reifschneider-Smith
Printed by Heidelberg Graphics, Chico, California, 95928

Association for Northern California Historical Research is an imprint of Heidelberg Graphics

Association for Northern California Historical Research (ANCHR)
PO Box 3024, Chico, California, 95927-3024 • (530) 636-0778
anchr.books@gmail.com • www.anchr.org • www.facebook.com/anchrbooks/

Contents

Photographs

Preface

This book could have been far longer and more detailed, but the park, like all public lands, demands attention now. I wrote it as a general overview of the park's human and natural history and an introduction to the controversies that have made it the special place it is. It would have taken me many years to describe every part of it and to include every issue. I see this book as a way for the park to regain the attention it deserves and to stimulate discussions that it needs.

As Roger Lederer said, information is scarce and scattered among many sources. To be honest, some of the documents and articles are sketchy about certain controversies. Also, no one with whom I've spoken remembers how some issues were resolved. Hopefully, others can share their thoughts, research, and memories to complement my work and include information on topics I haven't covered. I especially invite the current Bidwell Park and Playground Commissioners and other people who recently became involved with the park to the discussion.

I gathered facts and figures from newspaper articles, books, masters' theses, and other sources. The Bidwell Park and Playground Commission's minutes from 1918 to the present gave me a structure that helped me focus on the history. The descriptions of some of these meetings bored me to tears, but other reports reached the level of high drama!

Some of the minutes are rather technical, requiring familiarity with documents on land-use policy and other issues. Since readers might find some of the wording tedious, I chose to summarize the discussions' main points instead of including every detail. Again, debates around the issues sometime appear sporadically, and the minutes do not always indicate how an issue was resolved. I invite others to share information they may have. I summarized comments from specific meetings to provide basic information on the conflicts and issues.

Some information about issues became outdated while this book was being prepared for publication. With that in mind, I added an Afterword to provide updates, new information, and observations. I can do additional writing in the future, and I hope others will share more information.

Interviews and discussions form this book's backbone.[1] I share my thoughts and comments from scientists, city officials, activists, educators, volunteers, and others who love this special place. They do not always agree with each other, but I have tried to present everyone's thoughts fairly. I encourage readers to regard the quotes I share as reflections and perspectives rather than as statements of facts in all cases. The range of their passionate statements shows how complex Chico's feelings about this piece of land have become. I also strive to bring the park to life as I share descriptions of the marvels Kate and I discover as we wander through the park.

Paul Belz
Chico, California, 2023

---

1 Interviewees are listed in a special section in the bibliography.

Acknowledgements

The people I have to thank for help, feedback, and support on this book are uncountable; I couldn't have done it without all of you.

Thanks to Josie Reifschneider-Smith, Nancy Leek, Dr. Greg White, Dr. Eric Ritter, Lowell Thomas, Dave Brown, and Ron Womack of ANCHR Books and Rian Farley for editing, feedback, suggestions, and support.

I also feel grateful to the managers of the Bidwell Park Golf Course Clubhouse, where Josie Smith and I met for lunch and had a detailed discussion about revisions.

Also, very special thanks to Ralph Dranow and Naomi Rose, who read the whole manuscript meticulously and shared great ideas for improvements. I also want to strongly acknowledge my appreciation for people who read and commented on specific sections of the book. These include the late Wes Dempsey, Roger Lederer, Dave Nopel, Woody Elliott, Ann Polivka, Lise Smith-Peters, Jeanette Keables, Jean Varda, Sandy Makau, Linda Champanier, Norm Milstein, Kate Clark, David Ault, Doug Aiken, Genevieve Smith, Jennifer Bransky, Timmarie Hamill, Wren Tuatha, and Marcus Colasurdo.

Thanks also to the many people who I interviewed for this book (the names are listed in a special section in the bibliography), and particular thanks to Lise Smith-Peters who suggested this project.

My biggest appreciation of all goes to Kate Roark, who made wonderful suggestions and gave great feedback, kept a sense of humor through all this, and teased me when I deserved it.

December afternoon in Upper Park.

This Place and Its People

The Idea

I met Wes Dempsey on a death-defying New Year's Day hike up one part of an ancient volcanic mudflow. People named this formation "Monkey Face" because it looks like a primate staring down at hikers, dog walkers, and cyclists. Then in his 80s, Wes guided his adventurers to a spot where we could gaze over the park's wildland forms and rumbling creek. He told us about the Maidu, who lived in this region for thousands of years before European settlement and relied on the area's animals and plants. The journey up steep, dusty slopes showed us oak and pine-covered ridges just above chaparral plants' habitats. I'm a strong hiker but also a klutz. I turned back halfway so I wouldn't grab poison oak to avoid a fall.

This hike occurred during my second visit to Bidwell Park in Chico, California. My partner Kate and I stopped here several years earlier after a fine backpacking trip in Lassen Volcanic National Park. It had been cool in the high country, but we roasted in Chico, where the temperature reached 101-degrees Fahrenheit. A waiter in a sandwich shop told us how Big Chico Creek brought cold mountain water to the park's Sycamore Pool before continuing on its way to the Sacramento River.

After dinner, we settled into the pool's soothing chill. Dark blue pipevine swallowtail butterflies drifted above us while acorn woodpeckers shimmied up valley oaks and called "whacka, whacka!" Dogs ran on the lawn, and children of all ages splashed us while they and their parents tossed Frisbees and beach balls over our heads. Kate and I looked at each other and said, "Maybe we should move here!"

Other trips showed us the uncountable birds that visited the park in spring when galaxies of wildflowers covered the hills. Yahi Trail in rugged Upper Park led us past oaks, sycamores, and pines to Iron Canyon and its massive chunks of volcanic basalt. A lifeguard once told us how she and her colleagues cleared the well-loved Sycamore Pool of swimmers so a passing muskrat could have some privacy.

We moved from Oakland to Chico in 2016, and the park continues to charm us. We've been lucky to get to know Wes Dempsey and others who have loved and protected this semi-wild place for decades.

I talked with Wes, a retired California State University, Chico (CSU Chico), biology professor shortly after Kate and I settled in his town. His decades of research and experience leading more than a thousand hikes had made him an expert on Bidwell Park. Our conversations taught me about the area's complex geology, the Maidu culture, local plants and animals, and the some of the park's contentious history.

Dave Nopel, a fourth-generation Chico citizen, also welcomed me to his house, where he told me about his 1950s childhood. "I plugged into the creek early," he said. "We'd walk, bike, or swim down there." He and his friends explored more remote parts of Bidwell Park during his teenage years, and his relationship with this open space deepened when he came home from the Army in 1969.

Dave shared the extensive files of photos and articles that his father, a well-known Chico historian, collected for forty years. I learned about John and Annie Bidwell, the ranchers who donated parts of their land to this town as a public park, and the many controversies that make Bidwell Park the place it now is. Dave and his wife, Betty, operated a preschool in their home for many years. I can visualize them sharing the park's wildflowers, symphonies of birds and frogs, and unstoppable creek with their young naturalists.

I spoke with Shane Romain, Chico's Parks Services Coordinator, several times in his office. He coordinates volunteers who explain the park's policies to visitors, pick up trash in parking lots and other areas, and care for native plants. "Bidwell Park is in an interesting location because we are near the place where the Cascade range meets the Sierra Nevada," Shane commented. "A portion of the park is on the Sacramento Valley's floor, and it ascends to the foothills. The diversity of ecosystems is amazing. If someone is interested in the vegetation in the area, they can visit the ecosystems in a short distance. It's an urban park too—it runs through the middle of Chico!"

I had a coffee in a café with Roger Lederer, who had taught ornithology since 1972. He retired from CSU Chico and has led many field trips in the park. Two editions of *The Birds of Bidwell Park,* Roger's collaborative work with his wife, artist Carol Burr, are currently in print. They published two follow-up books: *The Trees of Bidwell Park* and *The Wildflowers of Bidwell Park.* "There are a lot more trees than we'll be able to include!" Roger told me, laughing. The couple teaches fascinating and humorous classes based on their books.

Roger added, "There's not a lot written on the natural history of the park. There's a book called *The Nature of Bidwell Park* by M. Jeanne Boze. There are also pamphlets on geology, wildflowers, amphibians and reptiles, and our books." He encouraged me to gather scattered information so Chico's people and visitors from other areas could understand this treasure. Other park lovers echoed that plea, and this book was born from our discussions.

What Is Bidwell Park?

John and Annie Bidwell often invited their guests and Chico's citizens to explore their land and agreed to give part of it to the town for a public park. John died in 1900, and Annie donated 1,900 acres to Chico in 1905. She left a series of instructions about her expectations, stating that this park belonged to all of Chico's people: they needed to care for the creek, the plants, the land, and the animals. Annie deeded other territory in 1911, and the city's later acquisitions led to the park's present 3,670 acres.

When Annie Bidwell died in 1918, people quickly argued about the park. These fights often pitted citizens who stressed Annie's desire to protect the park's wildness against those who interpreted her insistence that it belonged to all citizens equally to mean any idea people thought of for its use was fair game. The park has weathered many fierce battles, some of which are still unresolved. "Every organization would like to have its corner of the park and exclude everyone else. If it were a small property, it would have been used up. It's big enough that it did well," Wes Dempsey told me with a sad grin.

Shane Romain said, "Bidwell Park is not just a Chico park; it's a regional park. It gets more car traffic than nearby Lassen Volcanic National Park." Visitors on bicycles, horses, or on foot add to the cars' impact. The 2008 recession led to funding cuts and reductions in the city's staff, while Chico's growing population meant that the park demanded much more attention and care. With dedication and work, it can now become a model for other towns that want to have a thriving connection with wildlands and the history surrounding them.

· · · · · · · · · · · · · · · · · · ·

The hills and streambanks erupt with spring wildflowers. California buttercups and goldfields thrust yellow patches onto green hills, while other species thrive in rocks' cracks. Mountain lions hide in wilder areas; one unfortunate off-leash dog had a fatal encounter when it threatened a big cat. Clouds of pipevine swallowtail butterflies zip over trails in spring and summer, placing their dead-leaf-shaped chrysalises on railings, bridges, and State Highway 99's pillars. The creek flows among tawny suede hillsides in summer, and October's blazing colors prove that contrary to rumor, Northern California has a brilliant autumn! The bare branches of oaks and sycamores reach for the cloudy sky and dance during winter storms. Few towns of 100,000 people are lucky enough to have such a natural treasure. It is time to protect Chico's crown jewel!

Buck lounging on the Bidwell Park Golf Course.

CHAPTER ONE

Bidwell Park

Wes Dempsey's Path to Chico

Retired biology professor Wes Dempsey was Bidwell Park's walking encyclopedia. He was a thin man who liked to wear jeans and plaid shirts. His black-rimmed glasses contrasted sharply with his short, white hair. While he was a humble fellow who would rather talk about Bidwell Park than about himself, he laughed when he described his adventures along the trails. I once asked him about his favorite part of the park. He grinned and said, "Any part is my favorite part!"

Other park lovers who knew Wes well insisted that he was the first person I needed to interview for this project. We met several times in his split-level house on a tree-lined Chico street. One morning, he and I explored his files of park-oriented articles and newspaper clippings at his wooden dining room table. His wife, Phyllis, joined us that day and worked on crossword puzzles, stopping sometimes to share her thoughts.

"On one of my hikes, this kid was running around," Wes said. "He came back and told me, 'There is a nice snake down there!' It was a nice, big rattlesnake." Wes kept his hikers away from the rattler; it was only one of three that he saw during the sixty years he spent exploring the park.

Wes' explorations and education before he came to Chico prepared him for life as an expert on this region's natural history. "I grew up in Lexington, Massachusetts," he said. "Captain Parker, of the Massachusetts Minutemen, had a farm south of Lexington where he stored guns and ammunition. My family bought it, and I grew up there."

During World War II, Wes spent one and a half years as a paratrooper in the 82nd Airborne Division. He then studied biology at Cornell University at Ithaca, New York, and worked for a seed company in Troy, New York. A joint program at the University of California, Davis, and the University of California, Berkeley, awarded him a master's degree in plant genetics and later a Ph.D.

"I looked at my wallet and decided to move to Chico in 1954!" Wes said, grinning. "There were two of us who were instructors in the Agriculture Program. We taught essentially a junior college program; I had all the plant classes. I taught 22 classes the first two years. The saving grace was that some of the classes only had three students. I survived!"

"It didn't take me long to discover Bidwell Park," he added. He often brought field trips of thirty students or groups of Chico's citizens to explore the plant communities, wildlife, and geology. Wes grinned as he told me how more than 200 people came to the eightieth birthday hike he'd organized for Helen Bacon, one of the park's countless fans. The trucks delivering the sheet cakes were caught in a stop-and-go traffic jam. "The cakes were scrunched and flattened, but it was still a fun hike," Wes laughed. It is impossible to imagine a hike with knowledgeable and funny Wes as anything less than an adventure!

The Ground Beneath Your Feet

Wes's friend, the late geologist Phil Lydon, once described the park's geology as a wedding cake of three distinct layers, all slashed and disrupted by that boisterous and hungry guest Big Chico Creek (Urseny 2005b). Before the Coast Range rose, a warm inland sea deposited the Chico Formation during the Upper Cretaceous period, sixty-five to seventy-five million years ago. This formation usually lies buried, but it pokes above the surface near the far end of Yahi Trail and in neighboring Big Chico Creek Ecological Reserve. It lies upon a four-thousand-foot-thick shale and sandstone bedrock.

The clams, snails, and ammonites whose fossils lie in these layers tended to live in the calmer waters of shallow seas. These shells are not broken, meaning that large, powerful waves were absent here, which indicates that the Chico Formation originated near the ancient sea's coastline rather than in deeper, more turbulent water.

"You can run into the Chico formation," Wes told me as we sat at his dining room table. "Take the dirt road through Upper Park to the far end. There's a turnaround, and you can see sandstone deposits there. The Chico Formation is mostly several hundred feet below that. It runs [approximately 50 miles south] toward Yuba City; in the process, it creates a water reservoir. We're sitting on a wonderful lake!

"Chico would have an inadequate water supply without this underground water body. The Chico Formation is hard and does not readily absorb rainwater that soaks through the soil. The Sacramento Valley has an interior Mediterranean climate, with cool, wet (usually) winters and sweltering, dry summers. Spring and autumn are transition times between these extremes. We are lucky to have this underground water source in our arid region, especially during our parched summers!"

The Lovejoy Basalt, a fine-grained crystalline volcanic rock, forms the cake's middle section. This layer covers much of the Chico Formation, making it mostly invisible. Geologists think this lava flowed from Thompson Peak (near Susanville, CA) in the Cascade range eighteen million years ago (Boze 1991). These eruptions lasted somewhere between several hundred and several thousand years, a brief period in the earth's history. The formation contains many of the same minerals as lava flows in the Pacific Northwest's Columbia River Valley, suggesting that the two volcanic events are somehow connected (Teasdale 2009).

The Lovejoy flow covers 250 kilometers (155 miles), reaching Putnam Peak near the Sacramento Valley town of Vacaville. Much of it is now blanketed by later deposits that hide it from explorer's eyes (Teasdale 2009). "There is an outcrop at Black Butte Lake, over by Orland. Table Mountain, near Oroville, is another. And there's Iron Canyon, of course! This flow was two thousand degrees Fahrenheit when it reached here," Wes commented.

The lava cooled and contracted into hexagonal basalt columns (columnar jointing) as it hardened, but most have collapsed into rubble. Some of these blocks have a diameter of about ten to twenty centimeters, but there are columns at Little Grass Valley Reservoir that reach one meter across. The Lovejoy Basalt is much harder and more resistant to erosion than the Chico Formation. However, over time, Big Chico Creek has slowly eroded into these basalts to form rugged, narrow canyons (Teasdale 2009).

Big Chico Creek's white rapids contrast with these dark basaltic boulders and streambanks. Gray pines' pale needles look ghostly atop the nearby ridge. In April, orange fiddleheads and yellow buttercups thrive in the basalt's soil-filled cracks. Pacific Chorus frogs cry "ribit-ribit-ribit" so loudly that hikers sometimes can't hear the tumbling rapids.

The Tuscan Formation, the cake's top layer, covers much of the two older layers. These gray and brown hills and cliffs began as volcanic mudflows (or lahars) on Mt. Maidu (Mineral, California) and Mt. Yana (southwest of Chester, California) between one million and four million years ago. Successive eruptions melted snow on the mountainside, and vapor from super-hot underground water blasted through vents on the slopes. The scorching lahar of mud and debris careened down the mountains, carrying boulders and rocks all over ancient Butte County (DeCourten and Guyton 1978).

The mudflows hardened and left deposits that now hold sharp, angular rocks. Later, streams flowed over the Tuscan Formation, depositing water-tumbled smooth cobbles. The repeating sections of jagged and rounded rocks tell scientists that creeks and mudflows poured through this area several times (Boze 1991). I like to think of them as conveyor belts of mud and water following each other over and over again.

"These mudflows were seven hundred feet deep," Wes told me. "There were gaps in the eruptions; sometimes, the volcanoes were quiet. Most of the park is the Tuscan Formation. Over time, there's been uplift, and cracks have developed. You can see these cracks in the cliffs today."

Phil Lydon once commented that the Tuscan Formation would be the park's only visible geological feature if Big Chico Creek had not slashed through the area, exposing the deeper layers of the Chico Formation and the Lovejoy Basalt. The creek's forty-five-mile journey to the Sacramento River takes it from about 6,000 feet from its headwaters at Colby Mountain in the Butte Meadows/Jonesville region (Butte County) to 120 feet at its endpoint in the San Francisco Bay (Sacramento River Watershed Program 2023). Bidwell Park tilts gently at a one to three-degree angle from its eastern border toward the west. The creek races most quickly through Upper Park after snow melts in springtime.

The slope flattens slightly in Middle Park and more in Lower Park, where the slowing water deposits its sediment load on its floodplain (Boze 1991). The stream changed its positions many times here, creating flat areas in some spots between the volcanic ridges. It meanders lazily as the land becomes level in Lower Park.

Lower Park offers options to walkers who cannot deal with Upper Park's steep, rugged paths or only have time for a quiet stroll. Trails leave the paved roads at many spots and follow the creek, bringing solitude-seekers to quiet benches and picnic tables. The stream slides like liquid glass through groves of dark-barked valley oaks, western sycamores whose trunks look like brown and cream jigsaw puzzles, and bay laurels whose yellow flowers adorn late winter's cool days.

Lower Park and the town of Chico sit on a deep alluvial fan, an area created over millions of years when large rivers deposited sediments that eventually became the floor of California's Great Valley (up to ten miles thick in some areas). "This is one of the richest soils in the world, called the Vina Series, and the reason for our successful agriculture. Under my house, there are only rocks and clay. I have no Vina soil here!" Wes laughed.

The creek crosses CSU Chico's campus after it leaves Lower Park. It flows through agricultural land until it meets the Sacramento River. Big Chico Creek's water travels down that great course until it passes through San Francisco Bay and connects our region with the Pacific Ocean.

Grasses, Trees, Wildflowers, and Fungi

Many hikers follow the Upper Ridge Trail along the top of the volcanic Tuscan Formation hills and find great views of the Sacramento Valley and California's Coast Range to the west. Rugged rocks from the ancient mudflow challenge and sometimes trip them. They pass barbed wire fences that separate the park from the Bidwell Ranch open space. Cows stare at walkers, munch on grass, and rumble their "mooooos!"

Introduced grasses now dominate the park and all of California. These species arrived in the digestive tracts and coats of livestock that came with early settlers. They largely replaced purple needle grass and other local bunch grass species that grow in thick clusters from underground bulbs. The native species had survived grazing by antelopes and other migrating animals, which foraged but moved on seasonally before they could eat all the plants. Imported cattle and sheep that were present year-round often yanked grass bulbs out of the ground, creating spaces for introduced herbs. Happily, skilled observers like Wes can easily find and point out remaining patches of purple needlegrass and other indigenous species (Schoenhauer 1992).

These hills abound with springtime wildflowers. Frying Pan (or Fryingpan) poppies open four yellow petals in a flat plane to greet the sun. Tiny lupines hide among grass blades, but their dark purple color gives them away. Buckbrush, our local ceanothus shrub, glows with white blossoms while fiddlenecks curl and add yellow patches to the scene. Galaxies of milkmaids, sunflowers, Indian paintbrush, and Bird's-eye Gilia mix the colors white, yellow, red, and blue with the fields' dark green grasses.

The hills are also a habitat for blue oaks, one of the park's five common oak species. Valley oaks thrive closer to Big Chico Creek, while some black oaks, interior live oaks, and scrub oaks live near the ridge tops. Scrub jays, which love to eat acorns, gather and bury them to save them for times when food is scarce. Even these intelligent birds sometimes forget their meals' hiding places, becoming accidental foresters!

"Blue oaks, the shorter species, grow in cracks in rocks on the hillsides," Wes commented as we sat in his office. "They're blue because they have wax in their leaves that keeps them from drying out. They can survive in summer in the dry volcanic soil. There's little competition for water or nutrition once the roots are in the cracks."

Wes described the root crown, which is a structure between the roots and the first shoot that reaches toward the sun. Any of the many buds that cover the crown can begin to grow if this seedling somehow dies. The young tree produces a chemical that blocks its siblings' growth, and other buds won't sprout after the growing trunk reaches a diameter of six to eight inches.

"Blue oaks' roots store all the water they need in summer," Wes continued, "but you can kill a blue oak if you overwater it. They are not resistant to the microorganisms that grow in water around their root crowns. You get a lot of young blue oaks under older trees. Wildfires happen about every ten to fifteen years. Often, a fire will wipe the young oaks out, or cattle will eat them."

These native trees share the hillsides with Gray pines. These trees dominate the ridge tops, giving them a soft green tint when other trees are bare in winter. Their pale needles grow in sparse bundles. This adaptation and the needle's waxy coat means the trees lose less water than they might during their region's hot summers (Lukes 2019; Lederer and Burr 2019b).

"They live mainly on cooler north-facing slopes where they get more moisture," Wes told me. "They live less on dry, south-facing slopes where fires are more common. Fires happen every five to ten years, and the pines go off like a bomb!" Wes knows that occasional fires are healthy for these ecosystems, and the Maidu used them as part of their land management practices. Many caretakers now use prescribed burns to prevent large, destructive blazes.

Chaparral communities, composed of dry, sparse groups of shrubs, also thrive on the hillsides. Toyon produces bright red fruit in December, leading to its nickname, Christmas berry. Coffeeberry's very different fruits are shaped like a coffee bean, but I'm told if you brew a drink from them, it tastes lousy and gives you diarrhea.

Yahi Trail, which follows Big Chico Creek through Upper Park, is a much moister habitat than the hillsides. Wind spreads pollen from the fuzzy, yellow catkins that willows produce in late winter. Native people found a pain-killing chemical in white willow bark; this compound was later used to make aspirin. With their heart-shaped leaves, Fremont cottonwoods keep streambanks stable in times of heavy rain and erosion. Twigs were used for a variety of purposes: baskets, tools, and drums. The inner bark is high in vitamins such as vitamin C that can help people avoid scurvy.

These plants share their habitat with western redbuds that produce springtime clusters of pink flowers and autumn leaves of psychedelic oranges and reds. California buckeyes shed their leaves to avoid losing water during summer heat. Their creamy, candle-shaped blossoms reach for the sky in spring. They are not related to eastern buckeyes; their name comes from the fact Native Californians thought their nuts resembled deer's eyes (Lukes 2019c). Manzanitas' pink, urn-shaped flowers appear in January, showing that winter will soon end. The Maidu and other Native Californians make cider from the small, green fruits that appear in spring. Spanish settlers named this shrub "little apple" because of these berries (Joye n.d.).

Valley oaks prefer deep, damp soils. "The farther you get from deep soil, the big valley oaks can't live," Wes commented. "You find them mainly on soil that is six to eight feet deep or more." A valley oak's acorn initially produces a taproot that dips into the rich soil. "The first year, the taproot will grow four to six feet into the soil, but the shoot might only grow to be a foot tall. The valley oak needs moisture in summer, but it only gets it if the taproot hits the water table," Wes added.

Valley oaks grow quickly and can become thirty feet tall in eight years. Shade from their branches and leaves blocks sunlight from reaching plants that grow closer to the ground. These trees also produce tannin, a chemical that is toxic to plants that might otherwise surround them. These factors make these trees the dominant species in their damp habitats.

Thick clusters of mistletoe thrive high in the oaks' limbs. This parasite absorbs sugars from its host plant but rarely kills an oak. Round, bulging galls, which are apple-green when young, grow in groups on these trees' twigs and branches. An insect, usually a stinger-less wasp, lays an egg, and the oak responds by releasing a hormone that causes the spot to swell and form a gall that is at least as big as a golf ball. A baby wasp hides inside it to avoid predators until it chews its way out of its home and flies away.

Late autumn and winter are Northern California's seasons for wild fungi. Amanita, a fungus family that includes poisonous species, often thrives with oaks. The mycelium, the spider-web-like body that is the organism's main structure, intertwines with a plant's roots and helps it absorb water and nutrients. In return, the plant shares carbohydrates that it produces through photosynthesis. Researchers estimate that eighty to ninety percent of vascular plants have such a mycorrhizal connection with a fungus (Arora 1986).

Mushrooms and other strange, colorful structures produce spores that wind, rain, and animals carry to different spots so new mycelia can grow. Coral fungi look like they left an ocean habitat to decorate the forest's floor, while boletes resemble squashed, colorful balls with spongy surfaces under their caps. A mycelium can live for many years, but mushrooms, like wildflowers, have much shorter life spans; many only survive for a few days.

Other mycelia grow inside dead or dying plants. Some fungi break down the tissue and help return it to the soil. Turkey tails resemble those birds' banded tails growing in rows on lifeless trunks and branches. Pearl-colored oyster mushrooms blanket trees with their soft flesh. Some, like big, semi-circular artist's conks, are parasites on bay laurels and other trees. Witches' butter, a bright orange glob, grows from a mycelium that steals nutrients from other fungi (Arora 1986).

"Poisonous amanitas can get as big as a dinner plate," Wes commented. "Most years are too dry here to produce massive mushrooms unless you get successive rains. One year, it was wall-to-wall mushrooms, especially *Agaricus sylvestris,* which is edible. People filled the backs of pickup trucks with mushrooms!"

Wes stressed that many amanitas, especially the Death Cap, and some other mushrooms are deadly. An inexperienced person might mistake one of these for a delicacy. A forager must be very sure of a mushroom's identification before beginning the confusing task of searching for edible fungi. Other species, such as oyster mushrooms, are edible, although park rules discourage gourmets from gathering them. Some people might be allergic to mushrooms that are harmless to others and wind up with a bad stomachache. "I had one irate lady tell me she ate *Agaricus sylvesti* on my recommendation and got sick. It turned out she drank alcohol with it. That recommendation backfired on me!" Wes laughed.

Wildlife

Bidwell Park connects Chico with the Cascade range and many native animals. Black-tailed deer frequently visit Big Chico Creek and peer at hikers from the Bidwell Park Golf Course as dusk approaches. California ground squirrels, which live in spaces among rocks, also leave their prints. Male California quail perch on shrubs and call "chi-CA-go!" as females lead lines of bouncy chicks on foraging expeditions for insects and seeds.

Turkey vultures and red-tailed hawks often ride rising air currents, circling Upper Park's volcanic landscape. Red-shouldered hawks call rapid "pyo! pyo! pyo!" as they perch in oaks and scan the ground for tasty rodents or snakes. Hooded mergansers, ducks that snatch fish in powerful beaks, visit the creek and sometimes carry their young on their backs as they swim.

"With all the oaks in the park, acorn woodpeckers might be the most commonly seen animal species," Wes commented. These birds with dark backs flash their red heads as they zip among trees, breaking the silence with a call many people interpret as "whacka—whacka!" Others prefer to translate it as "I got ya!" Hikers often listen as they slam acorns into parallel holes on tree trunks. This strategy protects their food from squirrels, bears, and scrub jays. The nuts fit so tightly into their holes that other animals can't remove them. The woodpeckers shatter the shells with their beaks when they want a meal. These birds may feast on grubs they find in acorns but might also like the nuts' flesh. They also eat berries, seeds, and tree sap and zip out from branches to catch flying insects.

Acorn woodpeckers live in small groups, while their close relatives tend to be more solitary birds. Colonies can have as many as sixteen related members, sometimes including breeding pairs and their older offspring. Unrelated adults might also share this space and go through a free-for-all in mating season (Lederer and Burr 2010).

"Where Bidwell Park ends, Big Chico Creek Ecological Reserve begins," Park Services Coordinator Shane Romain told me one morning in his office. "That corridor is a very important area for migratory wildlife. Every now and then, you have a black bear that comes down that corridor through the park and into the city."

He described how California grizzly bears once dominated the Sacramento Valley, forcing smaller black bears to remain in the foothills and mountains. Once the grizzlies were hunted out of existence, the smaller animals began to move toward the lowlands.[1] Black bears' movement increased after development accelerated in the foothills, pushing them out of this habitat. These wanderers sometimes visit the park when acorns cover the ground or when berry shrubs' fruit call them. Black bears are omnivores who usually avoid people. They hunt for small animals, such as rodents, and might scavenge dead wildlife. They also tear downed logs apart to find ants, grubs, and other invertebrates.

Many people are afraid of these powerful animals, but I know from reading, talking with other hikers, and experience that a black bear will generally run away from people as quickly as possible. "They get into trouble if they get into the city," Shane Romain said.

Mountain lions are predators; deer are one of their favorite meals. Hikers must understand that wild animals consider the park their home and respect their presence. A mother mountain lion raised her young near Five Mile Recreation Area several years ago; park officials wisely made sure visitors stayed away from their spot until the family went on its way. Wes commented, "I've never seen a mountain lion in the park. I did find a half-eaten deer carcass at Five Mile Recreation Area. It looked like a mountain lion had killed it and cached it there."

Some people see rattlesnakes in the park fairly frequently; others encounter them more rarely. These rodent-eating snakes are less dangerous than many hikers think.

---

1 The last California grizzly bear was killed in 1922, and the last sighting of one was in 1924 at Sequoia National Park.

They use their venom to kill their prey and prefer to avoid wasting it to defend themselves. They rattle to say, "I'm here! Please don't step on me! Go away!" Wise hikers slowly back off and turn to walk in the opposite direction. Those who harass or try to catch a snake stand a great chance of being bit.

The park also abounds in spiders and insects. Webs cover every shrub on summer days and glisten like silver gems. Water striders, which have some of the highest libidos of invertebrates, skim across still pools in spring and summer. Dragonflies dart over wet areas and grasslands as they hunt for smaller flying creatures and avoid hungry cliff swallows. Grasshoppers begin to leap through dry areas in late winter, and centipedes leave narrow, winding trails in the dust.

Butterflies appear in late winter but become much more common as the weather warms. Western tiger swallowtails add a bright yellow flash to the park while mourning cloaks show their pale, black-fringed bodies. Dark blue-black pipevine swallowtails emerge from their chrysalises in March; they mate, and females lay their eggs on pipevine plants. They do not pollinate this species; their caterpillars only eat its leaves.

"The pipevine leaves contain a substance that is toxic to birds," Wes commented. "The caterpillars absorb it, and it protects them from predators. The larvae have an orange appendage on their foreheads, which serves as a warning to birds that get too close.

"Adults search for nectar," he continued. "Any flower will do, except for pipevine, which isn't in bloom when they leave the chrysalis. When the larvae emerge in springtime, they move to places where they can form chrysalises. They often build their temporary shelters on the pillars of the freeway that crosses the park, on railings by paths and short stairways. They also develop on branches where they are not so visible. The toxic chemical is transferred from the caterpillars to the chrysalises to discourage predators from feasting on them." The adult blue-black butterflies also have orange marks that tell birds not to eat them. They casually flit about in March and April, knowing predators will stay away.

Hikers must be careful to ensure they don't step on the caterpillars that frequently cross the park's trails. Since their chrysalises look like dead leaves, birds would probably ignore them.

Pipevine plants have a strange and important relationship with the park's fungus gnats. "The plant's flowers bloom before their leaves come out," Wes said. "There's a tiny gnat, a fly that lives on rotting mushrooms. It also pollinates the pipevine flowers in December and January. You can open a flower and see eight to ten gnats fly out.

Like all flies, they see in ultraviolet." They are attracted by the reflections from the flowers' purple veins and can spot these guidelines from fifty feet away.

Wes continued: "The flower also has a musky smell that's attractive to the flies and forms a landing pad for them. The pipe-shaped flowers create a dark chamber whose round 'skylight' transmits light that attracts the gnats to this pollen-producing area. The flower has a narrow throat and a musky smell that originates inside, at the flower's base. A hungry fly will be exposed to increasing amounts of the scent as it crawls down the dark tube. They reach the pollen and look back up the tube to see a donut-shaped window structure. Flies are attracted to light, so they will climb back up to head for that light, where they will find nectar and more pollen. They escape after the sun goes down, and there is no more reflected ultraviolet light." Wes laughed when he finished this tale, saying, "I used stories like this in my classes. Not everybody appreciated me. I was a demanding teacher; I stressed good writing. The good ones appreciated me!"

Invasive Plants

Bidwell Park's rugged geology and wild plant and animal species make many people think it is Chico's pristine wilderness. Sadly, invasive plants have always been one of the park's big problems. Nearby housing developments and other projects degrade the views of wildlands but, more importantly, introduce non-native, invasive plants from people's yards into the park.

These species spread quickly through their overabundance of seeds, taking over native plants' habitats, including the endangered Butte County meadowfoam's turf. Wind carries dandelions and Tree of Heavens' seeds, while mammals distribute privet, olive tree, and edible figs. Bicycle tires move Himalayan blackberry and puncture vine seeds. English ivy wraps itself around native oaks, blocking sunlight from leaves as it climbs to the trees' canopies.

The Dempseys and I talked about invasive plants as we sat at their dining room table and looked through a glass door to their backyard and garden. "The rancher John Bidwell had a plant nursery; it dates from 1870 until his death in 1900," Wes said. "He introduced 150 plants. That time, 1865-1870, marks a period of landscaping by the City of Chico. Bidwell introduced Bermuda grass for erosion control. It spreads underground through root systems, taking over local plants' habitats."

Wes responded to a red shoulder hawk's call and grinned wildly. "Sycamores were planted near the Esplanade, one of Chico's big streets, but they were susceptible to blight," Wes continued. "It spread into the park some years, and it affected bay laurels and sycamores there. The city tried spraying during blight years, but the spray landed on peoples' cars. That wasn't popular! The Tree of Heaven from Asia is another problem. Kids call it the stink tree."

An invasive plant can be beautiful and a nuisance at the same time. Scotch broom, a shrub that produces clumps of yellow flowers, and yellow star thistle, with its bright, star-shaped blossoms, are two rapidly spreading introduced species in Lower and Upper Park. "I spent fifteen years taking out broom with shears on my own. It grows by the creek," Wes said. "If you cut it off by the root collar, it's gone. A couple years ago, I was getting a thousand plants every spring!"

"There have been spotty and sporadic attempts to control yellow star thistle and broom. Star thistle can be controlled by fire if you get it while the plants are in flower and before they go to seed. They're surrounded by dry grasses then, and you can burn those noxious plants to the ground. Goats will also eat it; but them, they'll eat the clothes off you, too," Wes added, laughing.

Problems by the Score

Introduced plants are only one of the park's troubles. "I started fishing when I was seven or eight years old," local historian Dave Nopel told me as we searched his extensive files for articles about the park. "Pike was the most prevalent fish. There were schools of them in every pool, and there was no introduced smallmouth bass. Now, the introduced bass are taking over as the prevalent fish. Bass eat other fish and their eggs. There is still pike, but not as many as there used to be. Salmon populations are way down, too. California waterways have been diverted and polluted, and big-time fishing operations have affected them."

"Many people in Chico have a real connection to the park," he added. "Chico has always loved the park, but it is facing development pressures like never before."

Ornithologist Roger Lederer thoughtfully sipped coffee as we chatted in a local café. "If you go through Upper Bidwell and count the turtles, there are four to five per mile," he said. "In wilder Big Chico Creek Ecological Preserve, there are maybe 400 per mile. That isn't an exact count, but it is close. People in Bidwell Park catch the turtles and eat them, or do whatever they do with them."

"I used to take classes on bird walks near the Chico Creek Nature Center," he added. "I can't go there anymore. A lot of birds that were nesting in the area are being scared away. There were meadowlarks, horned larks, and Vaux's swifts. I don't see them much anymore. Now, I start at Hooker Oak Park and loop around to Five Mile Recreation Area, but not on weekends. There's just a lot more activity in the park, and where there's activity, there's misuse and vandalism. Birds are experiencing changes throughout the country. There used to be a lot of burrowing owls around here but not anymore."

Susan Mason, a co-founder of the advocacy group Friends of Bidwell Park, worked on that group's restoration projects and other activities until she moved to Southern California for family reasons. We discussed some people's attitudes toward the park and its issues in a downtown café/bakery several years ago. "A lot of people, when they walk in the park, don't see the problems. They think, 'If it's green, it's good.' When I worked in Lower Park removing non-natives, people yelled at me calling me a murderer."

"Nobody's really looking at the wildlife here, except for the Audubon Society watching the birds," she continued. "We know there are mountain lions, maybe a few bears, and we've seen bobcats. But we don't know about smaller creatures. Amphibians aren't doing too well because we have introduced bullfrogs that prey on other species. Also, people don't seem to understand that they shouldn't dump out their aquariums, so we have red slider turtles that don't belong here." These introduced reptiles crowd out native Western Pond turtles whose numbers are shrinking.

Phyllis Dempsey closed her crossword puzzle book as we sat at her table and mentioned the feral cats that once invaded the park, harming local birds and other animals. "Fifteen years ago, the park superintendent and park commissioners made an effort to get the cats out of the Park," she said. "I remember my bike group brought food for an injured cat. Domestic cats come into the park, and people drop off their unwanted cats."

"I'd find feathers from acorn woodpeckers, jays, and other birds," Wes added. "Eventually, the Bidwell Park and Playground Commission made it illegal to abandon cats in the park, adopting a policy of trapping and removing them to preserve wildlife. The Park Director had these raccoon traps he would use to catch cats and drop them off at the Humane Society. I think there's a fine for dumping cats in the park now. I don't see feeding stations anymore." The cats decimated California quail populations here, but these birds are much more common now that the feral predators are scarce.

"Feeding cats is against park rules, but people break rules all the time," Phyllis said. "People now put their dog droppings in bags but leave them all over the park." We all chuckled at peoples' behavior but agreed that the park deserves much better treatment.

Dave, Roger, Wes, Susan, Phyllis, and I pondered resolutions to these and the park's many other dilemmas and concluded that public education is essential. Chico needs to understand this treasure's natural and human history. Deep knowledge begins with the story of the Maidu people, who have lived here far longer than anyone.

Annie and John and Bidwell taken January 1897.
(Bidwell Mansion State Historic Park, CSU Chico Special Collections 14488)

CHAPTER TWO

Before the Park

Welcome to the Northern Sacramento Valley

After Kate and I moved to Chico, we became increasingly aware that while Oakland, California, is a fine city, we did not miss the congestion, traffic, and skyrocketing expenses. We were happy to have found a quieter place to live. Four ecosystems form the northern Sacramento Valley, the region we now call home. Ancient grasslands developed on deep river deposits; the valley's once extensive freshwater marshes formed from rain and streams that flowed out of the mountains. Riparian woodlands grow on a river's banks, and foothill woodlands are found on both sides of the valley. They cover the Sierra Nevada's and Cascades' lower western slopes and the eastern slopes of the Coast Range with oaks, big leaf maples, and pines (Schoenhauer 1992).

Settlement and development since the Gold Rush significantly impacted all these places. Introduced grasses crowd out native species, and most wetlands are lost to development. Almost all of California's rivers are dammed, and woodlands still hold scars from logging operations (Schoenhauer 1992). Nature lovers mourn this destruction and know how fascinating it would be if we could travel through time and visit these places when the Maidu managed them.

Maidu

California's mild climate and many resources gave the Maidu a comfortable home. The Maidu's range stretched from the Sacramento River in the west to the high Sierra Nevada in the east. The American River formed their southern boundary, while the areas around Rock Creek and Lassen Peak marked their farthest northern territory.

The Maidu based their lives on the abundant resources available during each season and knew how to manage the ecosystems around them sustainably. They carefully set small fires to clear grasslands to encourage healthier plant growth and provide better habitats for the animals they hunted.

Oaks gave the people acorns, the source of some of their most important foods. Acorn expeditions in autumn were a community activity for many Native Californians, including the Maidu. Women placed the acorns into a depression on a rock surface and ground them into a meal using a stone mortar. They leached the meal with water to remove the bitter tannins and made a kind of cereal as they cooked it in tightly constructed baskets that held water and hot stones. Women also used this high-protein acorn flour to make a kind of bread. Berries were often added to this acorn bread and cereal as a treat.

The coming of European Americans in the eighteenth to nineteenth centuries significantly impacted the way of life for all native populations living in California, including the Maidu and Mechoopda of the Chico area.[1]

John Bidwell Comes to California

"I think the story of Bidwell Park comes out of the story of John and Annie Bidwell, their times, and what prompted them to save part of their ranch, leave it as it was, and give it to the Chico," Dave Nopel commented. Dave is a thin man with a graying beard and wire-rimmed glasses. He loves to explore Big Chico Creek's banks with his two dogs whenever possible.

"I'm a fourth-generation Chico person," he said. "My first ancestor in California was Hugh Thomas Bell. He came overland to California and purchased a lot from John Bidwell. He built a house there in 1875–1876 and sold it so he and his wife could buy their first agricultural acreage west of Chico."

Dave's father, John, moved to Berkeley, California, in 1940 to get a credential as a school administrator from the University of California. He soon met his wife, a Butte County native who had decided she wanted to see the big city. They married and eventually returned to Chico to raise their family, and John became a school principal. "He was an amateur historian and photographer of the park for forty or fifty years. He began to give photograph-oriented programs from the mid-1960s

---

1   Editorial note: A more thorough discussion of Valley Maidu (which includes the Mechoopda) cultural history is beyond the scope of this work. The experts are the Valley Maidu and Konkow (Hill Maidu), and we do not wish to offend through ignorance or bias, conscious or not. We have provided a source list of more thorough histories in the appendix for readers who would like to learn more. The Valley and Hill Maidu have shaped Chico's history for thousands of years and continue to shape its present and future.

until the end of his trail in 2006," Dave said. He graciously shared his father's many files and his own deep knowledge about Chico's history, including John Bidwell.

Bidwell was born in Chautauqua County, New York, in 1819. His family struggled with poverty and moved to Ohio to seek a better life. Young John managed to support himself and get an education. "He distinguished himself from his teenage years by his desire to learn," Dave commented. "He had gone to a private academy and was soon the head instructor as a teenager."

Restlessness and curiosity drove John to move to the Missouri frontier. He worked as a teacher and tried to settle on a 160-acre piece of land. One day, returning from a trip to St. Louis, where he had bought books and school supplies, he found a violent squatter living on his farm. Bidwell was not twenty-one years old, had no legal title to his property, and was forced to leave. He read and heard descriptions of California as a paradise and organized the Western Emigration Society in 1840–1841. On May 18, 1841, they organized to emigrate to California. John Bartleson was elected president, with John Bidwell as secretary. Bidwell's journal is the best account of the group's travels, and the party has come to be known as the Bidwell-Bartleson Party, the first such group to set out for California.

The experienced guide, Thomas Fitzpatrick, accompanied them on the first part of the journey, but he left them when the party split at Soda Springs, which was then in Oregon Territory. John Bidwell stayed with the group that continued to California. The journey was arduous but filled with adventures, and John fell in love with the West's beauty.

"In his diary, he talks about how he and another man got so excited at seeing snow on a mountain that they set off thinking they could run up there and back before dark," Dave Nopel said. Their plan ended in disaster with them spending a freezing night on the mountain, and the rest of the party thinking they were either lost or dead (Gillis and Magliari 2004, 82). The journey climaxed with a harrowing crossing of the Sierra Nevada, and they arrived at John Marsh's ranch (near Mt. Diablo) fifteen miles from the San Francisco Bay in November 1841.

California was a shock to the newcomers. Two hundred thousand Native Americans composed most of the population. California was part of Mexico in the 1840s; 7,000 Spanish and Mexican settlers lived in a thin strip stretching from San Diego to present-day Sonoma County. Few ranchers were settled in the Sacramento Valley, and Russian trappers claimed Fort Ross on the northern coast as their base.

"There was no money in California at that time," John Bidwell wrote. "Practically, there was no doctor in California. There was no drugstore in California. . . . There was not to my knowledge, in all of California, a lawyer or law book, a post office or mail route, printing office, or newspaper. There were no roads, merely paths trodden by Indians and wild game" (Gillis and Magliari 2004, 82).

He deeply respected the Mexican settlers, whom he called Native Californians. "The kindness and hospitality of the Native Californians has not been overstated," he wrote. "Up to the time the Mexican regime ceased in California, they had the habit of not charging for anything; that is to say, for food, use of horses, etc." (Gillis and Magliari 2004, 90-91).

The Mexican government in California believed that immigrants from the United States and other countries could contribute to stability in the interior. Newcomers who accepted Mexican citizenship, converted to Roman Catholicism, married a Mexican citizen, and stayed for two years making improvements on their land grant could end up owning up to eleven square miles of property. These rules were poorly enforced, and many Americans who, like Bidwell, received Mexican land grants never fulfilled them.

John made his way to John Sutter's settlement, New Helvetia, at the point where the Sacramento and American Rivers meet. Governor Juan Bautista Alvarado felt that this community of immigrants from the United States and Hawaii with some peaceful Native Americans would act as a buffer to raids by more aggressive tribes. Bidwell remained associated with Sutter for years as a bookkeeper and property manager. He also helped recruit additional settlers to live at New Helvetia.

"In 1843, Bidwell lost two valuable horses he had borrowed," Dave Nopel said. "He came through this Butte County area with Peter Lassen, [Joe Bruheim], and an Indian guide looking for the horses. Bidwell wrote about how beautiful it was here and described the enchanting mountains with their springtime snowcaps. He celebrated the sparkling waters, the incredible growth of wildflowers, and the profusion of animals, including grizzly bears, antelope, elk, and deer.

"He drew the first map of the area that highlighted several creeks, including Chico Creek. The Mexican government used this map when it awarded land grants to William Dickey north of Chico Creek and Edward Farwell to the south who had arrived in the area earlier than Bidwell."

Inspired by Texas' separation from Mexico, settlers from the United States began their uprising for independence in 1846. John Bidwell participated in this movement, but his respect for Mexican culture led to his mixed feelings about the struggle. "If there ever was an unjust war in this world, it was that war," he wrote. "It was an unjustifiable war" (Gillis and Magliari 2004, 104).

John returned to New Helvetia after the war ended, which saw California ceded to the United States in 1848. He drew up a contract between Sutter and the carpenter James Marshall for a sawmill on the south fork of the American River. This was the spot where Marshall found particles of metal that he believed were gold on January 24, 1848.

"Bidwell was Sutter's most trusted employee," Dave Nopel said, "Sutter asked him to take the suspected gold to San Francisco for confirmation, which he did." The plan was to keep the discovery secret, but this proved impossible, and the California Gold Rush began almost immediately.

California changed drastically during and after the Gold Rush. The non-indigenous population grew to 380,000 people by 1860. Gold mining began as a collection of independent miners with shovels and pans, but the work was soon organized through miners' associations. Corporations that paid wage laborers dominated the scene by 1852. The powerful nozzles of hydraulic mining pounded hillsides with streams of water to remove topsoil so underlying rock and soil could be washed away to expose gold. This practice, which Bidwell came to oppose, led to streams being filled with sediments that destroyed fish habitat and disrupted navigation. These deposits caused water levels in streams to rise, leading to flooding and the loss of farmland. The Federal District Court in San Francisco eventually supported farmers when it banned hydraulic mining in 1884.

"Bidwell quickly organized a group of scattered Americans and began prospecting on the lower Feather River in spring 1848." Dave Nopel told me. "He found large surface deposits of gold at a place above Oroville, later called Bidwell's Bar. He had a crew of Native Americans and mined sacks of gold." His records show that he paid them with handkerchiefs, cigars, scissors, brandy, clothing, and beads. He also established a store selling gold pans, picks, shovels, clothes, flour, food, medicine, and whiskey. Bidwell's Bar quickly became a boomtown, with a population of six hundred. Bidwell's enterprise generated profits that may have exceeded $100,000 (approximately $4 million in 2023 dollars).

John Bidwell didn't plan to pursue a career in mining. His desire to be independent of Sutter led him to settle on a part of Edward Farwell's grant, where he herded cattle and began to plant fruit orchards. In 1849 and 1850, he used his mining profits to buy Rancho del Arroyo Chico from William Dickey. This property extended from the Sacramento River to the Sierra foothills and included 33,000 contiguous acres.

"Bidwell fell in love with this area and jumped at the chance to buy it when he had the gold," Dave Nopel said. "The soil was incredible here; there was a rich alluvial fan coming out of the canyon. He always wanted to be a farmer."

John knew miners would need a constant supply of food, and he used this property to provide them with beef, flour, vegetables, and other necessities. He owned 1,300 head of cattle by 1860 and 4,500 sheep by 1880, producing 45,000 pounds of wool in 1891. Despite his focus on livestock, winter wheat was his most important crop. He saw agriculture, rather than mining, as the basis of California's future.

John Bidwell's growing prominence in the area led him to political office on several occasions. He was elected to the California Senate in 1849 and to a term as United States Congressman in 1864. Bidwell was a strong supporter of the Union in the Civil War and a proponent of Radical Reconstruction. He identified with small farmers and prioritized agricultural policies that benefited them. He initially supported the development of railroads but became critical of the monopolies that controlled the transport of products and charged farmers high prices.

John ran for political office several times after his term in Congress but lost each election. His attention turned increasingly to agriculture. This era was the heyday of winter wheat production in California, and John's substantial holdings yielded 33,000 bushels of wheat annually by 1879. He also grew oats and barley and experimented with various other cereal crops. He grew wine grapes until his temperance-supporting wife, Annie, convinced him to shift production to raisins. He owned twelve thousand acres of orchards by 1891 and produced figs, olives, apples, peaches, and other crops.

"There was practically no cultivation of introduced crops during the tail end of the Mexican Era," Dave Nopel said. "Mostly, people were raising horses and cattle and selling the tallow and hides. But Bidwell had seen the mission's grapevines and fruit trees before the Gold Rush. He went to southern California on horseback to get cuttings. He planted them on land around Chico."

John met Annie Ellicott Kennedy, a charismatic member of Washington, D.C.'s high society, during his term in Congress. Annie, twenty years younger than John, had attended private schools where she learned to speak fluent French and studied philosophy and classic literature. When she was fifteen, she joined the Presbyterian Church and developed a strong moral sense that led her to work for women's equality and prohibition.

John had never met anyone like Annie, and he fell in love with her intelligence and ethics. He courted her through letters after he returned to California. She came to share his feelings. They were married in her parents' home in Washington, D.C., and she moved to Chico in 1868. Life in the California wilds would be difficult for a sophisticated Easterner, but Annie's growing love for the land led directly to her creation of Bidwell Park.

The Bidwells' Life in Chico

A life-sized portrait of John Bidwell hangs on a wall just beyond the Bidwell Mansion's front door. "You might notice that John is staring right at you no matter where you are in this hallway," mansion tour leader Noel Lopez said. "His eyes follow you throughout the room; his right hand will pivot and sway in your direction to point at you. This is an art style that was used in optical illusions, and later in cartoons. This is third graders' favorite part of the tour!"

John had built a two-story adobe house next to Chico Creek shortly after he bought Rancho del Arroyo Chico. He lived on the second floor; the first story served as an inn for stagecoach passengers. "He founded the City of Chico ten years after buying the Rancho," Noel Lopez said. The original settlement covered part of present-day downtown Chico, stretching as far as the railroad tracks. "He had a method for enticing people to settle on his land. He would give you a piece of land and a guaranteed job. You just had to move here."

The San Francisco architect Henry W. Cleaveland designed the mansion before John met Annie, and it was built between 1865 and 1868 for $56,000 (between $1 million and 1.2 million in 2023 dollars). It was one of the first modern houses north of Sacramento, offering gas fixtures for lights, flush toilets, and sinks with running water. It even had a toilet that resembles an elephant's trunk!

"The water came directly from Big Chico Creek; that's pretty cold, "Noel Lopez laughed. "The walls are brick, built for insulation. On the third floor, an opening to the roof acted like a house fan without electricity. Hot air would rise and exit there, and elaborate windows allowed a cross breeze."

John welcomed Annie to the mansion; it certainly made her life more comfortable than it would have been in a humbler house. "Annie's father was the first director of the United States Census Bureau, "Noel Lopez said. "Her family had been in the country for a long time. Both her grandfathers served under George Washington. John's origins were humbler. His family was poor; he only went to school a few months out of a given year. Who would have thought?"

Both Bidwells loved the mansion, which allowed them to entertain many prominent guests, like the environmental writer John Muir, President Rutherford B. Hayes, and General William T. Sherman. Susan B. Anthony visited Annie after John's death. The house's spacious rooms and refined decorations let them share their sophistication with visitors. The library, for example, included Native American baskets and books that ranged from history, science, and poetry to an autographed set of Anthony's *History of Women's Suffrage.*

How did the Bidwells feel about their land and the wilderness surrounding them? Their close friendship with the activist and writer John Muir offers some insights. Both Bidwells cherished Muir's charisma and his wild spirit. The two Johns were adventurous men who loved California's wild beauty. They identified as mavericks and outsiders who supported each other's unusual ideas. Annie was a devout Presbyterian, while Muir was more of a pantheist, but their spiritual connections to nature united them.

The three friends first bonded during an adventurous camping trip to Mount Shasta and the present Lassen Volcanic National Park in California's wild North Country. They shared their knowledge of botany, geology, and love for the remote and gorgeous area. Muir later spent many days at the mansion, where the Bidwells gave him space for his botanical studies. John Bidwell shared his expertise about agriculture after Muir became a rancher near the town of Martinez. Correspondence and visits continued through the decades, and Muir stayed in touch with Annie after John's death in 1900. He may have inspired her to turn part of the ranch into a public park.

"When the United States was created, the farmer was seen as the cornerstone of the new country and the embodiment of the new kind of person who would emerge," Dave Nopel said. While Bidwell shared Muir's love of wilderness, he also looked at the land in very practical and human-centered ways. He supported early environmental policies, such as opposition to hydraulic mining and deforestation that led to erosion in the foothills. Still, his positions mainly centered on his understanding of how damaging these policies were to small farmers.

John also believed wise farming policies could improve nature and transform California into a modern Garden of Eden. This land would be beautiful and produce profits from an extensive range of crops. John supported irrigation policies and the use of technologies and fertilizers that helped California become the super-agricultural state it now is.

"It was part of his vision that people could perfect this land," Dave Nopel said. "But I think he had a spark of something we don't have a name for. He saw this valley before people began digging, gouging, and changing it. Where many people only saw a resource, Bidwell felt something about the larger world. It continued throughout his life, and I think it came down to the creation of Bidwell Park."

The sophisticated city dweller Annie adapted surprisingly well to life in the rural Northern California wild country. The mansion's comfort, security, and elegance gave her a safe feeling that allowed her to develop an adventurous side. When John was occupied with business and political duties, she often rode a horse into the rugged grasslands and canyon country. Traditional women rode sidesaddle, and Annie sometimes did, but she also learned to straddle a horse when it was more convenient. Both she and John loved to swim in Big Chico Creek, and John built her a raft she used for her adventures.

The Bidwells often took guests on buggy rides around the ranch. In 1883, Bidwell was visited by an Australian journalist, Thomas Kirkland Dow, who wrote that Rancho Chico was "the most interesting and best-conducted farm in California." He was impressed by how Bidwell had preserved its natural beauty.

> An inspection of Rancho Chico and a study of its management soon convince a visitor that the proprietor, while seeking to work his estate at a profit, values some things in the world more highly than money. The ranch of this pioneer of California must not only make dollars, but it must teach the people how varied the productions of the state are; it must be "a thing of beauty and a joy forever," and not even the all-powerful American dollar would be able to bring about the destruction of a favorite oak, an avenue, or a bit of charming scenery. Not only have the natural beauties of the country been preserved, but the gold derived from its productiveness has been expended upon developing and increasing the pleasing appearance of the estate. The property of 25,000 acres is like a group of delightful parks, and one drives for hours in every direction along charming avenues, past farm-houses, orchards, vineyards, grain-fields, and pastures, among browsing cattle and sheep, and seeing busy fruit gatherers as well as quickly-moving harvesting machinery, without ever losing the sense of rural beauty. (Dow 1884, 42–43)

In 1877, the Bidwells took the English botanist Sir Joseph Hooker to see a valley oak over 100 feet tall. He declared it to be the largest oak in the world. It became known as the Hooker Oak in the botanist's honor. Annie's biographer, Lois H. McDonald, believed that the tree may have been a big part of the reason why Annie wanted to preserve part of the land.

"You could criticize John Bidwell for introducing invasive plants, but we live in the very lively situation he created. We have lots of food, and I enjoy it," Dave Nopel laughed. "Still, I have to wonder about its sustainability. You can find holes in what happened, including details about the Maidu's experiences, but looking back, I like the Bidwell story."

School children having a picinc in Bidwell Park in Chico, California, Butte County, ca. 1900.
(John Nopel, CSU Chico Special Collections 5910)

CHAPTER THREE

Vallombrosa and Beyond

Birth of the Park

Eighty-year-old John Bidwell had a sudden heart attack while cutting wood and died in 1900. "He and his wife owned 30,000 acres of land and twenty businesses. He left Annie in debt, and she had to get herself out of it," Noel Lopez said. "Toward the end of his life, John took out a loan to refinance the ranch, thinking he was healthy, but that wasn't the case. Annie was land rich after his death, but cash poor."

"They were about $350,000 in debt when John died," Dave Nopel commented.[1] "Franklin C. Lusk, the lawyer, sent Annie a letter that said, 'You better get to selling your land, or your creditors will come right to your door and usher you down the steps and write off your property.' I have a copy of her brochure offering land for sale. It sold like hotcakes, and she was out of debt by 1905."

"Annie liquidated much of John's land holdings, leaving her with twenty-five acres and the mansion, and financial security for life," Noel Lopez added. "This was when we saw the north side of Chico being developed. This was also when she began to donate land to family and friends, and to the city the land that became Bidwell Park."

Author Nancy Leek, a librarian who wrote the biography *John Bidwell: The Adventurous Life of a California Pioneer,* commented, "'Vallombrosa' is the name that John and Annie Bidwell gave to the strip of land running along either side of Big Chico Creek. The name first appeared in Bidwell's journal in 1876. It was a landscape that they loved and wanted to preserve in its natural state. Later, when Annie Bidwell donated the land to the City of Chico, it became Bidwell Park."

---

1   Approximately $13 million in 2023 dollars.

"I imagine it was Annie who came up with this poetical name based on Milton's *Paradise Lost* where he compares fallen angels to autumn leaves:

> *Angel forms who lay entranced*
> *Thick as autumnal leaves that strow the brooks*
> *In Vallombrosa, where th'Etruran shades high*
> *over-arched embower . . .*

"And where is that original Vallombrosa? It was a Benedictine monastery about 20 miles south of Florence in the Apennine Mountains. Milton traveled to Italy in 1638 and visited Florence in September. When he saw Vallombrosa, he was struck by the beauty of the thickly falling leaves and later immortalized the locale in *Paradise Lost*. The name Vallombrosa derives from the Latin (*vallis umbrosa*) for "shady valley.""

Annie surprised many people when she grew to love camping and other adventures in Vallombrosa and the wildlands surrounding it. She discovered her childlike side when she played pranks on her husband and when they walked off the trail to examine rocks and wild plants. When a visiting politician complimented her, calling her a sport because her hiking pace exhausted him, she bowed to him in a teasing way and replied, "Not too many people call me a 'sport.' Down there (she pointed to the valley spread beneath them), I have to be serious—everyone expects it of me. (She continued with a twinkle in her eye), I try not to disappoint them" (Hartsell 1992).

Photographs from the early twentieth century show how much Chico's citizens enjoyed visiting Vallombrosa. Buggies brought guests onto the ranch, and both adults and children loved to come for picnics. One of my favorite photographs feature fashionably dressed citizens having fun together on top of the elevated flume that brought Sierra Pacific's cut lumber from the mountains to Chico's lumber yard. Of course, very few of these visitors understood that this land had been the Mechoopda Maidu's home for millennia.

People familiar with the history have a range of opinions on whether John, Annie, or both were more influential in establishing the park. "Even though we see Annie as the person who left us Bidwell Park, it was John's values that left the park," Dave Nopel said. "It's said that there was nothing he liked better than to ride through the land on a horse or in a carriage. He had an extensive road and trail system that was immaculate and where no one could cut a branch without his permission."

"When John died, he left two wills," Noel Lopez said, "one for if he outlived Annie and one for if she outlived him. The second one says basically, 'Everything goes to my wife; she can do whatever she wants with it.' Annie decided to follow the first will as closely as she could. It mentions the property that became Bidwell Park."

The present Sycamore Pool and Five Mile Recreation Area were well-loved swimming spots. People shared the Bidwell's love for the Hooker Oak—it became the site of weddings and gatherings. When Annie sold enough property to free herself from debt, she decided the time was right to give Chico part of her remaining property as a public park.

Annie is referred to as "the party of the first part" and the City of Chico as "second party" in her July 7, 1905 deed.

> It is the wish of the Party of the first part, and it is to be fully considered and understood, that said park is the joint gift of herself and her husband, John Bidwell, to the City of Chico as a token of their love and affection and that that grand work of God may be preserved to his glory, and the happiness and pleasure of the people of said city for all time.

The deed states that she and John wanted the park to be used

> for the benefits of the citizens and residents of the said City of Chico. The deed also charged the city to preserve "as far as reasonably possible, for the beauty of said park as well as for the preservation and protection of Chico Creek, all of the trees, shrubs, and vines therein, and it shall sacredly guard the same and only remove such thereof as it finds absolutely necessary...."

The deed further stated that the city could rent pastureland to ranchers to help fund the park if they did not interfere with the public's enjoyment. Sierra Pacific Lumber could still use its flume to move lumber through the park. As a strong Presbyterian, Annie insisted that the city would not allow alcohol to be manufactured or sold anywhere in the park, and public picnics organized by "Orders, Lodges, Clubs, or Associations . . . " would be prohibited on Sundays. She did not mention gatherings by individual families in this statement. Annie also added a reversionary clause, which stated that she or her heirs would be permitted to take control of the park if the city's administration of the land did not keep any of its part of the bargain and went against her wishes.

Cindy Wolff, whose family has lived in Chico for generations, commented, "My great grandfather, William Robbie, was the mayor of Chico from 1907 until 1919. He and then-mayor O. L. Clark accepted the deed to Bidwell Park from Annie Bidwell in July 1905. He also accepted the deed to Children's Playground from Annie Bidwell in 1911. William Robbie took his identical twin daughters, Mary and Elsie, as early teenagers on a walk in what would become Lower Bidwell Park and said to them, 'The people of Chico need a road so they can see their new park.' Subsequently, he oversaw the building of roads through lower Bidwell Park so that the people of Chico could, in fact, see their new park."

The lumber flume at Iron Canyon in upper Bidwell Park, no date.
(John Nopel, CSU Chico Special Collections 4115)

Most of Chico's residents were overjoyed by Annie's gift, but no one could predict the disagreements that would later split the town over it. The city leaders planned a large celebration to thank Annie for the gift on July 17, 1905. An announcement in the *Chico Daily Enterprise* read, "The popular demonstration tonight on the Bidwell Grounds is not to be understood as a select affair . . . nothing should prevent it from being a popular assemblage" (*Chico Enterprise-Record* 2005a). The park belonged to everyone; no one needed to dress formally, and people of all backgrounds were invited to the party (Cassidy 2005).

The standing-room-only crowd gathered on the mansion's ground heard a performance by the city orchestra. Reverend William M. Martin offered a prayer, and the speakers included 85-year-old Susan B. Anthony. Annie told the grateful crowd, "little children, young men and maidens, men and women of all ages; the sad, the discouraged, the happy, should enjoy this Garden of God, because He had bestowed upon me the power and the wisdom to preserve it" (Cassidy 2005). She also said prophetically,

> From the first years of my residence on Chico Creek, a sadness has at times oppressed me as the thought has been borne in on me that someday the beautiful, beloved Chico Creek would be destroyed by the diverting of its waters and the slaughter of its trees. . . . It is of sufficient value to you to influence your choice of city officials, for if unworthy men be elected, it will become a thorn and a torment. (Boze 2004, 8)

The Park Grows

Annie's original gift included 1,900 acres of the ranch that included the basalt formations at Iron Canyon and Devil's Kitchen, and other sections of the present park. In 1911, she supplemented her donation with 301 acres in the park's far northeastern section. A road that was built for cars and wagons climbed the hills to spots where adventurers could find spectacular views of the Sacramento Valley. This was Annie's final donation before her death in 1918, but it would not be the only addition to the park (Boze 2004, 8).

In 1922, ten Chico citizens each gave $100 to the city so it could buy twenty-nine additional acres of land for the park, including sections of a development called the Forestry Station. John Bidwell gave this property to California's new State Forestry Board in 1888 for use as a nursery and a demonstration tree plantation. Forty-five thousand trees and saplings were grown here and in surrounding spaces by 1890. The Board distributed young trees and cuttings from willows, mulberry, maples, oaks, and others to local residents. These gifts included plants from distant parts of the world (Dempsey 2004).

Controversies rose over the Board's management of the land, and the state cut funding to the project in 1893. "The original forestry station commissioners were legislators who appointed themselves," Wes Dempsey reflected. "They were big on making money and just traveling around. After five years, the legislature caught on and took their funding away from them. The University of California had this land dumped on them. They had a budget of $2,000, which was nothing then." Johnson grass covered the area, gophers abounded, and only 2,000 healthy trees survived (Dempsey 2004).

Bidwell joined forces with the university to improve the site, and they planted about 4,000 trees, including coast redwoods, Scots pine, cypress, catalpas, cork oaks from Portugal, and others that were not native to the area. Later scientists worked successfully to hybridize Coulter pines and Jeffrey pines, yielding trees that were hardier than their parents (Dempsey 2004).

The University gave the land back to the state of California in 1898, and Chico later bought the twenty-nine acres and added them to Bidwell Park. Park headquarters and a maintenance building were located here; the Bidwell Wildlife Rehabilitation Center appeared around 1975 (Dempsey 2004). Today's hikers can visit this area when they walk on the World of Trees Nature Trail.

Kate and I walked down this path on a cool March day as a gray storm flowed toward us from the west. Poison oak grew so thick that a hiker might think people were planting and tending to it. We passed an orange-barked incense cedar, a native of the

Sierra Nevada and Cascade range and wandered through a grove of Italian cypress. English oak soon replaced this species followed by catalpas from the southeastern United States. These trees have heart-shaped leaves and long, cigar-like seed pods, which childhood friends of mine used to dry and smoke.

Pacific madrones, whose dark bark peeled away to reveal a smooth, orange surface, grew near introduced Portuguese cork oaks with deeply furrowed trunks. People made many products from cork before World War II until plastics took over.

In 1935, the city added a twenty-four acre plot that Annie's nephew Guy Kennedy had owned near Vallombrosa Avenue. The Bidwell Park and Playground Commission had agreed that Kennedy could ranch on this small plot if he paid $900 per year beginning in 1919. When Kennedy died in 1932, his will gave the land to his friend, Bidwell Park and Playground Commissioner Reuben Messinger. The Commission took over the land when Messinger died, but his widow was permitted to stay and work there for several more years (Boze 2005).

In 1995, the city added an undeveloped 1,417-acre parcel between Big Chico Creek and Highway 32. This acquisition, which included forty acres of Bureau of Land Management (BLM) property, brought the park to its present 3,670 acres (Lydon 1997). This also included a small disc golf course that was developed illegally on BLM land. As the course later became bigger and more popular, park lovers disagree to this day about its impact on native plants, and on the spot's thin, delicate soils.

Chico loves the park, but it's interesting to note that some citizens have always related to it more strongly than others. Cindy Wolff said, "My grandmother, Mary Brattan (William Robbie's daughter), used to take my three siblings and myself to picnic and swim in Big Chico Creek in Lower Bidwell Park when we were young. That would've been in the late 1950s and early 1960s. Her daughter, my Aunt Jean Brattan, was a lifeguard at One Mile for many summers as a teenager. . . . Five Mile was not a 'thing' in my life until I began to go there for swimming and events as a teenager, about 1970. My parents never took us into either Lower or Upper Park. Bidwell Park was just another outdoor country place like so many other places in and around Chico back then."

She continued with a story: "I started to go swimming with my cousin and friends in Upper Park, especially Salmon Hole and the Diversion Pool, while in high school. This same cousin and I cut P.E. in late spring of 1971 and went to the creek in what is now called Middle Park. We were swimming, laughing and splashing when we looked up and saw a young man and woman sitting on a huge sycamore branch arching over the creek. We were horrified to see that it was our P.E. student teacher. She called out that her younger brother was visiting from out of town, so she cut class to show him the park. She shouted, 'I won't tell if you don't tell.'"

Bidwell Park and Playground Commission

Annie Bidwell died in 1918, leaving no one to administer her gift. Chico continued to grow; its population reached 15,517 by 1920. Government policies promoted the production of grains and produce that would be canned and sent to World War I troops (Moon 2003). The city's expansion meant that Chico needed an organization that would closely monitor Bidwell Park.

Chico's Ordinance Number 155 established the Bidwell Park and Playground Commission (BPPC) in 1919 and charged it to ensure that the city and its citizens remembered the wishes Annie expressed in her deed. The Commission had the authority to enact rules and regulations, authorize roadways, and promote other improvements and upgrades to the park. With time, the commissioners' role broadened to include other city parks and open spaces including the Downtown Plaza (McGee 1983).

The City Council appointed influential Chico citizens who served without pay on the Commission. This policy gave them credibility, respect, and ensured they would not be seen as rabble-rousers or radicals with no connection to the Chico community (McGee 1983). Roger Lederer commented, "The Bidwell Park and Playground Commission is an advisory board. It makes recommendations to the City Council, which makes the final policy decisions. The Commission has no enforcement powers. They might have influence, depending on who is on it, but they must convince City Council."

The Commission's minutes indicate that the body mainly focused on funds for tools and maintenance and staff salaries during the park's early years. In January 1921, the commissioners agreed to send Dr. John Copeland to Berkeley to encourage the regents of the University of California to transfer ownership of the old Forestry Station to the City of Chico. These trees' health was an ongoing issue after the area became part of Bidwell Park. Commissioners also worried about the famous Hooker Oak's condition. Other matters that appeared periodically included the need for speed limit signs, maintenance of bridges across the creek, and the control of rodents.

Playground equipment at One Mile Recreation Area and lighting for the swimming areas there and at Five Mile Recreation Area needed discussion during June 1929. Sub-par conditions in these swimming areas and the lack of lifeguards were a topic in April 1946. The idea of amusement-park-type rides for children occasionally appeared in the Commission's minutes, but it is not clear from the records how far this idea progressed.

Local organizations regularly asked the Commission to approve their events in the park. A motorcycle club got permission to hold a scavenger hunt in the park in May 1953. The Girl Scouts and the Job's Daughters approached the Commission with requests for events in July 1964. One unique discussion in June 1964 centered on the fact that swimmers who wore street clothes in Sycamore Pool could become wet and waterlogged, making it hard for lifeguards to rescue them if they found themselves in trouble.

Environmental issues added storms and excitement to the meetings during the 1970s that continue even today. Commissioners also discussed the need for nature education programs in the park, and a proposal for a bird rehabilitation center appeared in October 1975.

The present body includes seven commissioners, each initially appointed by the City Council. The Commission had four sub-committees (Friends of Bidwell Park, n.d.-a):

1.   The Natural Resources Committee investigated and reported to the entire body on the management of vegetation, trails, and other resource and ecological-oriented issues.
2.   The Policy and Advisory Committee looked closely at present policies for possible changes to day-to-day park management. It also considered finances and connections between the park and the artistic communities.
3.   The Tree Committee discussed issues around trees in the park and other areas, such as neighborhoods.
4.   The City Bike Advisory Committee advised the Commission about biking-oriented issues.

The sub-committees have not met in several years; many park advocates look forward to their meeting again.

Agendas, minutes, and background reports for Commission meetings are available on the city's website and in printed form before the body meets on the last Monday of each month.[2] Citizens can request that items be included in future meetings and can speak to the gathered commissioners about their passions.

Some people also disagree that the Commission should only be an advisory body, stating that it should be independent of the city and have stronger influence over park policies. Long-time environmental activist John Merz, who once managed a recycling plant in Arcata, California, now serves as the chair of the advocacy group Friends of Bidwell Park. He commented. "One of the things that existed in

---

2   https://chico.ca.us/bidwell-park-playground-Commission

the Commission's charter is the Commission had the ability to hire and fire a park director. In the 1980s, the Plaza had giant elms giving shade in summer. We had barn owls nesting there; it was a very special place. The trees were trimmed severely because of concern about falling limbs.

"Some of us disagreed with this policy, and this was the end of the line," he continued. "The Commission fired the park director. The city manager was not happy about the commissioners doing what he thought was his job. To make a long story short, the issue was taken to the citizens as an initiative. The proposition passed; the Commission no longer has that power relative to the park director."

The Commission has always included a free-thinking group of people. Elaina McReynolds-Baird, whose term on the committee and position as its chair ended in late 2021, told me, "I worked on diversity and safety issues at Pennsylvania State University before I moved to Chico in 2010. I discovered the park, researched it, and saw it as a big environmental issue. I also became a leader in PALS, the park's volunteer program. When Bernie Sanders spoke in Chico before the 2016 election, he shared the perspective, 'I can't do it all; you need to participate!' I wanted to do something for the park, so I came to the Commission."

She continued, "The Commission had more governing power before my time. The council wants us to be an advisory board. If we had more power, we could deal with long-term contracts, staffing, and oversight of projects. But I don't see that happening right now."

Former Bidwell Park and Playground commissioner Lise Smith–Peters told me over an Octoberfest beer at a Chico restaurant, "I worked with Greenpeace and with Kentuckians for the Commonwealth's environmental work before I moved to Chico. I was the Development Director for the Chico Boys' and Girls' Club when I got here. We lived off Vallombrosa Avenue and loved being close to the park, and when the volunteer coordinator job for Bidwell Park came open, it was a dream come true! I later was promoted to be a management analyst, which included duties like overseeing Bidwell Park and Playground Commission meetings. I kept this job for years before I transferred to working for California State University, Chico."

She told me during another meeting, "The document states that we can create and manage contracts for projects like park maintenance and ecological studies. There are Commission members who have enough expertise to develop their own studies. At this point, we make proposals to City Council and, to some degree, rubber stamp their decisions. I kind of understand why they want us to be an advisory board. So many people have strong and conflicting opinions about the park that the situation could be chaotic! But the Commission could be stronger!"

Erroll Flynn and Olivia de Havilland standing next to unnamed seated woman, 1937. (Academy of Motion Picture Arts and Sciences, CSU Chico Special Collections 15773)

CHAPTER FOUR

Many Visions for the Park

Conservation Versus Preservation
Different Environmental Philosophies

I often wonder what it would be like to discuss Bidwell Park over a Cabernet Sauvignon with nineteenth-century environmentalists John Muir and Gifford Pinchot. While Muir, the nature writer and Sierra Club founder, and Pinchot, the United States Forest Service's first head, were often allies, they sometimes disagreed. Some people consider Pinchot, the conservationist, the more practical of the two. He loved wild places but usually emphasized policies that preserved them for human uses and the general welfare (Clayton 2019).

Muir is often called a preservationist. His deep sense of wonder and spiritual connection to the earth led him to believe that wild places and their creatures had every right to exist and must be protected from ongoing industrialization and development. He is the person who struggled to make Yosemite Valley and its surroundings a national park (Clayton 2019).

Pinchot's allies won a crucial battle with Muir's faction over whether Hetch Hetchy Valley, in the Sierra Nevada, should be preserved as a wilderness area or as a resource to benefit people. The conservationists' plan to dam the area's stream succeeded; the valley was flooded, creating a reservoir that serves the Bay Area's growing population (Clayton 2019). Some of Muir's admirers still work to have the dam removed so Hetch Hetchy's wildness can be restored (Restore Hetch Hetchy n.d.). Despite the differences in their philosophies, I believe Muir and Pinchot would find common ground over some of Bidwell Park's issues.

Preservationists and conservationists still wrestle and have a long history of arguments around Bidwell Park. These disagreements partly originated in Chico's population growth after Annie Bidwell's death. Agricultural activity, especially rice, grain farming, and the production of canned vegetables, expanded during World War I. As time passed, new arrivals included students, faculty, and staff who came to the growing California State University, Chico. Others worked in the growing industries and the town's regional hospitals (Boze 2004).

Chico's growth has always put additional pressure on the park and led to conflicts about its role in the community. Recreation and other human uses were the dominant themes during the park's first fifty years. The Bidwell Park and Playground Commission initially focused on funding and maintenance for buildings and facilities. It seemed primarily open to a free-for-all of development of recreational projects and other human activities. Preservationists gained much strength and influence on the Commission and community as the environmental movement grew during the 1970s, but some of the resulting issues and clashes remained unresolved.

Three articles in the *Chico Enterprise-Record* (1974c) help clarify each faction's position. An editorial stated,

> At the moment, a vigorous special interest effort is being waged for the adoption of unrealistic and undemocratic restrictions that would gravely diminish the rights of the average citizen and his family to use and enjoy Bidwell Park ... Such a restriction would turn Bidwell Park into a private nature preserve for hikers and environmental extremists while depriving the average people of their share of use and enjoyment of the park.

The editorial focused on the Bidwell Park Golf Course and a shooting range near Horseshoe Lake, both of which were sources of clashes at that time. The editorial suggested that the Bidwell Park and Playground Commission wanted to limit activities at the golf course, which the editorial called a beautiful and essential part of Chico. It defended the controversial rifle range, stating that it was important to citizens who wanted to promote safe gun use by adults and children. The editorial also claimed commissioners wanted to limit park picnics, swimming, and sports activities.

> Annie and General John Bidwell lived their lives for people. We believe they would deeply resent present efforts of the elitists to kidnap them posthumously and use them in a campaign against average citizens. ... Bidwell Park belongs to all the people and ideas of a proper park range all the way from bird watching and nature hikes through all the activities listed above and countless others.

Thus, no single restrictive and elite philosophy on Bidwell Park is acceptable. (*Chico Enterprise-Record* 1974c)

Commissioner Robert Dierdoff leaned toward the preservationist position as he criticized the idea that small groups should be able to use this land for their own needs and wants. He wrote in a December 6, 1974, letter to the editor ("E-R Rapped for Editorial Views"):

> You've certainly had your say on Bidwell Park, and it weakens your generally fair reputation as an editor. Referring to members of the Parks Commission as 'elitists' and 'royalists' may please some of your fans. At the same time, it is inconsiderate and thoughtless journalism. . . . Most major municipal parks in this country have been defended against encroachment. It is the legitimate function of a park Commission whether or not you approve. Special interest groups eye all that public land, and it can be eaten away over the years.

In the December 16, 1974, issue of the *Chico Enterprise-Record*, a letter from Irving Schiffman ("E-R Is Assailed for Park Views") of Chico agreed about the lack of recreational facilities in the park but commented on the idea that selfish environmental interests wanted to block development.

> It is unclear who these 'special interests' are, but I am willing to bet that they are the same 'selfish interests' who seek to protect agricultural land from being cemented over by urban development, who seek to protect our north coast redwoods from indiscriminate lumbering. . . . These 'selfish interests' realize that to protect the ecology, beauty, and solitude, a limit must be placed on the amount of public construction and crowd-inducing activities that can be allowed there.

Ornithologist Roger Lederer supplemented Dierdoff's and Schiffman's thoughts when he told me, "I learned that a group came up with an idea, and the Commission approved it. Groups came up with initial funding, and then they dropped it. The city had to maintain the projects then."

At the same time, people disagreed on the meaning of Annie Bidwell's insistence that citizens care for the creek, animals, and plants. Shane Romain once told me, "One person would interpret that as 'You can't trim anything because of Annie's wishes.' Another person would talk about how we need to remove non-native plants to promote natives. Someone else would say, 'It means we're not going to build more bathrooms in the park.'" Arguments and disagreements about this unique green space have rocked Chico for decades. A good look at some special places can reveal much about the park's troubled history.

Let's Take a Walk

Reader, let's imagine going for a hike that begins in wild Upper Park. We follow Big Chico Creek through the more developed Middle Park, ending near downtown Chico in Lower Park. I show you places involved in some of Chico's most contentious debates about the park. "Pinchot might have approved of some of the human-centered projects; Muir would probably have opposed all of them. Both probably would have been against the crazier ones," I comment.

We start on Yahi Trail, passing valley oaks, western sycamores, and rocky areas next to the creek. We have much ground to cover and choose to move to nearby Upper Park Road, where we can hike more quickly. A pickup truck passes us and creates clouds of aggravating dust. "It's so quiet and peaceful up here. I wish they'd keep the cars out of this area," you say, coughing.

"Some people think this road should be for hikers and bikers, but others love to drive on it," I say. "It leads to the most remote and beautiful parts of Upper Park, and some feel that families and people with disabilities should be able to see those places (Urseny 2018b). The problem is erosion along the road, and the city hasn't had enough money to repair it. You just noticed what happens when cars pass hikers. It would be great if some shuttle followed the road so cars would stay away, but that would take a lot of planning and money. Sadly, it seems like this isn't the time."

"Have people always loved Upper Park?" you ask.

"Not too many at first," I answer. "Some people thought, 'Sure, it's just wilderness; if it's not a popular area, why shouldn't we let people do what they want here?'"

"Where is the Easter Cross?" you ask.

"It's on a hillside a little to the west of Horseshoe Lake," I answer. "People have gathered there for sunrise services on Easter for years (*also* Epley 2010). Some citizens thought it was inappropriate for city property and thought it should be removed during the early part of the twenty-first century. They seem to have gotten a lot of opposition. The cross remains there" (*also* Boelens 2010).

"I heard that a ranch had cattle up here and that Annie's deed agreed to that so the landowners would help fund the park," you say.

"Yep, M&T Ranch rented land for cattle grazed in the hills with the Bidwell Park and Playground Commission's approval," I reply. "Pinchot might have liked that idea; I doubt that Muir would have supported it. Still, the Commission decided in 1962 that the rent the city received was less important than cattle eating and trampling the wildflowers. They decided to cancel the agreement, and no cattle have been in the park since then (*also* Moon 2003).

"We'd have to spend our whole hike in Upper Park to give us time to talk about all the projects that developed here," I continue. "There was this short, steep go-cart track where kids would race down the hillsides. The Commission never approved this idea, but since people thought Annie believed the park belonged to everyone, she would support any project people dreamed up. They just built the track in 1958 without the Commission's approval. Dave Nopel told me how he once saw a kid on a go-cart flip over and land upside down. There must have been a lot of other accidents; the track finally just faded away" (*also* Indar 2005).

We hike back to Yahi Trail and stop at a bench overlooking the Salmon Hole swimming area, where springtime wildflowers surround large chunks of black basalt. A Canada goose wanders through the poppies, buttercups, and fiddlenecks and seems to smell the lupines.

"There is a sign about something called Diversion Dam. Was it here?" you ask.

"People think the WPA built it around 1935 to channel creek water through a ditch to Horseshoe Lake," I answer. "The Bidwell Park Golf Course used the lake as a reservoir until the ditch leaked. The course decided this plan didn't work, so it let the lake go and started pumping water from the creek" (*also* Lydon 1997).

As we return to the rocky, dusty road, I ask, "Can you imagine people driving off-road vehicles and motorcycles through the hills or building unofficial trails through the wild areas? These paths and recreational drivers ripped up much of the loose, dry soil here, and rain carried it to the creek. I think Pinchot and Muir would have been allies around these issues. Wes Dempsey and Thad Walker told me that the city finally came down hard on off-road driving in the 1980s, but unauthorized hiking trails are still a problem."

We walk quietly for a while until we arrive at Horseshoe Lake itself. Ridges of the Tuscan Formation reach for the clouds just beyond the human-built lake's northern shore. Acorn woodpeckers thud repeatedly as they pound their food into a telephone pole, and ten turkey vultures squat in a dead pine that they sometimes share with a pair of bald eagles. We pass two silver-haired Chico folks fishing with their granddaughter. Three black Labradors splash noisily while a great blue heron ignores them.

"People came up with ideas for how to use the lake after the golf course turned it over to the city," I say. "The Commission approved water skiing here for a while. A group called the Chico Choppers got the Commission's green light to fly model airplanes in the 1960s. The commissioners told them they were fine if they didn't annoy motorcyclists, horseback riders, or get in the way of traffic. A few people were worried about how activities like these would affect the animals and plants, but a few years had to pass before they had the influence to raise a fuss about such things."

"What happened to the rifle range that was here?" you ask.

"The Bidwell Park and Playground Commission agreed they could be built in the 1920s," I said, "but they got to be less popular in the 1980s when people worried about safety and pollution. Imagine hiking around here while bullets whizzed by. The gun enthusiasts said Annie would have felt they had as much of a right to be in the park as anyone, but the Commission recommended that they relocate in the 1980s. They left a lot of toxins in the form of lead shot that the city had to clean up later" (*also* Gascoyne 2002)

Bidwell Park Golf Course sits across the road from Horseshoe Lake. Deer peer at us from one of the greens while locals in golf carts drift over the emerald grass. "You want a beer?" you laugh, pointing toward the clubhouse. "Prohibitionist Annie would be fit to be tied about that."

"Talk about battles!" I say with a grin. "That was a huge struggle for a lot of years. The golfers won that one, mainly because the sale of alcohol helped fund the course and made it less dependent on city money (*also* Hardee 2014). They had less luck with other fights, especially when they wanted to put in new greens by Horseshoe Lake in the 1980s. Some park commissioners and other citizens were against that idea. They claimed it disrupted wildlife habitat and let a small group of people grab part of the park for themselves. The whole issue seemed to fade after some years; I think everybody was too worn out to keep it up. Things seem calm between golfers and the Commission now."

We walk along the road, passing grassy fields with smatterings of oaks and came to the side route that leads to Five Mile Recreation Area. We stop at the picnic tables on the Big Chico Creek's north banks and watch squirrels leap through the oaks while acorn woodpeckers shout at them. Children and parents yell and splash in the creek while cliff swallows dart from their mud nests on a bridge to catch flying insects.

"Wasn't there a shepherd who used to bring his sheep to graze here?" you ask.

"Yes, that happened when the Bidwell's owned this land," I say. "People started to use his barn as a changing room. I'm not sure what he thought of that! John Bidwell eventually built a better structure where the swimmers could change clothes. Lifeguards were here after the park was created, and people came in droves to swim" (*also* Lydon 1997).

Big Chico Creek at Five Mile Recreation Area.

"I guess they stopped paying those lifeguards because there wasn't enough money," you say.

"Good guess. They seem to have enough money for lifeguards at Sycamore Pool," I answer. "Lots has happened at Five Mile, though. A miniature car club had a racing track here in the 1950s. It seems like the Commission approved this at first, but the city attorney said the city couldn't pay medical bills when accidents happened, and the owners had to get private insurance. That seems to be another project that just faded away; a field fills with spring wildflowers where the track used to be" (*also* Indar 2005).

We find the trail that follows the creek's southern shore and walk through Middle Park's oak and sycamore groves toward Lower Park. "Did the Bidwell Park and Playground Commission go along with all the ideas people suggested?" you ask.

"Oh no. Commissioners developed a lot of environmental consciousness beginning in the 1970s," I say. "They could also be wise in the early days. One of the first proposals someone made was for a car-based campground. The Commission rejected that one in 1919. They did change their minds and agreed to the campground in 1920, but it didn't get enough business, and it folded.

"The American Legion wanted to hold an auto show in the park, but that idea was lost because people would come from areas outside of Chico," I continue. "I am not sure why they thought this was a problem; maybe they thought the park would have been too crowded. Another group wanted a car wash, but that lost too. Imagine the suds, dirt, and other pollution that would have ended up in the creek!

"Airplane lovers wanted an airfield in the park in the 1920s. That one didn't fly," I add, chuckling. "There was a compromise where the airport was built on the north side of town, where it still is. The Commission also turned down a twenty-acre fish hatchery in the 1920s and a polo field project during the 1930s" (*also* Indar 2005).

"How many people would want to play polo during the Depression? It's a rich person's sport, really," you wonder out loud.

"Yep," I said. "The Commission also took back their support for a motorcycle club's track in the 1960s because it was loud and unsafe. The idea that really stuns me is the Air Force's proposal for a radar-based bombing range after World War II. This was at the beginning of the Cold War, and many people thought that our need to be militarily stronger than Russia was more important than anything. Imagine screaming fighter jets above the park and bomb craters on the hillsides! It is wonderful that the Commission rejected this one" (*also* Indar 2005).

The trail takes us to South Park Drive, which stretches from downtown toward Five Mile Recreation Area, and we reach some metal fences that stretch along the road. "The deer pens," you say. "I heard Roger Lederer talk about how the state set them up in the 1970s so people could get a good look at deer that lived in the park. But people fed the deer all kinds of junk; a fawn ate a bread loaf wrapper and died. So, the pens got phased out, too."

"It took a while, though," I say. "Some people teased the deer, and ducks and geese brought diseases into the pen. Writer Cindy Wolff told me, 'My father would take all four of us kids on the weekends to view the deer in the deer pens. He would give us cigarettes to feed them, saying that deer love to eat tobacco. Not sure if that was true, but they did seem to enjoy taking the cigarettes out of our hands and eating them.'

"The veterinarians for the deer and upkeep on the pens were expensive," I continue. "A lot of people thought it was great for kids to see the deer close-up and claimed that the animals were healthy despite everything. But the Commission voted to phase the pen out in the 1990s and send most deer to a wildlife sanctuary. A few animals did remain for a while. The last one died in 2005" (*also* Gascoyne 2005; Urseny 2012).

"Wasn't there a zoo?" you ask.

"Yes. In 1954, The Bidwell Park and Playground Commission allowed a couple from Oroville to build a small facility for thirty-five Native California animals. They justified it by saying people could learn a lot about local wildlife. After a few years, the owners brought a couple of capuchin monkeys to live here. How many of them do you find living in the hills around here? The Commission eventually recommended that the zoo close because the animals weren't healthy and the place smelled awful" (*also* Moon 2003).

We wander among the oaks that surround Sycamore Pool. "How did this place become a swimming area?"

"John Bidwell dammed the stream with sandbags here so people could swim for free," I answer. I love to swim here, but some wild things have happened. There were water skiing carnivals in the 1950s."

"No way!" you exclaim. "How did the boats keep from hitting each other?"

Sycamore Pool in Lower Park.

"You tell me," I say, shrugging. "A business also wanted to put in amusement park rides here. The Commission liked that idea because they thought it would help kids love the park. A lot of people don't understand that kids love to explore nature, and they don't need rides and things to have fun outside. But that's another idea that faded away from the Commission minutes."

Robin of Locksley in the Park

This would be a far longer book if I told you about all the issues that have defined Bidwell Park. One of the more unusual ones involved the park's starring role in *The Adventures of Robin Hood* in 1937. Warner Brothers Studios decided to use the park for the Technicolor movie's outdoor scenes, saying that its oak groves made it look like Sherwood Forest.

The studio also liked that while Chico was still a relatively small agricultural and university town, it had a rail station, developed roads, and a hospital. Actors and the film company could enjoy the town's restaurants, movie theaters, and stores. Warner Brothers and its employees eventually spent thousands of dollars in local businesses and hired local actors for small parts (Drennan 1970). The film was a massive stroke of luck for Depression-era Chico, but no one has studied its impact on the park.

The film starred Errol Flynn as Robin Hood, Olivia de Havilland as Maid Marian, and other famous actors in other leading roles. Warner Brothers filmed scenes inside castles and in the town of Nottingham at Hollywood studios but relied on Bidwell Park for forest scenes. Director William Keighley and his assistants picked a spot on the north side of Sycamore Pool for their headquarters. They set up tents as dressing rooms and storage areas for costumes and equipment. Filming began on September 27 with the scene where Robin and Little John became allies and friends after their quarterstaff duel on a log across Big Chico Creek (Ermini 1982).

The famous Hooker Oak served as Sherwood Forest's major oak in the film. It's here where Robin teases a napping Friar Tuck and where the banquet for the captured evil Sir Guy and Maid Marion was filmed (Ermini 1982).

While the park's sudden fame thrilled Chico, there were roadblocks. Housing the crew presented a problem since Chico had few hotels and apartment buildings. Hotel Oaks and Richardson Springs were filled to capacity for weeks with the Traveler's Hotel taking the overflow. Flynn and his wife, Lila Damitra, who had recently reunited after a separation, gave Richardson Spring's guests some high drama when a furious Damitra threw her shoe at Flynn in the dining room (Drennan 1970).

Crowds of out-of-town movie fans brought money and excitement to Chico. Visitors were not allowed to wander through the set during filming, but they visited and chatted with actors and got autographs when the cameras were shut down. The crew accepted local citizens' invitations to afternoon teas, and history buffs among them learned about the region's past. Richardson Springs welcomed Chico's people to dances planned for the actors and support staff. They forbade their waitresses and other workers to date the film crew, but couples avoided problems by going to the nearby town of Oroville (Drennan 1970).

It's unclear how the movie's crew and the thousands of film buffs who descended on little Chico affected the park and Butte County's other wild places. Flynn, Basil Rathbone, and Howard Hill enjoyed hunting; Flynn killed a wildcat with a bow and arrow. He and Rathbone were fined for shooting pheasants out of season and Flynn for racing his sports car on country roads.

The park got a makeover when the crew brought British ferns to make the scene look like England's Sherwood Forest. While valley oaks resemble English trees, the crew ran into a problem when trees, wild grapes, and grasses changed colors in autumn. Technicians solved this problem by using vegetable dyes to paint these plants green (Moon 2005). No one monitored the park's ecological state in those days, and it's unclear what impact any of this had on its plants and animals.

The park had small roles in other movies, including *The Red Badge of Courage, Gone with the Wind,* and *Friendly Persuasion* (Lydon 1997). It also appears in commercials and music videos, but none of these productions focus on it as an ecosystem, and producers are not required to pay fees. The land's appearance in these films is just one example that shows how much citizens' attitudes vary with this open space, its animals, and its plants. It used to seem that Chico could at least find consensus around the park's well-loved Hooker Oak, but the debates after the huge tree's death revealed the range of thoughts and feelings people in this town had about nature.

A Beloved Tree's Fate

I am looking at a photo of the Hooker Oak before its collapse. The massive trunk and huge branches supported a domed canopy that blanketed the ground with shade. Some limbs reached for the sky, while others bent so their leaves almost touched the ground, forming a huge green shelter.

"The creek splits just to the east," Wes Dempsey commented, "so the oak had a good water supply. It had good soil, brought there by the creek, and no competition from other trees, so it had a chance to become huge. Valley oaks grow fast when they have good water. It added two inches a year and was 111 feet tall in 1921. Its trunk had a circumference of twenty feet, and its longest branch was 111 feet long. The people of Chico, who kept an almost mythical connection with the tree, believed that it had lived in this spot for 1,100 years."

Annie and John Bidwell visited the oak frequently and often brought guests to see it. They called it "The Big Oak" and built a fence around it with a sign that stated, "Please do not mutilate this noble oak." Their guest, the British botanist Sir Joseph Hooker stated it was the largest valley oak he had ever seen and claimed it was the world's biggest valley oak.

Local folklore claims that John Bidwell described bigger oaks that lived on his land, and much larger ones have been found in other parts of California. Still, the Hooker Oak thrived as a symbol for Chico for many decades. It served as the site of marriage proposals, Easter egg hunts, uncounted picnics, and family photographs.

The great tree was named in Sir Joseph Hooker's honor. The Bidwells loved it, and the oak was part of Annie Bidwell's 301.76-acre gift to the City of Chico; this donation supplemented the land that was mentioned in her 1905 deed. In 1957, Chico Area Recreation and Park District acquired the spot and developed it for recreational purposes while preserving the oak (Moon 2005).

The great tree's problems began when a powerful rain and wind storm buffeted it on October 12-13, 1962. It seemed to withstand the onslaught until its major limb on the east side cracked and collapsed, practically cutting the oak in half. Experts worried the lack of nutrients from that section's missing leaves would weaken the tree (*Chico Enterprise-Record* 1977b; Moon 2005).

City workers removed the fallen sections and painted the stump yearly to keep destructive insects away. The limbs were linked to strengthen them and help the tree keep its shape. The city drilled 2,000 holes into the ground to add minerals and nutrients to the soil near the root system (Moon 2005). These efforts, strong though they were, could not prevent the Hooker Oak's collapse.

It happened on the evening of May 1, 1977. Neighbors who lived across the street reported a sound like thunder. Police got the first reports of the oak's fall around five p.m. It didn't take long for the community to gather. Children began to climb on the trunk, and some people tried to cut off pieces of wood for souvenirs. One unsentimental man showed up with a chainsaw, hoping to retrieve firewood from the tree, but he was told that since it was the city's property, he would not be allowed to do this (Butler 1977; *The Orion* 1977). The city quickly barricaded the area to stop these activities. The Horticulture Society built a fence around the tree and guarded it for three days to protect it and ensure visitors were not injured.

Other citizens brought garlands of flowers and wept over the fallen giant or took photos to share at public gatherings. Some said they couldn't visit the site because the experience reminded them of losing an old friend. A procession of mourning city officials and citizens lasted for three days (Moon 2005).

The question of what to do about the fallen oak appeared in a Bidwell Park and Playground Commission meeting in May 1977. Speakers noted that people ignored signs about respect for this area and stomped on seedlings as they gathered branches and twigs from the fallen tree. One commissioner suggested that people should be required to pay for a small piece of the oak and that this money should be used to fund the park. Citizens shared many ideas about what to do with the tree and the space. Some felt the city could build a band shell and a community-gathering place. They also felt craftspeople should get pieces of the oak to use in their work. Others suggested that researchers cut a section of the trunk and mark historical events on particular growth rings. Some citizens thought the fallen oak should remain in place so children could play on it. In June, many local people requested the city build a monument showing the tree's size (*Chico Enterprise-Record* 1977a).

Why did the community react so strongly to the tree's collapse? Its size and beauty offer good explanations and the fact that it was a long-standing symbol for Chico. It was one of the Bidwells' favorite landmarks, and a symbol of local pride. Its fall marked the end of an era for many people. Dave Nopel commented, "The valley oaks had a prominent place in the natural world here, and the Hooker Oak was a fine specimen. People came out in buggies and later cars to be photographed. They could find wonder in nature's grandeur, and the tree's size and longevity."

Therapists and others speculated on psychological reasons for the community's grief. Psychologist Steward Bedford commented, "When you have a tree that old, it begins to represent perpetual life, life everlasting. Its fall disrupted peoples' feelings about life going back generations and stretching into the future" (*Chico Enterprise-Record* 1977c). Others compared Chico's relationship with the oak with villages in India that sprang up around sacred trees. Some commentators reflected on Carl Jung's work, which resounded during the spiritually-oriented 1970s. They described the tree's roots as a symbol for the unconscious mind, one of Jung's central themes and suggested that the spreading branches were a metaphor for peoples' search for transcendence (*Chico Enterprise-Record* 1977c).

Dr. Kingsley Stern of the CSU, Chico,'s Biology Department stunned Chico in June 1979. He investigated cuttings taken from the trunk and determined that the tree was not one but two valley oaks. One sprouted in 1751, and the other grew very nearby in 1755. The two grafted together in 1785 when they were thirty-one and twenty-seven years old. Growth rings indicated that one tree was 226 years old and the other 222 years old when Hooker Oak toppled. Stern speculated that an underground water source may have contributed to the double oak's huge size. He commented that he did not know how the tales of the tree's advanced age of 1,100 years began but stated that his findings should not reduce Chico's love for the oak (*Chico Enterprise-Record* 1979).

Wes Dempsey shared another hypothesis with me, saying, "It wasn't necessarily two trees, but two shoots from the same root system. When an acorn germinates, it often has a double embryo, so the two trees grow side by side. Or the seedling might have been damaged, so two trunks grew side by side. It was quite traumatic when people discovered the tree's age. They couldn't eliminate the idea that it was over 1,000 years old; that was a bragging point for Chico."

This news did not quiet the debate about what to do with the fallen giant. Constant letters to the *Chico Enterprise-Record* offered suggestions. Some citizens felt it should be allowed to remain and decompose where it had fallen or that a historic display be created from a cross-section to memorialize it. One person suggested encasing the oak in glass and preserving it forever. Others suggested that some of its acorns should be planted and a picnic site could be built in the grove.

Some thought the tree could be cut into slabs and placed in the Bidwell Mansion, while others could be sent to CSU, Chico, and other interested universities. People suggested that it be made into furniture for the Bidwell Mansion, panels for offices in City Hall, or tables and benches for a picnic area where the oak once stood. A few suggested key chains or coffins. Many Chico residents opposed any plans to commercialize and sell the oak for profit. These debates raged for three years.

Hooker Oak.
(Eastman Studio, 1946/Randy Taylor, CSU Chico Special Collections 28373)

In 1980, the city finally contracted with Cal Oak Lumber Mill in nearby Oroville. The mills' owner, Gus Hall, agreed to keep and sell one-third of the wood. The city would keep the remaining two-thirds, which it placed in a west Chico warehouse. Hall found that the wood from two fused oaks seemed to be especially dense and that it was difficult to cut. The iron rings placed in the trunk to support it damaged some of Hall's equipment. A worker mentioned that the tree also held barbed wire and nails, suggesting it had fused with a fence (*Chico Enterprise-Record* 1980).

Hall did manage to salvage enough wood that workers with developmental disabilities at the Work Training Center could use it to make backings for clocks, tables and chairs, barometers, and small boxes. All these items were marked with the initials "HO" to prove they were real. The wood also became the frames for retirement plaques, the gavel used at Chico City Council meetings, and the pedal board for the Centennial Pipe Organ at Harlan Adams Theatre on campus. The 1980s were also the era of pet rocks, so some people jokingly mentioned that some wood could be made into pet blocks. Others found this idea disrespectful, and it never came to pass.

Guy Hall decided to return his remaining wood to Chico in 2005, a year before his death. His supply merged with the city's at a west Chico warehouse in 2010 (Urseny 2010a). The trunk joined the rest of the wood there in 2013. It had remained as a memorial to the tree but had burned in an unexplained fire. Children climbed on the ashy and decayed wood despite warning tape, and some people whittled at it for souvenirs. City officials felt it could be preserved and studied by future biologists. The city wanted to make a memorial model of the stump to mark the place where the oak grew so Chico would never forget it (Urseny 2013a).

Chico Area Recreation District now administers Hooker Oak Recreation Area, the section of the park where the oak once grew. It is a pleasant, grass-and-tree-covered spot with sheltered picnic areas, barbecue pits, playground equipment, and baseball fields. Families love to gather here on sunny weekends and after schools close.

· · · · · · · · · · · · · · · · · · ·

I searched unsuccessfully for a model of the stump, but I only found a small stone structure with a metal plaque describing the Hooker Oak. Cars zipped past on busy Manzanita Avenue while children played on swings and parents chatted nearby. It was a happy scene, but I wondered how many people remembered the great tree. Is it a ghost only rooted in a few peoples' memories? If people forget about Hooker Oak, I fear they can also forget how important Bidwell Park is. I hope details about some of its issues can help people focus again on this treasure.

Gregg Payne murals on Highway 99 support pillars.

CHAPTER FIVE

Roadways

Why Does a Freeway Cross the Park?

Imagine that one morning, you are in the mood for a bike ride. You pedal along South Park Drive, a one-way asphalt road that hikers and bicyclists take eastward from One Mile Recreation Area toward Five Mile Recreation Area. Depending on your energy level, you can choose among several bridges that cross Big Chico Creek and lead to North Park Drive. You can take that road back toward One Mile and downtown. You follow meandering Big Chico Creek as it wanders along its relatively flat floodplain and notice valley oaks, Fremont cottonwoods, and western sycamores on the stream's banks. English ivy clings to many of their trunks and grows toward their crowns, while Himalayan blackberry surrounds their roots.

You meet a good sample of Chico's people as you pedal. A woman walks a dachshund and a German shepherd who leap together like best friends. Children who skip in front of their parents grin at you and yell, "Hi!" Other bicyclists abound, and some riders have their hands in their pockets instead of on the handlebars. One carries big plastic bags of bottles and cans to sell to a recycling center. Skateboarders zip to the rhythm of loud rap music that joins the quiet creek in a unique duet.

The rumbling, groaning, slamming noise from California State Route 99 begins as a whisper, then grows to a roar as you approach the unexpected freeway about a half mile past One Mile. You can't miss the bare, rock-covered piles of dirt surrounding the thick, concrete pillars that hold this busy road above you. Sound barriers line the highway north and south of the park but are missing along the stretch directly overhead. Car horns blare and tires screech, disturbing walkers and cyclists who would rather listen to the creek and to acorn woodpeckers' calls, but there is no escape from this cacophony. The roar seems to stalk you as you wander away from the freeway, but it soon fades, leaving you and other walkers with the wind, the creek's hum, children's laughter, and bird songs. You reflect that it would be wonderful to imagine that Bidwell Park lives in a separate world from social, city planning, and economic issues, but Highway 99 just woke you from this sweet fantasy.

Road building for cars in the United States proceeded in fits and starts during the twentieth century. Both the world wars and the Great Depression interrupted plans for national highway development. By the 1950s, cars came to be seen as a symbol of affluence and mobility, along with televisions and picket fences. Cars transported people to their jobs, and trucks were seen as an efficient way to move products to markets. Raconteur and radio host Garrison Keillor noted the anniversary of the Federal Highway Act, which was passed in 1956, in his June 29, 2019, issue of the *Writer's Almanac*. This legislation resulted from President Eisenhower's admiration for the Autobahn highway system in postwar Germany. He decided that affluence and a growing love of cars in the United States meant that this country was ready for a similar project.

U. S. Highway 99, which was once considered California's main street, was the main route through the Central Valley for decades. John Steinbeck's *The Grapes of Wrath* mentions it as the route the Joad family followed during their search for work in the Great Depression. The road did not cross any state lines and lost its designation as a federal highway as Interstate 5 rose to prominence. That freeway is now the most direct route through the western part of the Central Valley and points north and south. California Highway 99 lies farther east, following much of US 99's route as far as Red Bluff. Unlike Interstate 5, it passes through large towns, including Chico (Historic Highway 99 Association of California n.d.).

The California Route 99-E Business Extension, the route California 99 took through downtown Chico, still follows northbound Main Street and connects with the Esplanade, then with California 99-E, which leads to Red Bluff and I-5 North. Southbound Broadway takes traffic to Park Avenue before it leaves town. Drivers on these streets pass motels, cafes, Mexican and Cajun restaurants, a well-loved used bookstore, the Chico Children's Museum, and the tree-surrounded city plaza with fountains where children splash each other in summertime. Traffic varies between sparse and heavy, but today's downtown area would be a true mess if Main Street and Broadway supported the hordes of vehicles that now move along the California Route 99 freeway.

Some Chico citizens worried about traffic and other dangerous conditions along the road through downtown before the larger highway was built. Writer Jane Ziad, who grew up in the nearby town of Willows, commented, "The major highways used to go right through towns, and Willows was like that. It was dangerous and serious accidents took place. In Chico, this was compounded by the train that used to go down Main Street well into the 1970s, I believe. It was a short spur that went by Northern Star Mills [toward the airport]. You'd be driving, and suddenly, a train was behind you. Very unnerving!"

Cindy Wolff added, "Highway 99 used to run right through Chico until the freeway was built. When my mother was a child in Chico, she rode horses down the bridle path between the two single lanes that comprised the old Highway 99 back in the 1930s.

"My school was Notre Dame on Fifth Street, so my siblings and I cut through the California State University, Chico campus," she continued. "That was well before bikes were restricted from campus. The railroad tracks ran along the highway, and we had to cross them in several locations. That was always tricky because someone's tire was bound to get caught between the parallel tracks and result in a crash. Those tracks were a real worry for us kids. All manner of trucks used that road. It became loud and congested before the freeway was built, much more so than it is now."

How Did the Freeway Get Here?

Like other California towns, Chico was still largely agricultural during the 1950s, but it was becoming more complex. John Bidwell donated his cherry orchard as the space where Normal School Teachers College was established in 1887. The college expanded over the years, and its student, faculty, and staff populations grew when it became California State Teachers College in 1921, Chico State College in 1935, and California State University, Chico, in 1972 (Moon 2003).

Butte County built its first airport near Chico in 1929. New schools and churches, drive-in-theaters, and radio stations appeared in the late 1940s. The growing number of stores, early shopping centers, and a television station showed that the town was expanding. Still, many of Chico's roads and other infrastructure needed repairs and upgrades, partially due to the lingering lack of funds from the Great Depression (Moon 2003).

Chico's officials had discussed rerouting a freeway and moving traffic from the crowded downtown area since 1949. A planning group recommended that the freeway should follow Sheridan Avenue, about one mile east of the city's center. It described this route as short and direct, allowing good connections to the city and was reasonably economical for such a project. Much of the community supported the alternative idea of a road following Forest Avenue, which passed through a less crowded part of town about a mile east of Sheridan Avenue (Woodward 1958).

These citizens who opposed the Sheridan Avenue route claimed it would break the city into two parts and isolate the developing eastern section. Children who walked to school would need to cross the freeway. Others felt overpasses and embankments planned to pass through Bidwell Park would destroy much of One Mile Recreation Area's beauty. A highway that followed Forest Avenue would be far from the well-loved One Mile Recreation Area and would direct traffic through Chico's more sparsely inhabited areas. The City Council agreed with this position and contacted California's Division of Highways and recommended the Forest Avenue route (Woodward 1958).

The Battle Begins

During the 1950s, the California Division of Highways based its decisions on where to place highways on engineering issues, such as the proposed routes' grades and placement of interchanges. They also considered present and future traffic patterns and safety issues, the economic value of the area that would be disrupted, and monetary savings to motorists. Impacts on schools, parks, and neighborhoods got less of this body's attention. Still, many people in Chico hoped the department would share their concerns about the Sheridan Avenue route and would agree to the Forest Avenue proposal. The City Council, increasingly worried about the freeway controversy, asked for a public hearing on the issue, and the state officials agreed (Woodward 1958).

The United Chico Committee, which supported the Forest Avenue route, appeared on the scene on June 23, 1955. Its leader, Attorney Robert E. Laughlin, and other activists published a petition opposing the Sheridan Avenue route in the *Chico Enterprise-Record* on June 23. Citizens showed up in front of grocery stores and other businesses with petitions and collected 3,734 signatures by July 13 (Woodward 1958).

Imagine a meeting between Chico's parents, businesspeople, city officials, lovers of One Mile Recreation area, and hundreds of other citizens with the Division of Highways on July 14. The state's officials shocked the community by supporting the Sheridan Avenue route. These officials based their decision on factors such as the placement of interchanges and the projected positive results for Chico's businesses. They also commented that a freeway close to Main Street would benefit local drivers and travelers passing through Chico. Property owners affected by the freeway would get market value compensation for their losses. The Commission commented that it had considered each route's impact on schools, parks, and neighborhoods but thought these were less important factors than the need for a more efficient traffic system (Woodward 1958).

Angry citizens believed the state had already formed its conclusions before the hearing and would not be moved by community concerns. Speakers questioned the state's figures and doubted that the Sheridan Avenue route would improve traffic safety as the state claimed. Others described how freeways had been routed around other towns rather than passing through them and stated that Chico should follow these communities' example (Woodward 1958).

Ted Meriam was Chico's mayor at the time. A *Chico News and Review* article that appeared after his death on August 5, 2001, described him as "quiet, unassuming, and unremarkable. He wasn't a showy speaker. He didn't try to impress." Despite all this, he served as mayor for five terms and was respected for his humility, integrity, and listening skills. It must have been hard for him to confront the Division of Highways, but he was the agency's adversary for several years (Speer 2001, 13).

Meriam stated at the meeting that the Sheridan Avenue route would significantly increase the traffic coming through more crowded parts of Chico. Robert E. Laughlin of the United Chico Committee got an enthusiastic response when he said the state hadn't thought carefully enough about Chico's schools, neighborhoods, and Bidwell Park. Despite all the passion that many of Chico's people expressed, a Division of Highways spokesperson said, "I haven't heard anything here personally that I think can change the picture materially with respect to the location" (Woodward 1958, 52).

The Sheridan Avenue route's opponents were not ready to give up the fight. On July 18, 1955, the Chico Public School Board officially opposed the Sheridan Avenue route, stating that it cut through four school areas and disrupted pedestrian traffic. The Board requested that the Highway Commission reconsider the Forest Avenue proposal and that any route stay at least one city block from school sites. The United Chico Committee continued its petition campaign and collected 4,229 signatures, representing one-seventh of the 30,000 people who lived in Chico (Woodward 1958).

The Fight Intensifies

On August 11, a state highway engineer recommended adopting the Sheridan Avenue route. Mayor Meriam quickly released a powerful statement that coincided with a public meeting on January 17, 1956. "We oppose the Sheridan Avenue route recommended by the Department of Highways," he said. "We do so, not because of any disagreement with the engineering concerns developed by the highway engineers, but because of non-engineering concerns which we believe to be of prime importance for the welfare of our community" (Woodward 1958, 64-65).

The mayor referred to the more than 4,000 signatures on the United Chico Committee's petitions opposing the Sheridan Avenue route. He declared that, to date, public opinion was mainly against that plan. His comments focused heavily on the impact the Sheridan Avenue route would have on One Mile Recreation Area in Bidwell Park. He described Sycamore Pool, where residents could swim for free in the hot summer. This area also had ball fields, horseshoe courts, and playgrounds. It was located close to downtown Chico and neighborhoods, making it the most accessible recreation area in the park (Woodward 1958).

"We feel that a freeway crossing the park at this point would seriously limit the further development of this activity area, a development we feel will be increasingly important as the population of this part of our county continues its rapid growth," Meriam said (Woodward 1958, 64-65). The Forest Avenue route would cross the park in a less crowded area. A plan to place the freeway there would allow One Mile's facilities to expand as the town's population grew (Woodward 1958).

Meriam also talked about other controversies, including that the Sheridan Avenue route would cut through neighborhoods served by Sierra View and Parkview Schools. He also mentioned that the Forest Avenue route was estimated to cost $2 million less than the Sheridan Avenue proposal. Many city officials and citizens believed that the state was trying to limit Chico's autonomy and rallied around the mayor (Woodward 1958).

"Ted Meriam was one of the most influential Chicoans of the twentieth century, and the freeway was one of the most contentious that came before the City Council in the 1950s," Dave Nopel told me as we sat in his living room. "Bidwell Park made Chico a more participatory community!"

Sheridan Avenue Gains the Upper Hand

The mayor's arguments did not change the state's position. On July 10, 1957, the Division of Highways met with the Butte County and Chico planning commissions in Oroville. The State engineers strongly requested an agreement so work on the freeway could begin. Despite friction, a contract was finally drawn up and submitted to Chico City Council on September 30, 1957. The Butte County Board of Supervisors also received a copy covering areas outside of Chico city limits (Woodward 1958).

The Board of Supervisors unanimously rejected the contract on September 30. Researchers had discovered that the freeway would have to be placed on a twenty-foot-high earth fill because of Chico's high water table. This possible "Great Wall of Chico" strengthened the town's sharp opposition to the state's plan. One letter to the *Chico Enterprise-Record* predicted it would be a large dirt wall bisecting Chico and the park and questioned whether an ugly freeway would actually solve traffic problems (Gage and Patty 1959).

Some Sheridan Avenue opponents reminded everyone that Annie Bidwell's 1905 deed included a reversionary clause, meaning that ownership of the park should revert to her heirs if the city violated her wishes. They argued that she would never agree to have a freeway cross her beloved Vallombrosa and that it was time to use this provision forcefully (Anderson 1983). But Annie's relatives no longer had the power to enforce her wishes. A court decision ruled that the reversionary rights were a type of property that Annie's heirs could sell if they needed money, which they did in 1934 to Wells Fargo Bank to settle her estate's debts (Pierce n.d.). The bank later sold them to a San Francisco insurance company, which deeded these rights to the City of Chico in 1947. This move canceled any claim the Bidwell's heirs had to the park (Pierce n.d.). "The reversionary clause were sold off to pay debts," Wes Dempsey commented.

"The City of Chico wanted to negate the clause that said the park could revert to Annie's heirs if her wishes were violated," Dave Nopel told me as we looked through his extensive files. "I've heard that development along Vallombrosa Avenue, on the park's north side, was getting underway in the post-World War II era. I think there was concern as to whether the reversionary clause could impede this. Could it stop neighborhoods' growth on both sides of the park? This is pure speculation, of course."

Resolution

The battle was long, and some weary citizens began to support the state's recommendations. Some wondered if the United Chico Committee's opposition came from a desire to protect its members' property values. In contrast, others saw the group as a sincere advocate for Chico and the park.

One letter to the editor called the road necessary as an evacuation route in case of a military attack. That's not too surprising with Cold War paranoia in mind. A pro-Sheridan Avenue organization headed by rancher Vernon Fish emerged in March 1958. Fish said that the freeway issue was a done deal, and the city should go along with the Sheridan Avenue route or lose the possibility of a freeway extension for twenty to thirty years. This group quickly gathered 1,000 signatures on a pro-Sheridan Avenue petition (Woodward 1958). Vernon Fish stated in a letter to the *Chico Enterprise-Record,*

> I am against the pressure of the Citizen's Committee which opposes the state adopted freeway along Sheridan Avenue. I see this group applying pressure to

the point where elected officials hesitate to make decisions based on facts for fear of creating disharmony. (Woodward 1958, 78)

The opposition to Sheridan Avenue soon began to weaken. Mayor Meriam and the rest of the Chico City Council seemed surprised that Chico was not completely opposed to the Sheridan Avenue route and indicated that the council and citizenry were changing their opinions. Dave Nopel commented, "Mayor Meriam had the spirit to resist the freeway crossing the park, but as a politician and business leader, he could see that the freeway was going to go somewhere and wondered, 'What is the best spot?' I'm sure it was a hard position to be in; he caught flak from both sides."

A special session of the Chico City Council met on March 31, 1958. The council stated that while it still believed the Forest Avenue route was the best alternative, nothing could be gained by opposing the Highway Commission's position. The council intended to sign the agreement with the State Highways Commission (Talbitzer 1958). The United Chico Committee agreed to abide by the officials' decision, but it continued to present petitions, newspaper ads, and mailings that opposed it (Woodward 1958; Moon 2003).

A few citizens finally focused strongly on the freeway's impact on the park's wild side. A Save Bidwell Park committee circulated petitions that opposed any route that crossed the park, including the Forest Avenue route. This move came too late. On May 12, 1958, the Butte County Board of Supervisors signed the freeway agreement (Woodward 1958). An election for the Board of Supervisors on June 3 seemed to diffuse the issue, especially since pro-Sheridan Avenue candidates were elected.

Chico's City Council approved the agreement with the state on June 1, 1958. Mayor Meriam used the town's strong opposition to the Sheridan Avenue route to pressure the state to fund improvements to the Esplanade, one of Chico's main roads, along with landscaping work on the highway. Skirmishes continued for years, but the issue truly ended in 1960. Judge Bertram James of the Third District Court of Appeals in Sacramento threw out Save Bidwell Park Committee's injunction to block the freeway. The first section of the road through Chico was dedicated in September 1963, effectively ending a local uprising that seems unusual for the conservative 1950s.

What Has the Impact Been?

Jane Ziad commented, "When I came to college in fall 1964, the freeway had been completed, but it was an anomaly. People didn't really know what it was for, and it didn't go anywhere except to the North Valley Plaza. I assume that the through traffic used it, but it was virtually empty."

The freeway's construction was probably inevitable; perhaps it did less damage than if it had crossed a wilder area, such as the section around Forest Avenue. "I don't think the freeway has had much ecological impact," Dave Nopel said. "Maybe it's best that it crossed lower down in the park. It is noisy and unpleasant, but where could it be? It couldn't be west of town because of railroad and agricultural land there. Also, the state agreed to elevate the freeway above the park rather than crossing through it because people were passionate about the park. That was something of a victory, but yes, it was a mess."

As you walk under the overpass, there are murals that artist Gregg Payne painted on the pillars in 2007. They show vibrant western sycamores that grow from the barren, rocky ground while a mallard and other birds fly past them. Payne said he did the paintings to integrate the structure with Bidwell Park. Sadly, some people have painted graffiti on the trees.

In some ways, the park and its wildlife have adapted to the freeway. Swallows cling to pillars in late spring and fly out to grab passing insects. Bats roost in the grooves on the bottom of the overpass, and pipevine swallowtails frequently build their chrysalises, which resemble dead leaves, on the pillars. These creatures seem undisturbed by the overhead noise and exhaust of traffic, but maybe they are more flexible than many hikers.

Traffic Jams

The bitter Highway 99 confrontation contradicts the idea that a small or medium-sized town can escape the intense political battles that often engulf bigger cities. Other confrontations began to pit many good people against each other. Some of these conflicts still have not been entirely resolved. A walk or bike ride through the park will take an explorer to battlegrounds, including the area where citizens clashed over the issue of traffic.

Cars sometimes move along the park's perimeter roads, although a gate blocks them between 11 p.m. and 8 a.m. South Park Drive is limited to one-way traffic moving eastward toward Middle Park. Cars are rare beyond the playground at Caper Acres, just east of Sycamore Pool. A bridge near Five Mile Recreation Area takes wanderers across the creek to Peterson Drive, also called North Park Drive, for the one-way return trip west toward downtown. While the traffic situation is calm now, it was once wild.

Gate closures are nothing new. Annie Bidwell closed access to her Vallombrosa and Chico Canyon in 1905/1906 over concerns of trash and vandalism "on the part of persons who would take liquors with them and thereby render themselves unthoughtful of what they were doing" (*Chico Record* August 28, 1908).

Citizens petitioned her to reopen the gates, offering to police the areas themselves. She responded that she would do so only if the City of Chico and Butte County "made the sale of intoxicating liquors unlawful within their borders . . . in the belief that if we have Chico "dry" and Butte County also, we need not fear the disorders which have obliged the closing of these grounds to the public." Additionally:

> Automobiles cannot be admitted because of danger along the narrow driveways in the canyon and because the comfort of the many cannot be sacrificed for the pleasure of the few. It will I think be generally conceded that the songs of birds, the fragrance and restfulness of the woods, and the safety of children warrant this restriction, especially as automobiles destroy all these blessings. (*Chico Record* August 28, 1908)

Annie would have been aggravated when Chico's growing population led to increased traffic in the park and the town. The Bidwell Park and Playground Commission first discussed the need for signs that clearly stated traffic rules in March 1929. Many autos showed up in places where they did not belong. In March 1933, the Commission discussed whether tow trucks should enter the park to rescue vehicles stuck in the mud. The officials also wondered if rescue vehicles should leave the established roads and venture into undeveloped places, tearing up hillside soil and grass. They considered the need for police on the park's roads in June 1951.

Many Chico citizens use North and South Park Drives responsibly and safely. Chico citizen Cindy commented, "Between 1968 and 1975, my sister and I used to borrow our parents' car, get a soft drink at Long John Silvers' on Mangrove, and drive (at a reasonable speed) through the park. We were familiar with Lower Park as our grandmother used to take us swimming there in the summer at various points along the creek. We also spent hours swimming at the One Mile, where my aunt was a lifeguard years earlier. My brother and I would go there at night to enjoy the cooling waters of the One Mile on hot summer nights. There were very few bicycle riders in Lower Park during those years. I rode my bike frequently in Lower Park with my flute in my backpack and spent many hours sitting along the creek playing my flute."

Sadly, the presence of responsible drivers didn't ensure that everyone would behave in the same way. Both perimeter roads were two-way thoroughfares, and some drivers insisted they had a right to drive as they chose.

"I certainly remember One Mile as a center of partying," Dave Nopel reflected as he handed me a glass of cold water in his house. "People were roaming the streets at night. It's a comment on the growth process. When I was a young person, Chico had 15,000-20,000 people; now it's five times that. The problem is magnified—more and more people, more and more cars."

Wes Dempsey commented, "Some people would use the North and South Park Drive to drive through the park. We had to shut down part of the roads, and there was resistance. Young people would use the roads as raceways. You can still see where South Park Drive hits the freeway; a car would miss the curve, hit an oak, and leave scars. People were killed at that point. We had to seek cooperation from the police and the courts and publicize the rules of the road.

"I was one of those people who wanted to see no cars on South Park Drive. You can still see where bark on trees is chewed away by automobiles. I remember my friend who lived on El Monte Avenue. He used to tell me about tremendous crashes at one or two in the morning. Kids were racing with drinks under their belts. There's a big oak where you can still see the scars."

Another Battle Gets Underway
North and South Park Drives

Dennis Beardsley held several positions with Chico city government, including Bidwell Park's director. He is a lifelong fisherman, hiker, bicyclist, and lover of other outdoor activities. He worked for the East Bay Regional Parks District in the San Francisco Bay Area and the Greater Vallejo Recreation and Parks District before moving to Chico where he served before retiring.

He commented, "North and South Park Roads are not in good condition. They are narrow, and people tend to drive too fast. Anytime you have vehicles (some slow, some fast, some smart, some stupid), walkers, walkers with dogs (on too long leashes), baby strollers, and bicyclists (some respectful, some not), you have opportunities for lots of conflicts and accidents. That is not what Bidwell Park is all about, in my opinion.

"We tried all sorts of ideas, but few were really effective and definitely were confusing for people to figure out. I am sure the problem of money to make opening and closing happen was/is a budget issue. We contracted and, other times, used Park Rangers. I am not suggesting closing any of the existing parking areas or closing One Mile or Five Mile to vehicular traffic. Those are all accessible and should be available."

Walkers, bicyclists, and nature advocates made strong recommendations during the highly politicized 1970s. These fights began in November 1971 when the Bidwell Park and Playground Commission and citizens discussed the idea of closing parts of South Park Drive to vehicles to make room for cyclists and walkers. The Commission recommended in April 1973 that North Park Drive be one-way and limited to westbound traffic; this policy was finally adopted in 1986. Arguments continued over South Park Drive for years.

Local families and swimming enthusiasts quickly objected to this plan. One mother stated that her children frequently swam at Five Mile Recreation Area. She needed to drive them to and from their favorite swimming area and also needed to drive there to check on their safety when they spent long, hot days in the water. The idea of closing the roads to vehicle traffic came up periodically but always found opposition. An editorial in the *Chico News and Review* defended drivers, motorcyclists, horseback riders, and bicyclists who respected the park, stating that problems only arose when people ignored regulations. The editors agreed that the city needed to concentrate on drivers and others who disobeyed park rules.

Still, the roads remained unsafe. "Dave and I witnessed a terrible accident," Betty Nopel told me as we sat in the family's wood-paneled living room. "We could hear a single car coming. We focused on our dog, and then we turned and saw two bicyclists flying through the air. I took off my jacket to cover one cyclist; he was in shock. Four more bikes came then. That driver could have hit all four. That was before the era of park rules and any attempt to bring rules about car use into the park."

Traffic congestion continued to grow, threatening smaller wildlife. Engines' roars drowned out acorn woodpeckers' calls and other birds' sounds. Cyclists and walkers had to watch out, too. South Park Drive was described as an accident-prone area in early 1978, with children's safety becoming a major concern. This was even though the road was now a one-way route.

The Bidwell Park and Playground Commission and citizens responded to this dangerous situation as they continued to argue about the idea of completely closing South Park Drive to vehicles and installing speed bumps. In March 1980, the Commission again proposed temporarily closing South Park Drive to vehicles and building a gate to keep them from this road. A gate was installed on a six-month trial basis, but in October, the parks' neighbors complained that people trying to get into the park at night vandalized it and turned it into a party spot.

People With Disabilities Enter the Debate

The reality that people with disabilities needed to use vehicles to reach picnic and swimming areas rose during the late 1980s. A speaker at the Commission's November 1988 meeting mentioned that Butte County had more people with disabilities than many other California counties and that limiting drivers' access to the park would prevent these citizens from enjoying it. Another citizen described how his three hearing-impaired children enjoyed riding through the park in the family car. Others who addressed this meeting supported the people with disabilities and opposed closing park roads to vehicles. One man recommended that the city keep the roads open to drivers but strongly enforce traffic regulations and increase fines for people who drove faster than the speed limit. The meeting ended inconclusively with the Commission deciding not to act on the traffic issue at that time.

An activist with a disability again raised this point at the August 1992 Bidwell Park and Playground Commission meeting. He also wondered if bicyclists and joggers damaged the park more than vehicles did. Nature enthusiasts replied that engine exhaust sickened plants so much that many leaves turned brown.

"Access for people with disabilities is a valid issue," Roger Lederer commented as we sipped black tea in a café, "but most cars you saw on the roads do not seem to include these people. They seem to be filled with teenagers."

"There could be other ways for people with limited mobility to get into the park," artist Carol Burr said. "Shuttle buses are one idea."

Something of a Compromise

Arguments flared through the 1990s, but the issue finally came to some resolution by the early twenty-first century. Vehicles were barred from the park before 9 a.m., so cyclists and walkers could use these routes without worrying about accidents. Regulations also prohibited drivers from parking in shady spots to avoid injuring oak's roots. North and South Park Drives roads became one-way routes for cars and bicycles. The maximum speed for both vehicles would be twenty-five miles per hour or less, and the park needed strict rules against reckless travel. Off-road parking was prohibited unless a driver had written permission to park in an area for maintenance (Eseaff 2013).

Park managers continue to work to improve access for families and for people with disabilities. Short trails that are easy to follow lead to picnic and swimming areas from parking areas on Vallombrosa Avenue on the park's northern borders. From East 8th Street, a paved path that a person in a wheelchair can follow connects the World of Trees parking lot with picnic areas.

Dennis Beardsley commented, "Restricting vehicular access and providing for people with mobility issues is a good strategy. We made arrangements to improve access to reservations and special events. Also, accessibility was improved in the restrooms at Five Mile and One Mile Recreation Areas and facilities throughout Middle and Lower Park in the 1990s to meet the Americans with Disabilities Act requirements. I do not believe that being able to drive throughout Lower Bidwell Park equates to ensuring accessibility. For example, people in wheelchairs enjoy the serenity and peaceful enjoyment of North Park Drive without vehicles as much as

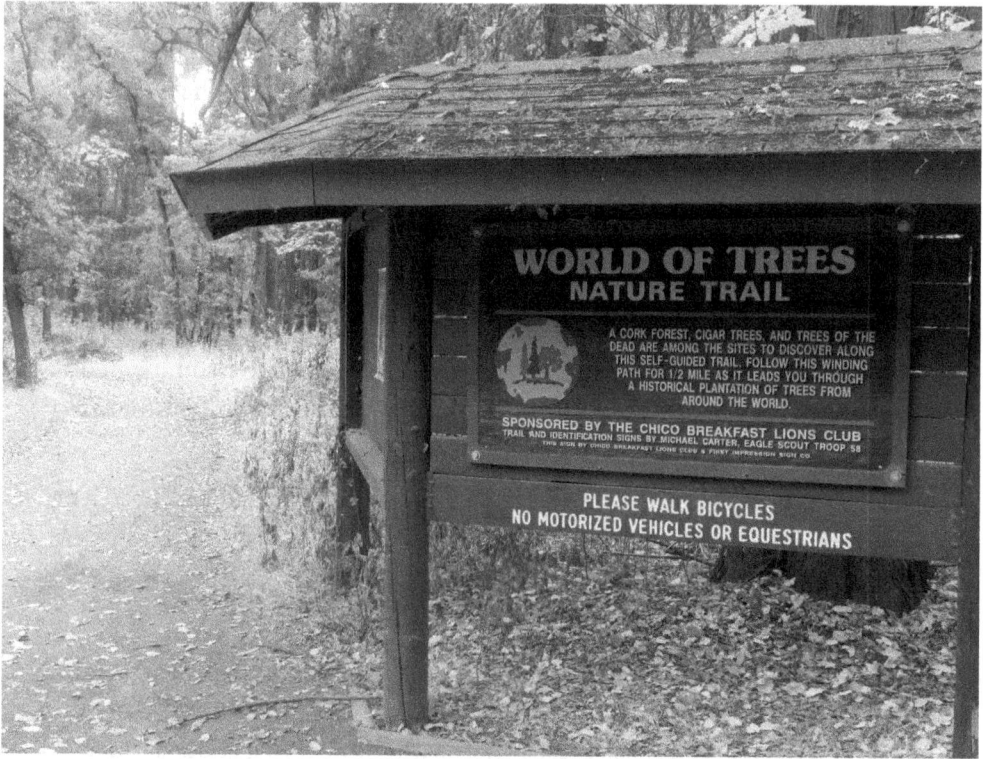

World of Trees nature trail.

people walking for the same experience. Everyone can access the family picnic areas, walkways, and restrooms at Five Mile, Cedar Grove, and One Mile."

Still, the Americans with Disabilities Act's passage came after most of the park's trails and facilities were built, and more work is needed.

The Bidwell Park and Playground Commission agreed with the idea of a human-powered shuttle in late 2019 when it approved a proposal for a pedal train on South Park Drive. Kate and I had to chuckle. We had recently visited Berlin, where we saw a train/bar customers pedaling around busy streets as they enjoyed beer. Commissioners laughed and promised no one would drink as they rode through the park. We look forward to joining other passengers who pump their feet frantically to move the multi-car, open-air train under the sycamores and oaks. This will be another kind of adventure in the park!

Upper Park
Invasion of the Off-Road Vehicles (ORVs)

When you walk along the Rim Trail, high on the volcanic Tuscan Formation hillsides, think about its strange history. You'll find yourself faced with cattle that stare at you over a barbed wire fence as they graze on the city's Bidwell Ranch open space. Your walk offers views of California's Coast Range mountains to the west, the extinct volcanoes called the Sutter Buttes to the south, and the nearby Bidwell Park Golf Course. Purple lupines grow on the trail's side, and flat frying pan poppies thrive between grayish-brown rocks that block your way. What would it be like to roar through this area in an off-road vehicle?

While the freeway and traffic issues divided the city, there was consensus about the problem of motorcycles and off-road vehicles in Upper Park's rough hills. These steep slopes only held three inches of topsoil. Damage from thick, powerful tires contributed to soil erosion when heavy winter rain hit the park. Plants and animals that thrived in these rugged areas began to lose their habitat; much of the displaced soil wound up in Big Chico Creek, clogging spots between underwater stones where salmon needed to deposit their eggs.

"ORVs were a problem in the 1960s and beyond until a policy of containing them was put in place," Dave Nopel commented as I petted his dog Tipper, who always demanded my attention when I visited Dave's house. "Eventually, a rule said, 'Look, you can't just head into the hills, you're going to get a ticket.' That's a part of natural values, letting some raccoon or quail have turf without these monster machines rolling down."

A Chico State recreation class asked the Bidwell Park and Playground Commission for permission to drive motorcycles and off-road vehicles in Upper Park in March 1971. The commissioners agreed with the proposal as long as the class did not advertise this activity to the public. Commissioners also said the club could drive off-road vehicles in the area if they entered it from the west side, which was close to roads. Their position and the community's changed as environmental consciousness grew in Chico. In January 1973, ornithologist and park defender Roger Lederer told the Bidwell Park and Playground Commission about the impact of off-road vehicles and motorcycles.

"If this unauthorized traffic continues, there will be nothing left but mud and rocks," Lederer told the Commission. "Just a motorcycle track. A rut takes fifteen years to return to its natural state." He added that strict rule enforcement was the only way to deal with this situation. Roger mentioned that he had tried to tell some offenders that their behavior was illegal and they could be cited. He stopped doing this when their aggressiveness made him fear for his safety.

He suggested that CSU, Chico, students could be hired at $1.50 per hour to enforce rules and keep motorized vehicles out of the hills. Other citizens recommended hiring a full-time ranger or regular park patrol unit. The park could install signs stating that vehicles could not go off the roads, and violators would be fined. Some doubted that education and warnings would have much of an impact on this behavior.

The issue intensified on February 12, 1974, as photos in the *Chico Enterprise-Record* showed vehicles' impact on destruction to vegetation on an Upper Park slope. The captions to the images described how off-road drivers removed warning signs a few hours after they were placed. Someone had removed a $1,200 gate installed to close Upper Park Road to vehicles at night and drove onto the Bidwell Park Golf Course. Violators removed "Road Closed" signs and barriers of logs, brush, and rocks. City council members stated that armed patrols might be the only way to curb illegal driving (Milliken 1974a, b).

The City Takes a Stand

"People would drive up into the hills in trucks and cut firewood," Wes Dempsey added as we examined his files. "If they had garbage, they'd dump it. High school kids would hold parties late at night. People put up gates and set hours to keep people out of the park. We had to hire people to lock and unlock gates. That shut down the party business and the trashing that went with it."

A joint meeting of the City Council and the Bidwell Park and Playground Commission occurred on February 14, 1974. Part of the discussion was about the ineffectiveness of signs and barriers to trails, and people wondered what could be done.

Some cyclists and off-road vehicle owners acknowledged that irresponsible drivers damaged the park but wondered why responsible people were targeted. Motorcyclist Jamie Payne wrote in a letter to the *Chico Enterprise-Record* commented that there were no places to drive. ORV registration fees funded spaces for off-road vehicle drivers, but one that had existed at Black Butte Lake closed, and nothing replaced it (Payne 1974). In March, commissioners reported a discussion with the Four-By-Fours. This off-road vehicle club understood the situation's seriousness and offered to help educate other drivers about the rules. They also asked the city's help in finding another area where ORV owners could drive. Suggestions included Bureau of Land Management territory outside of the park.

Citizens began to chime in with suggestions for solutions to the problems. One letter to the editor of the *Chico Enterprise-Record* recommended that anyone who saw an off-road vehicle report it to the police and take pictures of the license plate if they could. The writer also suggested one-way spikes, along with warning signs, could be placed where ORVs left paved roads. They would be sharp enough to puncture a tire but too dull to cut through a boot and injure a hiker's foot (Larson 1974).

Roger Lederer (1974) stated in a letter to the *Chico Enterprise-Record* that drivers frequently disregarded signs and warnings. If a park defender approached them, they ignored the information that the person shared or claimed they didn't know their behavior was illegal. The editors responded to this and other letters by suggesting that the city

> make park crimes expensive for vehicle vandals by arresting a few and assessing maximum fines. It is our belief that hitting the off-road vehicles where it hurts in the pocketbook to the tune of several hundred dollars will have more impact than warning signs, educational programs, etc.

Chico united to save the rugged hills. In March 1974, members of the Four-By-Fours spent a whole day moving logs and boulders to block paths created by other ORV drivers. Pressure from many sources made the city begin to take enforcement of the regulations seriously. Officials made an example of a young driver caught on the golf course with a $1,100 fine (*Chico Enterprise-Record* 1974b).

Wes Dempsey said, "The situation took a couple of years to resolve. That involved getting the Park Superintendent to contact the police. He would arrange for people to get a ticket, but the judge would not think it was worth his time. The Park Commission would make rules, but there was no enforcement. Finally, they got cooperation from the city, and the judge would get a handle on the situation."

The city's increasingly stricter policy finally encouraged ORV drivers and motorcyclists to stay away from the park's hillsides. A few people still considered it civil disobedience to drive into the hills and go around the gate that sometimes blocks rugged Upper Park Drive, while others managed to cut the bolt off and throw it into the bushes. This situation may have eased up; you don't see a single ORV as you wander through clusters of blue and white Birds' Eye Gilia, scarlet columbine, and goldfields. The hills have not completely recovered from reckless driving. Chico's park lovers will still need to protect them for years.

The iconic Monkey Face (top center of cliff) peering down at a
family of ducks on Horseshoe Lake.

CHAPTER SIX

The World of Horseshoe Lake

Humans Built This Lake

Horseshoe Lake sits at the base of hillsides where Middle and Upper Park merge. This roughly U-shaped water body looks like it was bent when a giant tossed it too hard at a post in a game of horseshoes. Visitors who think this is a natural lake where the Maidu once fished and gathered bird eggs are stunned to learn it has existed for less than a century.

Galaxies of wildflowers thrive on its grass and stone-covered banks in spring. Kate and I always find well-named goldfields gathering with yellow and white tidy tips, purple lupines peeking above the grass, surrounded by fiddlenecks' curling orange blossoms. Turkey vultures love to roost in a dead tree by the lake, and a pair of bald eagles occasionally join them while a great blue heron struts and forages among reeds. Lines of very young Canada geese drift past, led and followed by adults. Kildeer scurry along the rocky shore calling "KILDEE!" sometimes holding their wings in a bent, broken shape to distract predators from their ground nests. We're especially fond of a mallard trio: two males and a female we've named Jules, Jim, and Catherine. What kind of wild movie would French New Wave filmmaker François Truffaut have made about this love triangle?

"Many people were unfamiliar with the lake at first, but its popularity has grown over the years," writer Cindy Wolff said. "In my youth growing up in Chico, Horseshoe Lake was a known entity but nothing significant as an attraction. We were not fond of its proximity to the shooting range. I never went to Upper Park with my family as a child since there was plenty of outdoor access where I grew up in north Chico. As an adult, I am a frequent visitor to Horseshoe Lake for walks with my dog and friends. I have also taken my nephew to fish during the annual fishing events there."

Families gather to sit in folding chairs and fish for the catfish and other species that the city stocks. Dogs that come with hikers love to splash in the water and sometimes rush toward herons and geese, which ignore them. A small wooden building covered with acorn woodpeckers' stored food is usually silent, but it sometimes reverberates with metallic echoes when gun enthusiasts practice their skills behind its walls. This noise reminds walkers of the lake's history and the struggles that centered on it.

"There were all kinds of things that came and went, and nobody knows about them," John Merz said while sipping coffee at an outdoor café. "When we talk about these things, it's in the context of the population of the city. In the 1950s, when the city had a population of 20,000, the park was in many ways a wilderness."

"I wish I could see Chico and the park in those days!" I mused. "People thought the Forest Avenue area was part of our town's outskirts."

John nodded and added, "And Bidwell Park is not just for Chico; it's a regional park!"

The Lake's Birth and Youth

Official documents do not clearly indicate the exact date for Horseshoe Lake's construction. The Works Progress Administration (WPA) wanted to build a "restraining dam" in the creek in 1937. Later records show that a dam and reservoir provided the golf course with water by 1939. Water came via a ditch built at Diversion Dam near the Bear Hole swimming area in Upper Park (Lydon 1977).

"Up at Diversion Dam, you can find the initials '1938' on a weir," Wes Dempsey told me in his living room. "It was a WPA thing. Diversion Dam feeds into a flume. They protected the flume from winter flooding anytime it crossed a creek. There's a concrete structure where they could close it off with boards and regulate the flow. The ditch was dirt on top of volcanic rock. I don't think they got much water out of the creek; the ditch leaked all the time. When I came here, the golf course was pumping water from the creek, not the lake. The lake was used for fishing. The golf course had stopped using the lake as a water source by 1948, apparently because the ditch leaked, and they relied on a pump to provide water directly from Big Chico Creek. Golfers asked the Commission to take charge of the dam and the lake. The Commission replied that it was in favor of necessary repairs on the lake and stated it might agree to buy it."

The Lure of Boats, Waterskis, and Planes

Many Chico's citizens came up with creative suggestions for the lake's use, but these proposals reflected the idea that people had every right to develop outdoor areas in any way they chose. In September 1946, the Bidwell Park and Playground

Horseshoe Lake looking northeast.

Commission initially prohibited using boats on the lake since the waves they created damaged the shores. The Commission also banned swimming within 300 feet of Diversion Dam to ensure the current wouldn't hurl people over this structure. The Chico Rod & Gun Club offered to clean up the Diversion Dam area in June 1950 so fish could be introduced for anglers to catch. However, the club decided in July that this would be too big a project and decided to cancel it.

The Commission's thoughts about boating and other water activities gradually changed. In May 1955, a waterskiing club asked permission to hold a show on the lake and to sell ice cream. Club members planned the event to raise funds for a proposal to enlarge the lake for additional activities. The commissioners approved this idea in principle as long as it didn't interfere with activities at the nearby shooting range, although they hadn't agreed so far to a plan to make the lake bigger. In November, the body said they would favor this expansion if funds were available. Some speakers expressed concerns about how the plan to channel water from Big Chico Creek to the lake would affect downstream swimming areas. The Commission's minutes do not mention this project's ultimate fate.

"Around the time I came along, people wanted to enlarge Horseshoe Lake and One Mile so they could run these paddle boats," Wes Dempsey said. "They did some demonstration waterskiing. They lined the irrigation ditch with eight-inch concrete pipe so water could flow there from the creek. Evidently, that didn't work either. There was a big pile of pipe by Horseshoe Lake. I don't know where that went."

A group of outboard motor enthusiasts wanted boating on the lake in 1952. Water skiers also wished to use the lake for their sport and asked if they could use the golf course's old pump to keep it filled. The Bidwell Park and Playground Commission favored these proposals as long as the boaters didn't interfere with activities at the nearby rifle range. Commissioners and other citizens increasingly agreed that these activities would make the lake a more popular and fun place for Chico's citizens.

A hobby club asked permission to fly model airplanes over the lake in October 1979. They also wanted to level a field west of the lake for a landing strip. Commissioners wondered if this activity would impact hikers and others using the area. Could accidents, collisions, and the possibility of a fire starting in dry times be possible outcomes of this activity? Some commissioners preferred by then to maintain the park as a natural area as far as possible. They described Horseshoe Lake as an area with fragile soils that were not conducive to the landing field's construction.

Horseshoe Lake looking west.

Gunshots by the Lake

Gun culture is and has always been popular in the United States. The number of guns has grown with the population. People use them for hunting, target shooting, and other outdoor recreation as well as for personal safety (Yamane, Yamane, and Ivory 2020).

"The National Guard had a shooting range near the lake since World War I," Wes Dempsey told me. "These were army rifles, so the shooters were a quarter mile from the targets."

The Bidwell Park and Playground Commission renewed the initial lease for an official firing range in November 1929. The National Guard and Chico Police Department solely used this range for years, but local gun clubs increasingly wanted to share it. In May 1951, the Commission decided that the Guard would have priority over civilians for use of the shooting range, but affiliated gun clubs could use a smaller area. An illegal skeet-shooting range, where people shot at discs flung through the air, appeared in 1947. This ran the risk of shooters not seeing hikers and others in the area.

Wes Dempsey commented, "The Chico Rod & Gun Club set up a rifle range where the parking lot is. They expanded that to six or eight shooting stations. They even had a shade over the stations. They fired into the hills east of Horseshoe Lake. I remember hiking above the lake. I ran into this tearful mother with two little kids."

John Merz added, "I remember hiking on North Rim trail on the ridge top. There were guns going off, and I heard something moving in the trees. I don't know if it was bullets; the gun range supposedly posted signs warning people of their presence, but hikers were coming from all directions and didn't always see them. People questioned whether the gun range should be in the park at all. Part of the justification was historical precedent; it had been there for a long time."

Dave Nopel remarked, "In the 1950s, when you went beyond the Hooker Oak and Horseshoe Lake, you were outside the city's limits. You had so few people hiking and biking in that area that a person could just drive out there and start shooting. I don't think you needed permission. In the post-World War II era, the military still used its old shooting range. Targets popped up and down out of bunkers."

Commissioners and citizens became increasingly concerned with safety of the shooting range during the 1970s. In January 1975, commissioners discussed the need for earth-filled bunkers made from soil and rocks that could block flying bullets. They also recommended fences and signs around the range to inform hikers about the danger of being near gunfire.

The Chico Rod & Gun Club and Archery Club

An archery range was established in Upper Park in 1947. "The archery range was a growing concern in the 1950s and 1960s," Wes Dempsey said. "The archery people decided to consolidate with the gun range and move the targets to the lake. They wanted to cut down trees to improve the appearance of the range."

The Archery Club approached the Commission in August 1976, stating that its members would volunteer to build a new range by the lake. The old range had been vandalized, and they needed to move. The group requested $200 per year from the Commission for the facility's maintenance and upkeep. Some commissioners stated that they should not agree to this idea before the archers cleaned up the site they planned to abandon and that the city should not subsidize private interest groups that wanted to sponsor activities in the park.

In September, some commissioners raised questions about potential liability with a new archery range and asked if a master archer would be present to maintain safety. Would there be a fence that could block hikers and others from wandering onto the range? Would the archery and shooting ranges require police protection? Opponents began to feel that all organized recreational activities should be phased out around Horseshoe Lake and that the area should be restored to as natural a state as possible. But the Bidwell Park and Playground Commission approved the ranges, and they remained by the lake for years.

During the following years, the Chico Rod & Gun Club continued to defend its presence in the park against mounting concerns over safety. In July 1987, gun enthusiasts told the Bidwell Park and Playground Commission that the shooting range existed to train children on safe hunting practices. One local child had even won a national championship in marksmanship. Shooting range supporters called the facility part of Chico's heritage and claimed it was safer than when people shot from any place they chose in the park.

The National Rifle Association told the Commission that shooting was America's safest sport. They added that Americans have a Second Amendment right to bear arms but stressed that people must be trained in safe gun practices. Other gun owners said the range should stay in its present location since hikers and other park users were scarce near the lake.

One shooting enthusiast who attended the same Commission meeting recommended beautifying the shooting range and making it an important part of Chico. Gun owners stated that some local children had received awards for their shooting and might be able to participate in the Olympics if they could practice and get more training. Another talked about how difficult it had been to maintain the

The indoor-shooting range with acorn woodpecker holes on the outside wooden walls.

range and described the difficulty of moving boulders so bullets would not ricochet from them. Gun enthusiasts mentioned that shooting ranges were dangerous when houses and neighborhoods were nearby, but this range was far from where people lived.

Commissioners and others increasingly favored finding another location for the shooting range after viewing a critical slide show that presented images of the range in disrepair. Speakers called the range an eyesore and recommended that it be removed. Gun club members responded that the Commission did not represent their interests and that hikers harassed them and stood in front of them when they wanted to shoot. Some took a more conciliatory approach in August when they suggested that the gun club could be used as a soccer and baseball field when shooters were not present. Some claimed the shooting range was less damaging to the park than cars or bicycles.

Commissioners continued to support the idea of relocation, mentioning that ricocheting bullets were a safety issue in the area. A motion supporting the range's relocation passed in March 1988, and the Commission recommended that the issue appear on the City Council's agenda. The council called for the removal of the rifle range in July 1988 and formally canceled its license in August. They recommended that it should move by the summer of 1989. Commissioners suggested that the archery range should also be moved but said it might be possible for the indoor-shooting range to stay.

"There was a mountain of shotgun pellets and pieces of the clay pigeons they shot at, "Wes Dempsey told me. "They had to decontaminate that early in my time, in 1958. The rifle range was eventually shut down because people worried about kids fishing in the lake. There's still an indoor-shooting range."

"The outdoor-shooting range ended in the late 1980s," Dave Nopel added. "The city had to do the major clean-up of lead and broken skeets. Bleachers, bunkers, and other facilities needed to be removed at city expense."

"When you get down to it, common sense prevailed, "John Merz commented. "The City Attorney's attitude toward the gun club was, 'Are you guys nuts? You're going to get your asses sued!' That would have happened with a ricochet or something."

The wooden building by the lake still offers people chances to practice shooting skills. Shots sometimes ping against its walls with metallic echoes, but the building is usually silent.

Guns Again

The issue of guns in the park, one of the 1980s biggest controversies, returned in March 1995 when the Chico Rod & Gun Club proposed installing a new skeet-shooting range near Horseshoe Lake. Gun enthusiasts commented that shooting helped kids gain confidence, and it was a better activity than the use of drugs. The club offered to place signs and warning cones near the shooting range, although they claimed there was no history of accidents at the old shooting range. They also suggested that there would be no environmental damage since the skeets would be made from clay that would break down to form good fertilizer. Migratory birds were uncommon at the lake, and the skeet shooting would not disturb resident birds.

The Bidwell Park and Playground Commission again questioned whether a shooting range was compatible with the park and if gunshots would impact hikers and bike riders. At the same time, gun club members claimed that the concentration of lead in the lake and soil around the lake was low. The commissioners mentioned that even a small amount could hurt children's nervous systems and wondered who would be responsible for cleaning up the toxins. Club members replied that pollutants were not present at other skeet ranges that used clay targets, and no one had needed to remove them. In October 1996, the Commission rejected these arguments and voted to deny the request for the skeet-shooting range, but they would help the Rod and Gun find other facilities near the airport or elsewhere. The club reluctantly agreed to this move.

Discoveries near Horseshoe Lake in 2002 supported the Commission's attitude toward the skeet range. Dennis Beardsley described the contamination in a dirt bank that blocked bullets on the outdoor rifle and skeet-shooting range between the 1930s and 1984. Researchers worried that pollution might find its way to fish in the lake (Gascoyne 2002).

The Butte County Department of Public Health said that frequent visits to this area could hurt young children's health. Officials expressed concern about the impact on Chico Rotary Club's annual Hooked on Fishing event, which tries to offer young people an alternative activity to drug use. The cleanup was declared to be nearly complete by September 2003, but leftover shells, arrows, and toxic glue from skeets remained until 2005.

How's the Lake Today?

Horseshoe Lake is now where people gather to hike, walk dogs, and fish. It remains a shallow pool, fed by winter and spring runoff. While it loses water and shrinks during the summer, it never turns dry. A report in the late 1990s described it as a water body where phytoplankton, tiny photosynthetic organisms that drift in the water, form a basis for the food web. Very tiny drifting animals called zooplankton eat these and are themselves food for fish and other larger creatures.

Many non-native fish have been introduced to the lake over the years. Golden shiners and several other species breed here (Maslin 1997). The Commission instituted a catch-and-release policy for people twelve and older in February 1976. The city and the Chico Rotary Club bring several thousand pounds of channel catfish for Hooked on Fishing, an annual event encouraging children to fish instead of experimenting with drugs. Fishing enthusiasts who are fifteen years old and younger can fish for free and without a license. Children between one and five years old get to visit a "Huck Finn" pond. Rods and reels are available, and children can take the fish they catch home. Kate and I walked by the lake the day after one of these events and were impressed that trash was practically absent.

Chico Community Observatory

People will probably always disagree about how the lake area should be used. Some park enthusiasts even criticize the Chico Community Observatory, which sits near the lake's western shore. They feel the building blocks views of the hills and is out of place. I love astronomy and ecology, and the observatory is an excellent addition to the area. Astronomy is a type of nature study requiring a night sky that is relatively far from city lights.

Kate and I made our way to the observatory in 2019, on the fiftieth anniversary of the first moon landing. A large group took turns gazing at Jupiter, Saturn, and the Swan Nebulae through telescopes and munched on Moon Pies and Milky Way bars.

Chico Community Observatory.

The moon wouldn't rise until 11 p.m. that night, but one volunteer led us outside at 10 p.m. for a tour of the summer constellations. He used a laser pointer to show us Cassiopeia, Hercules, Pegasus, and many others. The crowd was quiet as a church's congregation until he named a small constellation, and a thrilled child repeated, "Delphinus the Dolphin!" The observatory is far healthier for the Horseshoe Lake area than waterskiing or skeet shooting. Still, we can never forget the wild battles over the lake, so we can make sure this area will stay as healthy as possible.

• • • • • • • • • • • • • • • • • • •

The lake becomes quiet at dusk as the sun rushes westward toward the Coast Range mountains. These ridges turn purple and then brown as darkness comes. The autumn moon slowly appears and grows strong, greeted by the chirps from thousands of crickets. A few dogs still splash in the lake, but their owners call them, and they walk toward cars together. Parents and kids who love to fish fold their chairs as they prepare to go home, and the world grows peaceful and chilled, comforting many people in these troubled times.

CHAPTER SEVEN

Fore!

Commissioners Meet the Golf Course

A sign across Upper Park Road from Horseshoe Lake announces everyone is welcome in Bidwell Park Golf Course's clubhouse for breakfast or lunch. I drink mint tea at an outdoor table on a warm October afternoon. The irrigated greens are emerald, but the introduced grasses that surround them have turned golden brown. Most of the course is flat, but oaks crowned with mistletoe surround the greens.

Men wearing dark shorts, T-shirts, and caps advise each other on the best strategy to tee off. Nearby women match each other's black pants and pink tops, making me think they are part of a club. People seem responsible about caring for the area, although I note one large group of balls that someone left on one of the greens. I will be honest; I have never played a round of golf. I wondered how far these good-natured peoples' right to relax can fit with the preservationists' point of view.

Dave Nopel told me, "I don't think people knew what it meant to have a public park in a community or what it meant to people bent on taming the natural world. Annie dies in 1918, and she's not there to see over the park. Two years later, people say, 'Let's build a golf course!'"

Five golfers petitioned the Bidwell Park and Playground Commission to allow a nine-hole golf course in remote Upper Park on March 1, 1920, saying they would cover all expenses. While the Bidwell's friends, guests, and employees used this wild area for picnics, swimming, and carriage rides, few other people seemed to wander into the park's undeveloped regions. They often limited their visits to Sycamore Pool, Five Mile Recreation Area, and other popular spots. The Bidwell Park and

Playground Commission probably felt that little-visited Upper Park would be an excellent area for the golf course.

Work on the nine-hole golf course began in 1920 when people removed rocks and weeds and did other work on the site.[1] Local families brought picnics and shovels to help work on the construction project. Many later stated that their work deepened family connections to the course for years to come. Children probably ran and played while adults laughed and talked as they worked. Golfers played their first rounds on the course in 1921; the first tournament occurred in 1922 ("This Is Our Story"—Bidwell Golf Course Clubhouse exhibit). Payment was fifty cents for a game with an annual membership fee of twelve dollars.

While there were disagreements over the course's funding and administration, the Bidwell Park and Playground Commission seems to have generally supported its presence for many years. In September 1925, the Commission agreed to cooperate with the Chico Golf Club on building a clubhouse, with the club's request for a deep well pump to replace the inadequate facilities and to fund its insurance. In September 1929, commissioners favorably discussed sharing the park's revenue to maintain the course because of its importance to the community. They also supported funds to improve one of the hills on the course and paid for gasoline and operators for equipment to repair erosion by Big Chico Creek in 1936. The Commission regularly discussed the course's operations and several notes in the minutes show that they were generally satisfied with its performance.

The course's popularity and the revenue it raised increased dramatically during the 1940s and 1950s. The commissioners agreed to fund a barbecue pit and to install tables and benches near the clubhouse in April 1950. They discussed the possibility of the Commission's funding maintenance for the clubhouse in May and considered installing signs directing traffic to the course at the October meeting. When Horseshoe Lake proved to be an unreliable water source, commissioners authorized the park supervisor to take bids to install a pipe that would deliver water from Big Chico Creek to the golf course in July 1951. They accepted bids for a tractor to maintain the course in February 1952 and discussed the vegetation that would be planted on the course in June 1952.

In January 1953, a women's golf club proposed constructing a swimming area on the course. The commissioners considered this idea but decided at the March meeting

---

1   The golf course became 18 holes in 1957. A bulldozer was hired for $5,000 to "carve fairways through the olive groves across the creek. Some golfers sprinkled grass seed in the loamy soil as they played, and the fairways grew rapidly. The greens were another story. They were built by the Parks Department with sawdust and dirt, and some were like putting on a washboard until the traffic helped smooth them out." (Murray 1999a, b).

Bidwell Park Golf Course greens.

that construction on that part of the creek would be too expensive and that winter rains could flood and damage the spot. They also noted at the March meeting that the course had received 150 tons of manure for the fairway and greens and that staff had removed fifty-five trees from a new driving range. Swimming became an issue again in August 1955 when the Commission agreed with the golf club that people who swam in the creek near the course brought too much traffic to the course's parking lot and the nearby road. Commissioners agreed to post signs saying the lot was closed after 9 p.m., except when official golf club events occurred.

Tensions over how the golf course's land would be used arose in the early 1960s when California State University track team members requested access for practice runs. The Commission disagreed, stating that golfing in the area made other activities dangerous—no one wanted to be hit by a stray golf ball! Several years later, the park's advisory body agreed to restrict swimming in Big Chico Creek within two hundred yards of the course to avoid accidents.

Like the controversies centered on Horseshoe Lake, these spats show how divided Chico's people felt about Annie Bidwell's condition that the park belonged to all the town's citizens. Would she say that each private organization could use a part of the park for its favorite activity and exclude others from that area? Others felt that Annie would insist that people had to share the park and require that no one group could exclude others from the territory it claimed. These disagreements were mild compared with the long argument over the golf course's plan to sell beer.

The Battle Over Beer

Americans have always had a complex relationship with alcohol. Many early colonists loved to drink and saw their favorite beverages as healthy and invigorating. Drunkenness was a failure of an individual, and it could not be attributed to alcohol itself. The later temperance movement confronted these ideas. These activists saw booze as addictive, and possibly poisonous, even if one drank moderately. Drunkards were victims of that devil alcohol and were not just people who used a healthy pleasure irresponsibly (Gerstein and Dry 1985).

Alcoholism weakened families, which prohibitionists saw as the base of American society and culture. They claimed that if bars and distributors closed, alcohol would be unavailable and the problem would vanish (Gerstein and Dry 1985). Annie Bidwell expressed this attitude when her deed forbade the production and sale of alcohol in her Vallombrosa and when she temporarily closed part of the park in 1908 because of the piles of beer bottles. She stated that people who had drunk too much were "unthoughtful of what they were doing" (*Chico Record* 1908).

Prohibitionists triumphed when the Eighteenth Amendment to the Constitution prohibited the manufacture, sale, and distribution of alcohol in the United States beginning in 1920. This spawned an underground market controlled by ruthless gangs, and the frequent violence that erupted withered support for Prohibition. This led to the adoption of the Twenty-First Amendment to the United States Constitution, which officially ended Prohibition in 1933. Many peoples' attitudes changed, and some saw the manufacture of alcohol as a way to create jobs during the Great Depression (History.com Editors 2009).

Gradually, many Americans came to believe that alcoholism was a disease but that most people could drink without experiencing harmful effects. Alcohol and people who enjoyed it were not evil, but some people's body chemistry reacted badly to wine, beer, and spirits and they needed help for this condition (Gerstein and Dry 1985).

Golfers may have shared this perspective in August 1975 when they approached the Bidwell Park and Playground Commission saying that a businessman wanted to serve food over the counter but would only do so if he could sell beer. They commented that most golf courses in California served alcohol, so they should also have that right. The sale of alcohol would make the course self-sufficient and less dependent on the city for funds.

Some citizens worried that the presence of alcohol could make conditions dangerous when people who had drunk beer drove on the park's roads. Many people who opposed the sale of booze agreed that the course needed to increase its revenue source. Commissioner Wes Dempsey proposed in October 1975 that a restaurant be established but that all of the profits would go to the golf course and none to the city. He was careful not to endorse the sale of beer.

As the situation grew tense, some citizens wondered if Bidwell Park was an appropriate spot for golf. They called it an activity that appealed to one part of the community but not everyone. Golfers and their supporters defended their presence, countering that they could not understand why golf was singled out among all the activities in the park.

In November 1975, golfers proposed the golf course should become a semi-private facility that could control its affairs. The non-profit Bidwell Park Golf Club agreed to take charge of the course's management and leased it from the city in 1982 (Bidwell Park Golf Course Mission Statement 1982). This body eventually hired Empire Golf to manage day-to-day operations in the park, including a café in the clubhouse in October 2012. This group oversaw cafés at other courses in Northern California that served alcohol (*Golf Course Trades* 2015).

The Battle Brews

In January 1983, golfers said they only wanted to sell alcohol in a small part of the clubhouse where it could be controlled, and the profits would help fund the course. They argued they could manage alcohol consumption better by selling it than if individuals brought their booze. Some Bidwell Park and Playground commissioners agreed and stated that values had changed since Annie Bidwell's time. They mentioned that swimming pools, rifle ranges, and asphalt roads were also not part of her vision. Besides, Annie's wishes were violated when businesses on the downtown property she had deeded to the city started selling alcohol. This seemed to make the sale of beer at the golf course less critical than if Chico were an alcohol-free town.

Some opponents of beer sales responded by again questioning the course's existence and asking why a private group should be able to take over part of the park for its own use. They mentioned the reversionary clause in Annie Bidwell's deed, which stated that Annie's heirs should claim possession of the park if policies that violated her wishes came to pass. The arguments remained heated, and the Commission and City Council opposed the sale of beer in 1995.

The City Council asked the Commission to revisit the issue of beer sales after Empire Golf began to manage the café in 2012. Empire Golf stated that it had difficulty competing with other courses whose cafés sold beer and that while alcohol was not allowed in the park, drinking was very present and out of control. Beer cans were visible in the park, including those some golfers brought to the course. A license to sell alcohol would empower golf officials to control consumption on

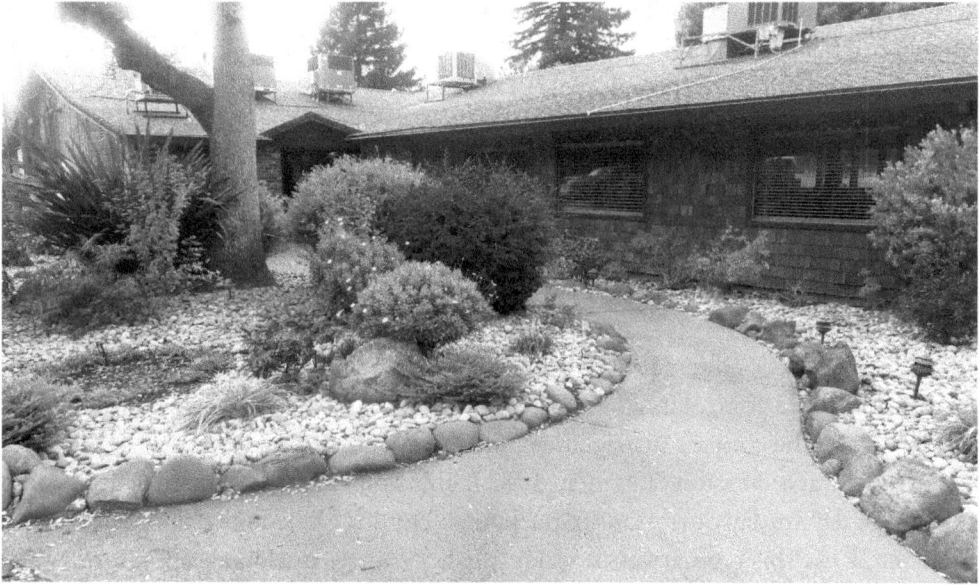

Bidwell Park Golf Course clubhouse.

the course. Golfers commented that the café would only sell beer when responsible golfers played during the daytime, and the café wouldn't become a late-night hangout or a party scene (Bidwell Park and Playground Commission 2013).

Many people got tired of this issue. In October 2013, the Bidwell Park and Playground Commission recommended sales occur only during the day when people played golf and did not happen away from the course, that beer be sold from a tap and not from glass bottles, and that the clubhouse staff be trained in California's recommended safe ways of serving alcohol. The City Council agreed to the sale of beer in January 2014 (Hardee 2014).

"In light of our current culture, we can see that Annie was a bit much," Dave Nopel told me. "We can see what a failure the Eighteenth Amendment was."

• • • • • • • • • • • • • • • • •

The indoor part of the café, which occupies a large room in the brick clubhouse, is empty when I buy my mint tea, although I have seen it full of talkative people. The pandemic probably means that customers have to sit outside. I notice a color TV tuned to a sports talk channel, which featured a discussion of the COVID-19 pandemic's impact on the 2020-2021 football seasons.

The morning menu offers breakfast burritos and hotcakes. Lunch includes hot dogs, grilled chicken sandwiches, and a range of burgers, including vegetarian garden burgers. Several Sierra Nevada beers are on tap, along with Jack Daniels,

Irish Mist, and other liquors. I ask the friendly, masked café worker what today's special "pumpkin spice Boston mule" might be. She describes it as a vodka-based drink, an October treat. Things sure have changed since Annie's time!

I don't see anyone drinking during the afternoon when I sit on the patio. Several older men talk about issues like retirement funds and materials they used for house repairs. I don't notice scattered beer, wine, or whiskey bottles as I do in other parts of the park. Still, this issue raised the question about a private group's role on public land like Bidwell Park. This was far from the only situation where this question exploded.

• • • • • • • • • • • • • • • • • •

The Golf Course's Condition

The battles over the golf course's physical condition began around the same time as the debate over alcohol sales. As far as I can tell from my observations from the clubhouse's patio, the course seems in good shape, but this wasn't always the case. Tensions blew up in June 1976 when golfers told the City Council that the course's beautiful location contrasted with its poor condition. Piles of abandoned pipes on the fairways, leaky drainage ditches, bathrooms in poor condition, lumpy areas, tall grass, and mud holes that often limited their play where just a few of the complaints (Butler 1976).

In December 1976, local men's and women's golf club members led City Council representatives on a course tour (the golfers leased the city-owned golf course that was responsible for its upkeep). They stated that they were only asking for improvements, not the establishment of a fancy country club-type facility. They complained about the poorly maintained bathrooms and the bad food quality in the vending machines. In March 1977, golfers complained that the Commission had ignored a letter describing problems on the course and had done nothing to improve the situation, while commissioners insisted they were concerned with the problems (Mowry 1976).

Water was pumped directly from Big Chico Creek to irrigate the course, but the inadequate sprinkler system resulted in dry spots around some of the holes and did not break up the water into a fine mist. The resulting large drops packed the grass into clumps in small areas, blocking some shots. Some citizens criticized the ways the golf course used these sprinklers (Mowry 1976). "They wanted to water those greens every day," Wes Dempsey reflected. "If a valley oak gets watered more than twice in a summer for fifteen years, you kill them. They pretty much killed the pines and oaks on the golf course; the ones that survived were pretty much out of reach. They're watering more conservatively now."

In 1987, golfers complained that the fairways were too close to each other and were becoming more dangerous by the day. Enthusiasts now played 77,000 rounds yearly on a relatively small, compact eighty-acre course. These crowded conditions led to golfers being hit by other players' golf balls; some claimed this happened as much as twice a week. Some golfers and other citizens suggested that the safety issue could be resolved if the course expanded onto territory near Big Chico Creek by the course's present borders (Toussaint 1987d). Another reason was that Golfco wanted to make the course usable for "championship-caliber" golf tournaments (Farrell 1991)

Critics replied that this would require removing some of the trees on the course, affecting deer, foxes, and over 150 bird species. Wes Dempsey, who explored the area, sent the Bidwell Park and Playground Commission a letter in January 1985. He wrote,

> We found a lush jungle of oak, sycamore, ash, willows, alder, and wild grape, which obviously supported a wide variety of birds, mammals, insects, and so on. There is no doubt that the area is a rich wildlife sanctuary, and it is quite evident that it would also be a welcome addition to the golf course. Obviously, you have the classic conflict of values over the use of public land. With careful planning, perhaps we can have both a fairway and yet keep many features of the wildlife area.

At a March 1985 meeting, golfers and some Bidwell Park and Playground commissioners agreed that the one solution could be for two holes to be added to an area near Horseshoe Lake. The golfers wanted to build holes in specific areas to ensure that balls wouldn't hit hikers. They claimed that off-road vehicle drivers would be less likely to drive in nearby hills after the two holes were complete. Also, the course would add water to Horseshoe Lake to supply the whole course, so there would be no more need to pump water from Big Chico Creek. The Chico Rod & Gun Club objected to this idea, but the Commission initially favored the golf club.

Preservationists and hikers also disagreed with the decision. Some felt that the golfers should raise funds, find another course, and forget about asking for more parkland. Some golfers shared attitudes that enflamed the situation. Ornithologist Roger Lederer told me, "In the 1980s, people wanted to expand the golf course to the other side of the road. One of the golfers said, 'There is junk out there.' He was pointing at the grass and trees." The debate intensified as some golfers wondered if the city needed to preserve wildlands by the lake since few hikers and dog walkers used the area. Their opponents worried that the park might become less wild if human use got more emphasis than preserving undeveloped areas. Some felt that the golf course and the shooting range were inappropriate uses of the Horseshoe Lake area.

Free for All

In February 1988, critics of expansion came to a Commission meeting and said they worried the unresolved proposal would make traffic unmanageable in Upper Park. These citizens wondered who would pay for road repairs and if realignment would make the course safer. Cars might run over golfers who cross the busy road, and golf balls might now hit hikers by the lake. The golf club replied that the widened road would make things safer for joggers, bicyclists, and golfers, and it offered to pay $25,000 a year to maintain the course.

The battle intensified. In November 1988, the Butte Environmental Council opposed using a natural area for the expansion since pesticides and other chemicals would poison wild animals. Golfers replied that they saw deer, raccoons, and foxes on the course, and expanding it would give them more habitats. They also mentioned that the course wasn't the only developed site in the park; picnic areas and playgrounds were other types of development. They couldn't understand why anti-expansion activists didn't criticize these facilities.

In January 1989, many of the Bidwell Park and Playground commissioners stated that they supported the realignment because of the safety issues but questioned the impact of the irrigation on Horseshoe Lake. The Sierra Club replied that runoff, irrigation water not absorbed by grass, would carry toxins to the lake. At the October Commission meeting, tree enthusiasts questioned irrigation's impact on native plants and mentioned that fungi grew on blue oaks' roots when they got too wet.

Tree No. 50
Acorn Woodpeckers Enter the Fight

Preservationists at the October meeting also mentioned that an acorn woodpecker granary, a blue oak where these native birds stored acorns and raised their young, grew on the expansion area. In November, the Bidwell Park and Playground Commission passed a resolution that supported removing granary Tree No. 50, suggesting that parts of it could be saved and attached to other trees so the woodpeckers could rely on these new sites.

The issue reached a pitch in January and February 1992 when dissenting commissioners stated strongly that they had not supported the oak's removal. Golfers resented being called woodpecker killers. They claimed that the tree's removal would not hurt the birds, and many other animals could find habitat on the log that would be left behind. They stated that other woodpecker colonies in the park would be fine if the oak were cut. They said that acorn woodpeckers stored their food more frequently in pines than in oaks, and they offered to plant pines to replace the granary tree. One golfer stated that he didn't think woodpeckers were important enough to risk people being hit by a stray golf ball.

I asked ornithologist Roger Lederer about his memories of this issue. He replied, "Regarding planting pines to replace oaks—nonsense. The acorn woodpeckers need oaks, not pines. They will put their granaries in pines or even telephone poles, but they much prefer oaks, which is where they get their food. And that's where they prefer their colonies to be. To say they will just join other colonies is also nonsense. Sure, leaving the log helps the mammals and insects, but not the birds."

Many bird lovers commented that displaced acorn woodpeckers were generally not absorbed into other colonies and might die if forced to live alone. Seven hundred people signed a petition that insisted that the oak should not be cut, and the Commission rejected a proposal to remove the tree.

More arguments dominated the meeting. John Merz stated what while the golf club had done a good job with its land, the Commission needed to respect Annie Bidwell's wish to keep the park in a natural state, and that a golf course was not a natural feature. He recommended that the golf course reconsider its design instead of expanding and make the best use of the land it acquired in its original lease.

Acorn woodpecker (courtesy Kate Roark)

One golfer countered that he had heard Annie's arguments for sixty years and that there would be no college in town or One Mile and Five Mile recreation areas if her restrictions had been followed. The golf course had removed other trees. Why was there such a fuss over one? A golfer angrily said he wanted to live long enough to enjoy his favorite game near the lake. One commissioner replied at the February 1992 meeting that she hadn't seen statistics relating to the course's safety and wondered how much of an issue it actually was.

The Last Twist

After ten long years of intensive public debate and heated arguments, an agreement allowing the expansion plan and required road relocation to go forward was almost complete—it just needed to be approved. The estimated $700,000 cost for the project would be entirely paid for by the golfers, bike and horse paths would be built, and more trees would be planted (at a ratio of 25 to 1) to make up for the ones that would be removed (Milan 1992).

As reported by Elaine Gray (February 11, 1992), the expected approval by the Bidwell Park and Playground Commission was a "done deal" at its Monday night meeting. Instead, in a shock 3-3 split with no recommendations, the Commission handed the issues of the acorn granary tree removal, the golf course expansion on twenty acres of parkland, and subsequent road relocation over to Chico's City Council for approval, which they did.

However, hard feelings remained. Some park advocates considered the realigned Upper Park Road, with its speed bumps and reflective warning signs, an eyesore. Park and Playground Commissioner Malowney strongly implied that these new features were ugly and out of place at a July 1993 meeting. Commissioners discussed the idea of a committee to look for more appropriate, un-traditional signs. Commissioner Gibbs asked if this seemed like an appropriate use of the commission's time and energy but agreed to support it if this group also considered the fiscal impact of its proposals (Urseny 1993).

"Into the 1980s, the road to Horseshoe Lake was different, "Dave Nopel said. "You had a beautiful little roadway, a windy road that followed the contour of the landscape. It was wide enough and went through a series of twists and turns. Now we have that road with the series of speed bumps. I hate those because they stripped away the feel of the landscape."

John Merz added, "In the 1980s, the issue that affected Upper and Middle Park the most was the extensions to Upper Park Road. It was a gentle way to get into Upper Park, and now that road is pathetic. There were plans for planting blue oaks along its sides, but that never happened."

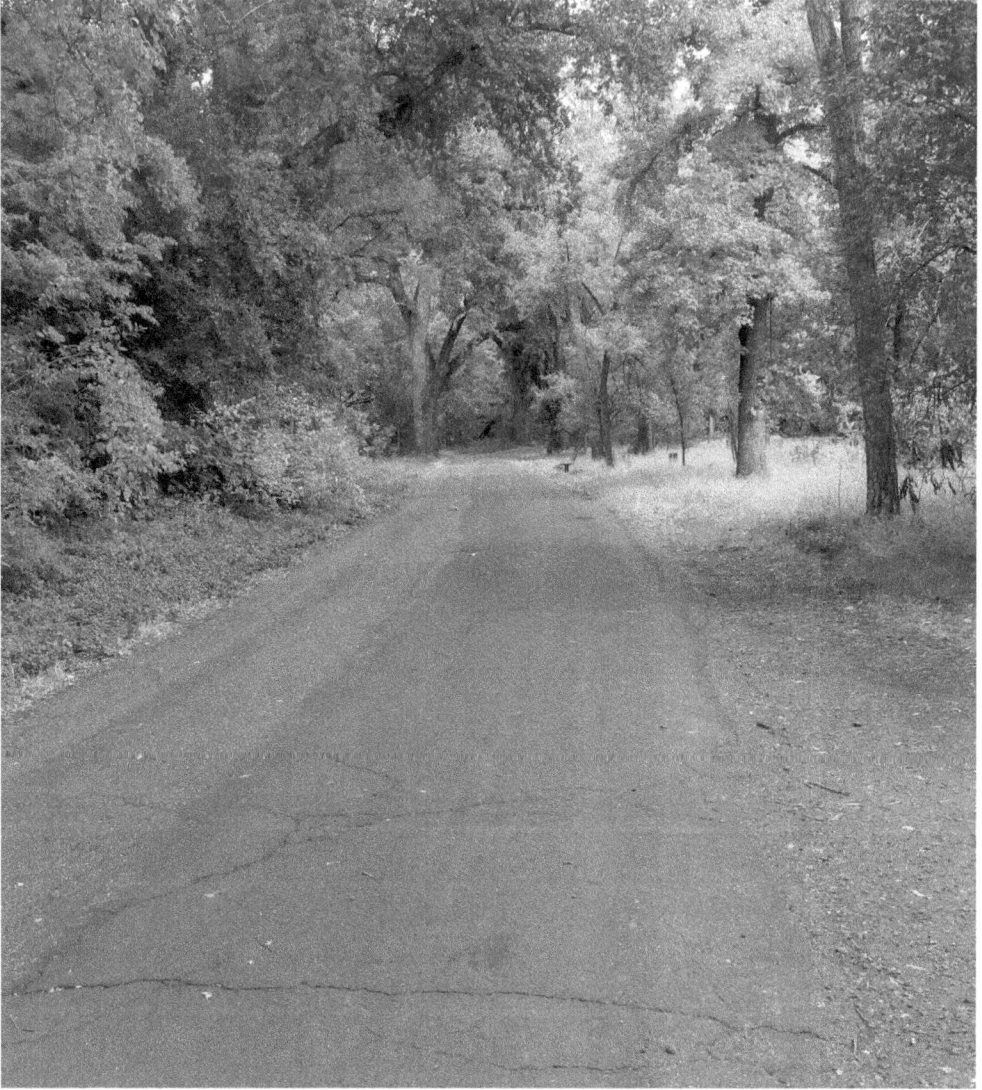

South Park Drive in Lower Park.

CHAPTER EIGHT

The Cacophonous Years

Chico Grows

Chico continued to grow as the twentieth century moved into the twenty-first century. At least 100 enterprises, including aviation-based industries, developed near the Chico Regional Airport north of town. Big Chico Creek flows through an arboretum at the tree-lined campus of California State University, Chico, passing a big student union, many classroom buildings, and performance arts centers that many students and community members love. Butte Community College expanded from its main campus in Butte Valley, near Oroville, and opened its Chico campus in September 1984. This state-of-the-art building, which sits near Highway 99 in south Chico, became the area's second institution of higher learning.

Tourism developed as a significant enterprise by the 1980s as nature enthusiasts discovered that Chico was a gateway to the Cascade range and Sierra Nevada. The Sierra Nevada Brewery began in 1980 as a hand-built brew house that utilized recycled dairy equipment. It grew to offer many jobs at today's modern brewery, restaurant, and concert hall. These and other employers enabled Chico's population to reach 86,187 in 2010 and 102,661 in 2023 (World Population Review 2023). New people in the area were inevitably not always familiar with Bidwell Park's history and needs.

Many Chico's citizens increasingly identified with the Sierra Club, Butte Environmental Council, and other environmental movements. Nature-loving locals suggested that city-managed open spaces in other areas could relieve the new pressures. Some focused on where Teichert Construction removed gravel from a southeastern Chico area to build Highway 99. This construction ruptured an underground aquifer whose water flowed into the pits, creating oak-surrounded Teichert Ponds. Hikers saw great blue herons, Canada geese, river otters, and other species who made this place their home (Cory n.d.).

Verbena Fields is a twenty-acre preserve in a central Chico neighborhood next to Lindo Channel's floodplain. It includes grasslands, wetlands, and a Maidu Interpretive Garden, where visitors learn how native people use local plants. Activists suggested that Chico's people would grow through educational and recreational programs at all these open spaces, and the newer open areas would lessen the growing population's impact on Bidwell Park (Lukes 2020).

Other citizens continued the idea that Annie Bidwell gave the park to everyone and that recreation was vital. They stressed the importance of ball fields, the golf course, and swimming areas. One mother emphatically told the Bidwell Park and Playground Commission that her golf- and baseball-loving son and her horseback-riding daughter had as much of a right to the park as her nature-loving son.

Community-Based Management Plan

These ongoing debates convinced many people that the park needed a community-based management plan that met as many people's needs as possible while balancing recreation with the park's ecological fragility. In 1987, Hardesty & Associates (Menlo Park, California) looked for some degree of consensus when they coordinated a series of conversations and meetings during the mid-1980s. A citizen's committee joined park staff members, commissioners, and environmental and recreational groups to oversee the Hardesty & Associates' work.

The goal was to develop guidelines for future projects, management strategies, and compromises that might resolve conflicts and strengthen the park's health. Advocates told Hardesty & Associates about problems like the erosion of Big Chico Creek's banks, vulnerable picnic spaces where twenty drivers could suddenly park their cars, and wild grapevines that could fuel wildfires. They also described how the park's staff constantly had to repair vandalism in bathrooms and other facilities and had less time than they needed for educational projects.

People discussed how some of Chico's neighborhoods bordered on the park. Non-native plants that grew in yards could spread their seeds into wilder areas and displace long-established species. Other problems included disturbances caused by the gun range, off-road vehicles, domestic cats, and unauthorized trails. Many citizens insisted that the park needed a visitor's center where visitors could learn about the park's human and natural history.

Chico's response to the project was enthusiastic, but the large number of participants sometimes made consensus difficult. Dave Nopel, who joined the Conservation Committee as a Sierra Club representative, reflected, "There were about five people, including a guy who owned an almond orchard. He came forward with an idea to dam Big Chico Creek for agriculture and recreation. He seemed to think the rest of us would support it, but we quickly turned that idea down and moved on. After three or four months of discussions, all the participants developed the Master Management Plan. Hardesty & Associates included a lot of viewpoints in the discussion, and most people were satisfied with it."

Hardesty & Associates published the management plan based on these discussions in January 1987. The introduction described how the park suffered from growing use as Chico's population increased. Bidwell Park and Playground Commissioners had complained for a decade that inadequate funding kept them from dealing with these issues. The plan supported these claims and sought solutions for long-lasting problems.

Hardesty & Associates noted problems that hurt all parts of the park. Automobile accidents became more likely as drivers increasingly raced the park's roads. Big Chico Creek needed greater care to avoid pollution that would harm plants and wildlife and reach Chico's underground water supply. All areas suffered when invasive plants took over native vegetation's territory.

The plan also described issues that were specific to each section of the park. The growing number of people who walked through One Mile Recreation Area compacted the soil around valley oaks' roots, making it difficult for the trees to absorb water and nutrients. Hardesty & Associates noted the raging fights surrounding the gun and archery ranges and agreed that the city needed to move these facilities from the park. They also focused on Upper Park's thin soil and stated that off-road vehicles and motorcycles must stay out of the delicate hills.

Hardesty & Associates recognized that some citizens would think these and other proposals would limit how they used the park. They knew the management plan would fail if Chico didn't create strong educational programs supporting their recommendations. The city needed to post signs that explained policies like traffic regulations and the need to keep dogs on leashes in some places. Hardesty & Associates also encouraged Chico to set up education centers at Chico Area Recreation District headquarters, the Chico Creek Nature Center, the Hooker Oak Recreation Area, and near Horseshoe Lake.

The report was an idealistic statement, but dreamers often can't find the money their plans need. Some citizens described the 1980s as a time of limited expectations and insisted that visionaries develop more realistic plans. They pointed to the fact that voters had passed California's Proposition 13, an initiative that cut property taxes in 1978 and described how that law slashed the funds available for parks and other public projects.

Also, low-interest rates meant that Chico needed to make more money on its investments, and the Bidwell Park and Playground Commission began to look for outside sources of funds. An endowment fund was one idea; another was a "gift catalog" for the park, where businesses and individuals could donate anything from a fifty-cent bag of seeds to a $2,000 fence. Creative ideas flourished. Some commissioners noticed cars showing up in Lower Park's designated car-free areas. They proposed a fence to limit this parking in late 1987, but the city denied this request because of a lack of funds. The innovative commissioners worked with sympathetic maintenance workers, who dug a ditch to block the cars so they couldn't enter these spots. Sadly, creativity can't solve all problems when money can't be found, and some of the management plan's proposals, such as the four educational centers, never left the dream stage.

War Games in the Park

Chico is a complicated town. Deep philosophical and political issues also impact the park, along with funding and administrative problems. These even include citizens' feelings about war and peace. A group of anti-war activists gathers at noon each Saturday in downtown Chico. They stand on sidewalks by Main Street holding placards with slogans demanding "No War with Iran," "Defund the Military," and "No Nuclear Weapons." These blue jean-wearing and plaid shirt-clad dreamers, who are gray- or white-haired, wave at passing drivers, many of whom honk to show their support. How many people know this is the United States' oldest ongoing peace vigil?

This gathering began when a group of citizens founded Chico Peace Endeavor in 1960 to counter a proposal for missile silos and storage facilities in Chico. Their weekly event grew when new people responded to the Vietnam War, the threat of a Central American war during the 1980s, and the conflicts that followed the 9/11 terrorist attacks in 2001. Activists opened the Peace and Justice Center as an umbrella group for Chico's progressive groups in the 1980s. The storefront office closed during the COVID-19, but the group has since reemerged and now uses the name Chico Peace Alliance.

The military's long-standing use of the park for training exercises led to fierce disagreements during the 1980s. Company G of the 184th Infantry got the Bidwell

Park and Playground Commission's approval to camp in the park in 1921. The military regularly asked for permission to use the park but did not always receive it.

Exercises often took place during the Vietnam War. In November 1966, the army requested permission for maneuvers that would include 180 men bringing vehicles and camping in Upper Park. They suggested that the park be closed during this event since soldiers would use blank ammunition; the sound of gunshots could scare horses and hikers. Citizens objected to the idea of the whole park being closed; the army agreed that the activities would be restricted to Upper Park, and soldiers would warn hikers to avoid those trails. The Bidwell Park and Playground Commission approved this idea.

With time, some citizen support for military training in the park faded. In March 1987, an Army Reserve unit and campus ROTC asked the commissioners to allow them access to Upper Park for training exercises. They agreed to use model guns rather than real ones that could upset the public and stated they would not dig ditches or foxholes in the fragile habitat. These practices would work, they said, since the session's focus would be on developing leadership skills among young officers instead of strengthening their fighting skills. Also, they said there was no other large area they could use for this kind of training near Chico.

At the March 1987 Bidwell Park and Playground Commission meeting, a speaker read a letter opposing the appearance of military uniforms in the park. Many community members supported ROTC, saying cadets volunteered to provide services to Chico. One anti-war citizen agreed that while ROTC helped the community in crises such as floods, she worried that skills soldiers gained from the training could be used against peasant movements in Nicaragua and El Salvador. Others objected to the closing of Upper Park during exercises. They also described the park as a well-loved place where families could hike and play, and many parents could encourage their kids to appreciate nature and engage in peaceful, non-violent games.

The minutes are unclear whether the Commission agreed to these particular exercises. Commissioners later approved requests for military training as long as these exercises respected community needs. In January 1988, they approved ROTC's request for a day of land navigation and orienteering training as long as the number of participants was limited. The Commission also agreed to a training session in rappelling from cliffs in February 1988.

Ironically, even though the military's popularity was at a height after the Gulf War, the California State University's Faculty Counsel recommended in 1991 that ROTC be removed from the system's twenty campuses because of the military's discrimination against gays and lesbians. CSU Chico adopted this policy in January 1992, and military training activities have faded from the park (Pyle 1991).

Kitty-Kittys

Some people were passionate about issues of war and peace, while others focused on homeless cats. I am indeed a kitty fan. One of my pets shared my love for tomato juice; others gave me needed breaks from my writing as they knocked my pencil from my hand or crawled all over my computer keyboard. I will never forget how I once tried to trick a kitten by twirling a string above her head. She ingeniously climbed to the top of a couch, took a flying leap to grab the yarn and landed in my lap.

Many cat owners know that cats need to be indoor pets. Feral cats have no home or reliable food source and decimate small wildlife such as quail. Over the years, some irresponsible pet owners who got tired of their furry friends abandoned them in Bidwell Park and students would dump them there at the end of a semester. Some may have thought the cats would find a good home there; but, sadly, these house cats were now exposed to diseases, injuries, wild predators, and forced to prey on smaller creatures if they even knew how to hunt. The ones that survived led hard, brief lives. Still, some animal rights activists defend feral cats.

When the homeless cat population skyrocketed in Bidwell Park during the 1980s, some animal rights activists questioned whether wild felines caused problems, stating that feral cats had led happy and healthy lives in and around human communities for thousands of years. One group recommended that they be trapped, neutered, tested and vaccinated for rabies and other diseases, and then released. They felt this would be both more a humane policy than one of removing and possibly euthanizing the cats. They claimed that a trapping strategy would cost $70 per animal, while their plan would cost $14 per cat.

"I'd see women drive up and lay out rugs and towels," Phyllis Dempsey told me one afternoon in her living room. "They'd put out spreads of turkey and tuna for the cats. You'd see ten to twenty cats eating. An animal rights group wanted the city to adopt a policy of setting up cat feeding stations. They thought if you fed them, they wouldn't bother wildlife."

This became a surprisingly contentious issue and sharp fight. Animal rights advocates claimed that feral cats live less than three years and the population would fall since neutered animals can't reproduce. The surviving animals would control the rodent population and chase new cats who wanted to enter the park. They asked again for the city to install feeding stations for cats, stating that denying them food would be cruel and might encourage them to attack wildlife.

Supporters of removing feral cats continued to counter that they were dangerous to birds and other wildlife. The City Council agreed and adopted this policy that recommended the cats be trapped and removed from the park in 1990. The Bidwell Park and Playground Commission selected a no-tolerance policy for cats in the park by January 1992. The Chico Cat Coalition was formed in 1998 and began to address the issue of feral cats. The city gave this group a $10,000 grant and, in 2000, approved a fine of $ 1,000 for people who abandoned cats. In January 2002, the Chico Cat Coalition reported that it had been a year since anyone had been caught dumping a cat in the park.

In 2014, the Chico Cat Coalition stated that it had removed 900 cats from the park in 1998, and the numbers continued to shrink in subsequent years. The group continued to discourage releases and offered $500 for information about someone who abandoned their pet in the park. Neighborhood Cat Advocates continues to trap feral cats in the park, and the Chico Cat Coalition shelters them until they can be adopted.

Salmon in Bidwell Park?

Kate and I kayaked on a warm October morning on the Feather River near Oroville, California. Chinook salmon swarmed in areas where males fertilized eggs that females left in redds (gravel nests) along stream bottoms. Some slid through the water like otherworldly shadows, while others leaped quickly above the river's surface and quickly vanished as they splashed downwards. Turkey vultures circled the area looking for dead salmon, and a hungry osprey watched from a valley oak.

These spectacular fish, which can grow almost five feet long and weigh 129 pounds (depending on the species), begin their lives when they hatch in freshwater streams and rivers. After they hatch, the young salmon travel downstream. In Northern California, populations travel to the Sacramento River and the Pacific Ocean. They eat and grow there and are ready to mate when they are between one and eight years old. Each fish finds the route back to its birthplace and struggles to swim upstream, passing rapids, waterfalls, hungry bears and raptors, and people fishing. They do not eat during this journey and die after the female lays her eggs. They once thrived along the West Coast, but climate change, overfishing, and dams that block their migration routes have reduced their populations (NOAA Fisheries n.d.).

People sometimes build fish ladders that guide salmon past dams and other blocked parts of their streams. A fish ladder is a series of pools the fish pass through as they move upstream. They jump through cascading water that connects these ponds, rest for a while, and jump to the next pool. Chinooks are now far less common in Big

Chico Creek than in neighboring streams, but their needs once pitted their advocates against other park enthusiasts.

During the early twenty first century, the California Fish and Game Commission proposed repairs to the damaged Iron Canyon fish ladders along a one-quarter-mile stretch of Big Chico Creek above Salmon Hole. Salmon eggs need deep, cool water where they can develop and hatch. The salmon couldn't leap between the ladder pools when summer's blasting sun and decreased runoff reduced the creek's water level. They became trapped in shallow spots where water warmed up and evaporated.

The Fish and Game Commission proposed using explosives to remove big rocks and other obstacles, hoping that fish could then make the trip far upstream to spawn in the cool waters of secluded Higgins Hole.

Salmon Hole is a remote area. Rugged cliffs surround its basalt boulders that create Big Chico Creek's rapids. The rough terrain would make it difficult to bring explosives and other needed materials to the spot. A crane could deliver supplies, but workers would have to transport it along rugged Upper Park Road. Many park lovers worried this equipment could damage roadside trees near the Salmon Hole parking lot and the fish ladder.

Iron Canyon (courtesy Kate Roark).

Officials decided that since black bears and other animals fed on salmon, and nutrients from the dead fish added to the riparian forests' health, repairs on the fish ladder should go forward. The crane could be transported without damaging the road, and the work would not harm the creek.

The issue remained a subject of hot debate in 2008. Some citizens still questioned whether the repairs would damage Upper Park. Mechoopda tribal representatives strongly requested they be included as consultants on a policy impacting salmon and the park. The City Council initially approved funds for the project, which appeared to be moving forward, but again, the project failed because of a lack of money.

Aquatic biologist Timmarie Hammil coordinates the Stream Team, a citizen's science-based project that regularly tests Big Chico Creek's water quality. She reflected on the fish ladder issue, saying, "There was a feasibility study funded by the Big Chico Creek Watershed Alliance. All of the money was there, but one part was missing, and it all fell apart. Big Chico Creek is not as big a priority for salmon runs as other streams in the area; the populations are lower than in Butte Creek."

Currently, there are efforts to remove the damaged fish ladders and restore the area to a natural salmon run (Gebb 2023).

Invasive Plants, Be Gone!

The only word for a prescribed burn is surreal. I once saw the last stages of one when I arrived for an educational program at Big Chico Creek Ecological Reserve. Patches of the ground smoldered, sending small smoke columns skyward in areas far away from the places kids would soon visit. I knew that at its height, flames from this burn removed dry underbrush, fallen branches, and logs that could contribute to firestorms and helped clear the land of introduced plants. Workers with water tanks patrolled the area to ensure flames didn't grow out of control. They were careful not to set fires during times of strong winds.

California's hot, dry summers make our region fire-prone; however, landscapes have adapted to fire's presence. Some plant species, such as gray pines, only release seeds after high temperatures or a blaze. But Native Californians knew that fire could be preventive medicine for the land. The Maidu and other tribes carefully set fires to encourage certain plant growth, to provide habitat for animals they hunted, and to prevent larger fires.

Debates raged over methods that could control the growth of introduced plants during the 1990s. Botanist Josephine Guardino (Fall 2005, 1) wrote,

> By allowing residents adjacent to Bidwell Park to landscape with noxious weeds
> such as ivy, brooms, and olive, the city is encouraging the spread of these highly

invasive non-native species into the park…. An example of an ecosystem now dominated by non-native species is Lower Park, which is surrounded by urban development.

Researchers noted herbicides did not affect the deep roots of non-natives such as star thistle and Himalayan blackberry. They did conclude that controlled burns could be more useful in Upper Park with its open grass fields. Some park officials supported using herbicides and controlled burns to remove star thistle, which produces a huge number of seeds that spread quickly and make control by other means difficult.

Critics commented that some proposed herbicides were associated with cancer. They could hurt wildlife and humans, including people camped in the park. Others wondered about their impact on birds that ate berries from shrubs that had been sprayed, fish in the stream, and burrowing owls. Citizens presented a petition with 450 signatures recommending banning herbicides in the park. Many park advocates suggested that the city use prescribed burns to control introduced plants, as native people had done. People who opposed this policy commented that the Maidu who lived in the region before 1860 did not need to worry about creating air pollution or setting a bigger fire in an area filled with dense towns and neighborhoods.

People's fears of polluting smoke and high winds that could spread prescribed fires into neighborhoods led to the end of prescribed burns during the 1990s. In 2010, Wes Dempsey sent a pro-prescribed burn letter to the Bidwell Park and Playground Commission. He discussed how these fires had eliminated the star thistle in most of the plots researchers studied and that the burns also reduced the number of non-native grasses. Brodiaea and other species that grow from bulbs thrived on the nutrients from plants that had burned, and the return of native plants helped birds that loved to eat their seeds.

California's wildfires have become an increasingly serious threat in recent years, and officials in many areas now see the wisdom of prescribed burns. The Chico Fire Department burned 100 acres west of Horseshoe Lake on May 17, 2021. Park volunteers helped in this effort, carrying out tasks such as telling park visitors about the fire, which observers agreed was well handled and a success. Officials planned this burn to reduce the fuel load and to eradicate star thistle and other introduced plants such as medusa head grass. Other fires are planned to occur on this spot over the next three years, and additional ones are projected for other parts of the park (Mash 2021).

This burn didn't come a minute too soon. A 402-acre fire began near Bear Hole in Upper Park on June 17, 2021. Firefighters contained it by June 19, although some trails were closed for a few days to make sure the area was safe. Shane Romain

Prescribed burn in Upper Park.

commented, "The controlled burn by Horseshoe Lake could have been a potentially critical fuel break if the park fire had spread farther west. We are very fortunate that the park fire did not escape us. It could have been much worse. Actually, the result of it resembles a controlled burn."

Kate and I walked through the area about a week later. Grasses were blackened, and some trees appeared to be damaged, but this was mainly a grass fire, and the damage would not be visible after several good rainstorms. Conditions during future spring times will tell the tale.

The Park's First Century Party!

Bidwell Park celebrated its 100th birthday with a party in July 2005. There were presentations, organized hikes, a festival with live music at One Mile Recreation Area, and movie screenings at the Blue Room Theatre of *The Adventures of Robin Hood*, *The Red Badge of Courage,* and *Gone with the Wind,* all of which were partially filmed in the park (*Chico Enterprise-Record* 2005a).

The festivities climaxed with a July 10 reenactment of the 1905 ceremony where Annie Bidwell deeded the park to Chico. Chinese lanterns adorned the grounds of the Bidwell Mansion as they had on that evening long ago. Chico resident Helen Martin performed as Annie and shared her speech with the happy crowd. Afterward, participants danced to live music and feasted on ice cream (*Chico Enterprise-Record* 2005a).

Best Debacle Ever

The celebrations did not reduce Chico's ongoing concerns. The Park only received $3 million annually from the city. Other community parks of similar size, such as New York City's Central Park, received well-needed funds from community groups. Bidwell Park had no large supportive organization, although community groups such as Butte Environmental Council, Friends of Bidwell Park, Altacal Audubon, neighborhood groups, and others gave what they could. This situation led to inadequate staffing and the park's increasing need to rely on volunteers who could help with its upkeep.

Traffic and illegal parking remained problems. Some hikers seemed frustrated with the park's official trails and took it upon themselves to build others that brought them where they wanted to go. Sadly, these paths slashed through native plant communities and loosened thin soil, which flowed to the creek during the rainy season. And there remained, of course, those invasive plants!

While these problems remained unresolved, the city realized a 20-year-old dream when it acquired 1,380 acres of land to add to the park's south side in 1995, nearly doubling the size of the park (*Chico News and Review* 1990; Ek 1995; Speer 1995).

Looking west toward Coast Range from a point on the 1,380-acre addition.

"The acquisition ended a long and difficult process for the city," Dave Nopel recalled. "There had always been a possibility that the land would remain in private hands. One developer had an option for building housing on that property. But he came to the city and said, 'I'd like this to become part of Bidwell Park. I'm a local boy. But you'll have to pay development rates.' The city wasn't prepared to offer that much money. It wanted to pay the rates used to buy grazing land; there was a difference of several million dollars."

When negotiations broke down, the city filed an eminent-domain lawsuit to take the property, which it lost. A judge ruled the city had to pay development rates, which amounted to almost $3 million, on top of paying related legal expenses, including those of the defendants, which amounted to another $1 million (Ek 1995, 20-21).

Some citizens were not happy about the acquisition. Dave recounted people saying, "'We don't want to pay $4 million for the park, and we never go up there!'" But the purchase took place, and the property became the city's latest addition to the park. Despite that costly debacle, that beautiful piece of land is now safe from development.

● ● ● ● ● ● ● ● ● ● ● ● ● ● ● ● ● ● ●

We travel Highway 32 east into the foothills, catching glimpses of distant snow-covered peaks as we approach a parking lot near this new park section. Kate and I hiked here with our friend Ann one warm November morning. The South Rim Trail leads through the higher country and connects with other paths that hikers can take downslope toward Iron Canyon. Gray pines (or California Foothill Pine) thrive on the slopes next to blue oaks that cling to late autumn's golden leaves. The dusty trail leads to many viewpoints where hikers can see Iron Canyon's gray, rugged walls. The canyon channels Big Chico Creek's roar upwards to mix with the sighing wind while fluffy cumulus clouds float lazily eastward toward Big Chico Creek Ecological Reserve.

● ● ● ● ● ● ● ● ● ● ● ● ● ● ● ● ● ● ●

The Place Where Frisbees Fly

The United States Bureau of Land Management (BLM) originally owned a small piece of this property. The Bureau's land included a small, illegal Frisbee golf course. This game, also called disc golf, was born in the 1970s. The rules are similar to traditional golf. Players start at an area where they throw a Frisbee at a target, often an elevated metal basket, and they need to hit it with the fewest possible tosses. They must hurl the disc from any spot where it lands after they "tee off," and they need to avoid trees, boulders, and other objects (Disc Golf Association n.d.). While many love the game, this Frisbee golf course led to bitter fights.

"The first course was a bootleg course on the BLM land. I don't think it was ever coordinated with the city," Dave Nopel told me. "The City Council didn't want to include Frisbee golf on the new land. But there was such a strong contingent supporting it that they carried the day under the umbrella that they would police it and protect natural features."

A second disc golf course appeared in 1997 on the parcel of newly acquired land on the park's south side. Some park advocates worried that the course might impact the area's population of Butte County checkerbloom, an endangered wildflower. They also commented that disc golfers might damage vernal pools, and erosion would damage the area's thin soils, affecting its plants and animals (Abbot, 2005).

Disc golfers commented that as Chico's population grew, the city needed to focus on activities that had relatively small impacts on the park's wildlands. They believed that their family-friendly game could be offered in environmentally sensitive ways. They also called the course's critics strict and rigid elitists. They pointed out that the area was not pristine: cattle once grazed here, and hunters had stalked wild animals on these slopes. Citizens who questioned the course's presence replied that while they were not necessarily against disc golf in the park, they felt the Bidwell Park Master Management Plan and the city's General Plan did not receive enough attention in discussions about this project (Baldwin 2003).

On-going discussions between disc golfers and Chico tried to come to a consensus about how the course could fit into the park in an environmentally friendly way. Park Director Dennis Beardsley commented that no one had guessed how popular the disc golf course would become.

In 2010, after years of heated debate, the city and a disc golf group called Chico Outsiders reached a compromise. The Outsiders raised money for environmental reviews and agreed to place signs describing the etiquette players must follow to protect the land and plants. A barrier would block and close the course's entrance in wet weather when heavy foot traffic might speed up the erosion of thin soils. Disc golfers also offered to plant gray pines that would create a barrier between the course and the native oaks (Gascoyne 2012). This agreement remains in effect today.

Peregrine Point Disc Golf Course

Woody Elliott retired as a land manager with the San Simeon District of California State Parks. He worked closely with Friends of Bidwell Park and the Chico branch of the California Native Plant Society before his move to Inverness, California. When we met for coffee at a Chico bakery, he told me, "Friends of Bidwell Park works to promote the cultural and ecological nature of the park. We strive to keep Upper Park wild and work to control invasive plants." The group contracts with the city to remove introduced Scotch broom shrubs and other invasive weeds and collect trash in the park. It advocates lessening automobile traffic on rugged Upper Park Road and promotes hiking and bicycle travel along that route as alternatives.

Woody continued, "Friends of Bidwell Park was organized in opposition to a proposal to officially sanction and install a disc golf course at the place we now call Peregrine Point. Before this proposal, disc golfers were trespassing with unsanctioned play in this place." Many citizens felt that a course that contracted with the city would follow environmental regulations more easily than one where people played without restrictions, but others felt the course's contract with the city was flawed. The city had initially arranged for Chico Outsiders to cover funding for the tasks of maintaining and monitoring the course, but the city now covers most of this cost because the area is also used by bikers and hikers."

Woody began to monitor the course in 2011. He looked carefully to see whether all parts of the course met the requirements of its environmental impact report. At first, Woody worried about the peregrine falcons that lived on cliffs near the course. "After several years of monitoring the pair of peregrine falcons using the cliff, I found that they occasionally fledged young and seemed compatible with human use of the area." His conclusions led him and others to emphasize the course's impact on wild plants and to accept that these birds seemed to be doing well.

In 2014, the city reported that disc golfers had completed efforts to protect the land and that the disc golfers were behaving responsibly with signage and barriers that protected trees (Hardee 2015a). Woody noted that disc golfers sometimes need to search for discs away from the official fairways but acknowledged that was part of the game and did not blame them, but foot traffic around the baskets and tee-off areas caused soil erosion and compaction. Wood chips and seeded rice straw could lessen the impact in these areas. He also commented that flying discs probably did relatively minor damage to oaks (Hardee 2015a).

Parks and Natural Resources Manager Linda Herman told commissioners that lack of staff limited the city's ability to supervise the course, but she supported Chico Outsiders' efforts. She noted that the group had paid for biological studies every year between 2011 and 2016, even though the agreement with the city asked for this to be done every two years. They also contributed money and volunteers to improve the course. She stated that the city needed to take a stronger role in monitoring the area since hikers and other guests also had an impact there (Scharaga 2018a; Urseney 2018c). Friends of Bidwell Park commented that Chico Outsiders needed to mulch areas to protect trees and clearly mark the trails so golfers and others would respect sensitive areas by staying out of them.

City officials agreed that the efforts by the Chico Outsiders had led to good conditions on the course. The city hoped to install information signs and a bathroom

A view to the east from Peregrine Point Disc Golf Course showing erosion-controlling wood chips around a frisbee golf target.

to make the area attractive to others in addition to disc golfers. The city also stated that it needed to work harder to monitor the course and to educate the public about the area (Urseny 2018c). Woody Elliott and other park advocates remained skeptical about this perspective, and they strongly referred to the city's lack of funds and the necessary staff needed to keep an eye on the area.

In August 2018, the Stony Fire burned almost 1,000 acres in Upper Park. The city decided to keep sections of Upper Park, including Peregrine Point, closed so they could assess hazards. In April 2019, the city Parks Department and the Bidwell Park and Playground Commission recommended that the course reopen in May since damaged trees and debris piles were gone (Urseny 2019a). The officials and commissioners agreed that the course needed more work; a fence around a sensitive plant area needed to be replaced, and native oaks required better protection. Some targets and teeing areas should be moved so native plants could regenerate. The city agreed to monitor the course better and praised disc golfers for all their efforts to maintain it (Urseny 2019a).

Lise Smith-Peters reflected: "Should the course have been there? Originally, disc golfers were running all over the place when it was not an official facility. The course's environmental impact report placed restrictions. It's better to have a dedicated group like Chico Outsiders that can take care of the course and live up to agreements."

Shane Romain commented, "I think the Peregrine Point Disc Golf Course is an asset to Bidwell Park and the Chico community. Frankly, I think this debate of the course that has gone on for over ten years is ridiculous. I remember what it was like before the course was established up there. The area is in much better condition now in many ways." Time will tell if controversies around the disc golf course rise again.

Park Rangers

Shane Romain, a powerful-looking and soft-spoken man, once told me he'd wanted to be a rock star in his youth and laughed that his name would have fit well with that role in life. He now serves as Chico's Park Services Coordinator, a position that includes a lot of roles. He began his career as a Bidwell Park ranger, working with the late, beloved Ranger Bob Donahue.[1]

---

1   Editor's note: In 1987, Byron Brace became Bidwell Park's first official park ranger. Before that, the Chico Police Department's reserve officers and community service officers patrolled the park. Ranger Brace quit nine months into his job over frustrations that the City continually ignored his suggestions to improve park conditions for users, prevent crime and vandalism, and improve the safety of his job with proper training. However, by 2023, thirty-five years later, the City has implemented most of Ranger Brace's prescient recommendations and is currently considering some of his other suggestions (Aylworth 1988; Brace 1988; Thoms 1989; Scharaga 2017a, b).

Lise Smith-Peters remembered Ranger Bob, saying, "He wanted to educate people and encourage them to comply with rules before issuing citations. He was an expert on the park. I was amazed. I once asked him to describe areas where people had burned star thistle. He came back with a colored map that he did by hand!" Ranger Bob's staff served as public relations officers who educated people about reasons for rules and encouraged them to follow these regulations. They shared information on the park's plants, animals, geology, and history with visitors and managed the teams of inmates who did maintenance work and removed invasive plants.

Shane Romain's life path made him a natural candidate to become a ranger. He reflected, "I remember being about four or five years old when I really discovered my love for nature and wanting to be a park ranger from that point. I would set up stuffed animals in the woods around my grandparents' house and take my family on nature safaris.

"Of course, life takes many twists and turns along the way," he continued. "It was not until I moved to Chico from the Bay Area in 1996 that I would revisit the idea of becoming a park ranger. Ultimately, I would complete my general education at Butte College and obtain my BA from CSU, Chico, in Recreation Administration/Parks and Natural Resources Management in 2005.

Shane paused and continued, "My work as a ranger was incredible! I was fortunate to be trained by Ranger Bob for about a year before he retired [2008] and really learned the art of what he called obtaining voluntary compliance with park regulations.

"There are a lot of stories I could tell! Everything from giving CPR to a young man who made a fatal jump off the rocks at Salmon Hole only two weeks into my ranger position, to wading out to the middle of Horseshoe Lake to save a dog that was drowning because it was wrapped up in fishing line, to educating school children on the wonders of the natural world, to tracking a mountain lion that had killed a dog, to engaging with a whole cast of characters from the public from gentle, elderly people to unpleasant felons.

"The ranger position was changing, and I found myself dealing with more unruly people and having to make more law enforcement-type contacts. I was always more interested in helping to educate people to appreciate and care for the park than to play more of a police role," Shane concluded.

Each of the three rangers' work changed as many citizens began to worry about public safety in Chico. In 2017, over 2,000 park-related calls were made, ranging from 9-1-1 hang-ups and being locked in the park after closing hours to assaults, fights, drugs, and warrant arrests, to name a few (Scharaga 2017a).

Faced with these statistics and concerns about crime in city parks, the City Council voted on June 2017 to make park rangers armed sworn officers (Waddell 2017a, b). Under the sworn ranger program, rangers must complete 664 hours of law enforcement training through an academy. They must also complete an additional five- to six-month field training with the Chico Police Department (Scharaga 2017b).

Iron Canyon from Peregrine Point.

Meadow at Five Mile Recreation Area where Happy Acres Forest School
and (sometimes) Earthbound Skills meet.

CHAPTER NINE

Park Volunteers

First, A Story

There are a million stories in Bidwell Park. In July 2019, Shane Romain shared a good one at a meeting of PALS (Partners, Ambassadors, Leaders, and Stewards), the umbrella group that unites the park's volunteer projects. A Chico man whose dog had recently died took some magic mushrooms and ventured into Upper Park to mourn and center himself. Later that day, the stoned hiker called his roommate and said, "I don't know where I am."

His friend panicked and alerted park officials, who organized search parties. The following day, the grieving man wandered out of the hills and found himself surrounded and baffled by people who had been looking for him. Happy endings are welcome and wonderful, and we volunteers laughed and clapped.

Money Makes the Park Go Round?

It's great that Chico could mobilize so many volunteers to search for this fellow. The recession of 2008 hit Bidwell Park hard. The 1995 addition of additional land in Upper Park grew the park's size to 3,674 acres, a sixty-percent increase, but a $50,000 cut in the park's 2012 budget shrunk staff. Fourteen full-time staff worked in the park in fiscal year 1988–1989, which was cut to twelve people in 2012. At the same time, park lovers remained aware of the land's desperate ecological needs. Facilities were also deteriorating—the park's restrooms were among California's oldest and least maintained (Cassidy 2012).

Park advocates and staff passions run high about staffing and funding issues. I spoke with several of them in 2017 when I worked on an article about the park for a British travel website. Woody Elliott commented, "Since the crash of 2008, there's not been funding. The city's model now is to focus on infrastructure—things like opening and closing gates, filling potholes in Lower Park Road, picking up trash."

Former Bidwell Park and Playground Commissioner Lise Smith-Peters added, "The budget for the Parks has been cut every single year. In 2013 when I was still there, it went from ten maintenance workers to half that. Now they're down to four."

Susan Mason, who worked with Friends of Bidwell Park until she moved to Southern California, commented, "The money comes from the General Fund; there is no dedicated funding source. Most of this money comes from the sales tax. It depends on how the economy is doing."

"Bidwell Park is really a regional park, not just a Chico park," Shane Romain reflected. "We get more traffic than Lassen Volcanic National Park. Right now, our biggest issue is a lack of funding. For 3,670 acres, we have a staff of four maintenance people. We're the only park of this size I know of that charges no user fees or parking fees."

Former Commissioner Tom Barrett said, "The problem is the Park was a donation. Because of that, everybody seems to think maintenance is free." He agreed that the city needs a consistent fee schedule for the park. "If you want reserve a larger picnic site in the park, you need to pay a fee, but if you want to make a film or a commercial, you don't. If people are making a profit from the park, they should give back."

He continued, "Bidwell Park is a treasure on a statewide level. If Chico targeted the Park and encouraged guests to visit it, that would contribute to local tourism. Biking, hiking, running, birding—there are many ways for guests to enjoy the park and bring resources into Chico!"

Welcome PALS!

Everyone agrees that Chico must take more financial responsibility for the park, but they love and appreciate the volunteers who actively care for it. As Park Services Coordinator, Shane Romain oversees the PALS program, which contributed to removing invasive plants, planting native species, collecting litter, and maintaining trails. Volunteers contributed 22,896 work hours in 2014; the total number of hours has since averaged 20,000 per year.

Volunteers' importance became evident in 2014 when observers noted that park users were ignorant of regulations. Vandalism was growing, particularly in washrooms. Alcohol was prohibited outside the golf course, but drinking increased all over the park. Dog owners did not understand leash laws, and bike riders frequently rode on sensitive trails without helmets. Everyone knew that public education had to be addressed immediately. Park Watch picked up much of the responsibility for this work (Bash 2015).

"I've been involved with volunteers since I was a ranger," Shane Romain told me one day in his office. "Park Watch, the original volunteer group, came out of the neighborhood watch idea. Ambassadors would be the eyes and ears of the park. They would go out on patrols and report things."

Park Watchers reminded dog walkers to keep their pets on a leash on some trails and warned smokers they could be fined for puffing in the park. These volunteers did not have the authority to cite people who ignored the rules, but they could call park rangers if the illegal behavior continued.

"The world has changed," Shane reflected. "There were situations where people could have been hurt. The protocols have gradually been rewritten to get away from patrols toward Park Watchers being ambassadors—giving directions and information more than warning people about infractions. Instead of telling smokers, a ranger might cite them, they could remind people, and 'You know, you can't smoke in the park; you might start a fire.' The high visibility of the ambassadors wearing bright yellow vests often lets potential rule violators know they are being watched. They are also present to help people who lost their car keys, need to find a bathroom quickly, or who have questions about a bird or a wildflower."

Shane feels respectful discussions with park users is more effective than warnings and infractions. He sees ambassadors as a visible presence that reminds people to treat the land respectfully. Most park users are more likely to cooperate if volunteers approach them respectively. This is also true for people who camp in the park. Their numbers have increased in recent years, and some leave sleeping bags, clothes, and food around their illegal campsites. Shane believes that many of these lonely people need to talk with someone about their lives, and most will maintain a clean camp if they are approached kindly.[1]

"We need unity among groups that are doing their own things," Shane continued. "When I became Park Services Coordinator, I wanted to bring them more into unity—Park Watch, Friends of Bidwell Park, university students, Chico Velo trail works, and others.

"PALS, the group I now coordinate includes volunteers who talk with visitors, but it also connects volunteers with restoration work, trash removal, and cutting of ivy

---

1   The issue of homelessness in Chico and its impact on Bidwell Park and greenways is an ongoing controversy beyond the scope of this book. While important, the many issues and feelings surrounding it could be a book of its own. Recent issues that have impacted the park are touched upon in the Afterword (pp. 173-175).

from oaks and other trees. Many volunteers feel more comfortable in these roles than as ambassadors who deal directly with the public."

PALS meetings give Shane a chance to share current information about the park with a range of volunteers. In September 2019, he told us how the algal bloom at Horseshoe Lake had ended for the season and how goats had returned to graze on plants that might contribute to a wildfire. He also expressed concern about how some people saw Lower Park as a commuter stream, using it as a crowded path leading to work or school. PALS volunteers make him feel hopeful. They come from many political perspectives but work cooperatively toward a common goal in these times when some people thrive on screaming at each other.

Trash, Trash, Trash!

Kate and I count ourselves as part of PALS' cleanup team. We carry our trash pickers and large plastic bags to Horseshoe Lake, Five Mile Recreation Area, World of Trees, and other spots, and sometimes leave lost teddy bears in visible places so sad children can retrieve them. The garbage we remove includes plastic bags and soda cups, empty beer cans and liquor bottles, shoes, deserted blankets, confetti, and countless cigarette butts.

We have also joined many other PALS volunteers at several Butte Environmental Council's (BEC) park and waterway cleanup days. BEC was born in 1975 when Wes Dempsey, who represented the Sierra Club, and activists from four other environmental groups united under one tent. The group founded a recycling center in 1977 and later focused on education and advocacy around groundwater issues, endangered habitats, and climate change. BEC also sponsors the annual Endangered Species Faire each May and invites hundreds of children to make puppets of threatened animals and carry them in a parade through Bidwell Park.

Hundreds of community members, including many PALS volunteers, gathered on a September 2018 weekend at Hooker Oak Recreation Area and waited to be assigned an area to clean. Kate and I were directed to sections of the Yahi Trail that lay close to Upper Park Road. A hidden Nuttall's woodpecker drummed on a tree as we scoured the ground beneath the naked buckwheat blossoms, mid-September's only wildflowers, and poked at crimson poison oak leaves while being careful not to touch them. The season's last few pipevine swallowtail butterflies slowly drifted past us, turning abruptly as they flew to avoid hungry birds. Big Chico Creek's water level approached its yearly low point as summer slid toward autumn, but it hummed as it flowed toward the Sacramento River.

We suddenly spotted a beer can between a tree's forked branches. It looked like some poor drunk's idea of art, but we decided that someone in a passing car had used the tree as a target. Kate gently grabbed the sapling with her trash picker and shook it until the can fell, and I could fetch it without walking through poison oak. I also found a deflated inner tube, which easily fit into my trash bag.

We stuffed pieces of plywood, Styrofoam and plastic cups, cigarette butts, broken glass, and the remains of a joint into our trash bags, filling each of them halfway. We'd found far more during the 2017 effort when we joined a team that cleaned Lindo Channel in a west Chico neighborhood. That group found smashed chairs and tables, computer monitors, wine boxes, and a wide collection of small whiskey bottles. Upper Park was comparatively empty of trash, but we found enough to make us lose some faith in our species.

Celebrating the Clean-Up

After the cleanup, hundreds of participants went to the Sierra Nevada Brewery. A melody from a saxophone and electric guitar duet whirled around us as people ate veggie and beef burgers, enjoyed Sierra Nevada Brewery's Octoberfest Beer, and shared stories. I spoke with Monica and PJ, a woman and man who had volunteered for the day. "We found a lot of cigarette butts, beer bottles, beer cans, and Styrofoam. We filled two five-gallon buckets and pulled a T-shirt from the bottom of the creek," PJ said.

"There were butts everywhere, wherever smokers go. I found a lighter. I was surprised by the number of socks!" Monica said. "What about that weird bomb thing we found?"

"It was like a PVC pipe, with a stick and cherry bomb," PJ said. "I've heard about people throwing plastic explosives in a swimming hole to kill and gather the fish."

"I like to think about nature when I see it, even if it's little," Monica commented. "Today, where I looked, there were feathers—owl feathers and turkey feathers. I once saw a bear near Bear Hole, a big one! The dogs were chasing it, and it crossed the creek. Then there was the rattlesnake today."

"I was about to pick up a plastic cup, and there he was, rattling," PJ said. "His instinct was to scurry off into the woods. I took one giant step back and screamed like a girl! He was still rattling a few minutes later, telling us to stay away."

"I don't think Chico would be Chico without the park," Monica said.

Kate and I worked near the Caper Acres children's area during the 2019 cleanup. We found less trash here than in other areas, making us think parents and others wanted to set a good example for the kiddos. Still, we returned with a bag of bottles, plastic forks, crumpled paper, confetti, and cigarette butts.

Five hundred fifty-six volunteers showed up for this thirty-second annual cleanup of Chico's waterways, including Big Chico Creek. Many of these people participated for the first time. The day's haul included: 27,720 pounds of trash and landfill, 2,053 pounds of scrap metal, and 929 pounds of recyclables.

Other discoveries included ten shopping carts, two couches, and one mini-fridge for a total of fifteen-and-one-half tons of stuff (Butte Environmental Council 2019).

Some groups discovered abandoned campsites where they removed clothes, bottles, and used syringes. One team gathered three used syringes in an hour. Others found larger objects such as mini-fridges, bike parts, and couches. I chatted with fellow volunteer Aaron Logan over burgers and chips at the 2019 community barbecue. "Some people think homeless people make most of the trash, "I said. "What do you think?"

"When you're witnessing all the trash coming in from the creek, it's clear it's not just our homeless population contributing to the problem," Aaron commented. "You find everything from car parts to construction materials to refrigerators and household products. You can't target one part of the population, especially a marginalized group. People need to take personal responsibility instead." We worked with Aaron and other volunteers to clean up a spot near Little Chico Creek in 2020. Our discoveries included furniture, piles of discarded clothes, whiskey and wine bottles, and used hypodermic needles.

Watching Out for the Creek

I joined another project one warm June 2019 afternoon and quickly discovered how quickly my feet could get wet. "Maybe I should have brought better shoes for this," I laughed, standing on Big Chico Creek's shores just east of Sycamore Pool. Like a clear, sparkling snail trail, the creek wandered slowly through this flat area. The oak and sycamore leaves had reached full size, protecting us from early June's sun.

I'd come with Timmarie Hamill, Anton Dressler, and Michael Bruin, members of the Stream Team. This group is associated with PALS and affiliated with the State Water Resources Control Board's Clean Water Team. We came to monitor Big Chico Creek's water quality condition and health. "We have ten monitoring sites on the creek," biologist Timmarie said. She described how they begin in remote areas in the creek's upper watershed and stretch downstream through Big Chico Creek Ecological Reserve, the park, downtown Chico, and the CSU Chico campus, to where the creek hits the Sacramento River.

"We often work with Cal State students and local elementary schools, and we set up tables at events to recruit other volunteers," Timmarie said. "The volunteers actually come from a range of backgrounds—librarians, chemists, retired professors, people who want to learn to test the water so they can go out on their own to protect the water in their own creeks. It's a community-building project—you might work with someone you see at the grocery store but don't know!"

Anton, a credentialed high school teacher, and I often worked as environmental educators at two sites near Chico. Today, he measured the time it took a few sticks to float between two outstretched measuring tapes so he could determine how much water the creek held today. "The sticks are small enough to float but big enough to not be affected by the wind," he commented. "We use oranges as floats when we work with elementary school students."

Michael is a chemist who plans to work as an English teacher in Japan to become fluent in Japanese. "We are friends, and friends of Bidwell Park!" he laughed. He and I measured the creek's depth at different points between its north and south shores. The amount of water always grows as the winter storms fill it with rain and snowmelt and decreases during the summer's hot, dry season. This is an important factor for researchers to remember when they measure the concentration of potentially harmful chemicals in the creek.

Michael stretched two measuring tapes between the creek's banks and marked the twenty-foot stretches off at one-foot increments. He waded through the tumbling creek and used a meter stick to measure the depth at each mark. I stood on the shore, making sure I didn't get my feet wet. I repeated his measurements when he called them and marked them on a chart. They ranged from zero centimeters at the creek's bank to twenty-two centimeters near its middle.

The creek's depth and speed were average for early June. Anton tested the water to discover the dissolved oxygen concentration that fish and other creek creatures needed. He found it low, but we speculated that the constant direct sunlight had warmed the water, making it harder to hold as much oxygen as in cooler weather.

The pH scale measures the presence of toxins that impact water quality and affect organisms that live in the creek. Acids and bases are scientific terms that describe a range of pollutants. If a test shows that water has a pH of seven, it is considered neutral, meaning no acids or bases are present. A pH lower than seven shows that acids are present; their concentration strengthens as the test shows lower values until it reaches zero. Values above seven show increasing concentrations of bases, with 14 as the highest. We found that the creek's pH was slightly above eight. The water held some bases but was within the healthy limits for fish and other aquatic creatures.

"The city washes Sycamore Pool weekly on Thursdays in the summer to get rid of algae and pollution," Michael remarked.

"They drive trucks and other vehicles around to do this," Anton added. "They could spill pollution if there were a wreck."

The Stream Team collected three containers of water from the same spots for later tests in a laboratory. They would measure the concentration of dissolved solids in the water, discover which bacteria were present, and document whether the water was safe for swimmers. Timmarie noted that they also counted the insects and other invertebrates that lived in the creek. "We're in the healthy range for aquatic life and for people who go swimming," she commented. "Still, bacterial levels can get high during the warm months when there is less water, and the aquatic insect diversity declines in the urban zones of the creek when compared with the upper reaches of the watershed, indicating impacts from the urban environment."

"The city closed the dam at Sycamore Pool this year because of salmon trying to swim upstream to spawn. Do you know what happened to them?" I asked.

"We don't know how far they made it," Anton replied. "We are hoping they will show up in the cooler parts of the Big Chico Creek Reserve." None of us knew this then, but people spotted them at Salmon Hole in Upper Park a few months later.

Why Monitor Water Quality?

Michael and Anton left after we completed the tests, and I talked with Timmarie for a while. "This creek is terribly important for the state," she declared. "It is a groundwater recharge point, meaning its water soaks through the soil down into the aquifer underneath Chico. We have wells; we get our drinking water from them. It flows into the Sacramento River and supplies water for people downstream. The city is on its second year of being mandated by the state to monitor water quality. We have opportunities for the city to utilize citizen's monitoring efforts to help track the creek's health."

Timmarie initiated the Stream Team in 2000 as a citizen science project where people from all backgrounds could participate in research. One of the group's goals was to educate people about how stormwater, rainwater that falls on their yards and nearby roads, can carry pollution to Big Chico Creek. Timmarie strives to educate people on how to keep these contaminating chemicals at a minimum. The state provided the City of Chico with several $1 million grants toward this goal and to promote the stream's health. Volunteers have gathered data on the creek for years and have contributed thousands of hours of services annually to track the effectiveness of these grant projects in improving water quality.

"Right at the edge of the creek, homeless camps are a problem," Timmarie said. "Also, sprinklers in lawns go all summer, and the water can bring pollution to our creeks, but the creek is holding its own. We are in a healthy range for aquatic life and safe swimming. The bacterial levels can get high in the summer months, though, when the water level is low. We must get better and better at what we do to prevent pollution, and we strive to encourage informed stewardship actions to help.

"I'm a biologist. I went to Chico State. I also have a teaching credential and a master's degree in science education. Many of the grants I have helped write support projects for teachers to bring kids out to learn about stormwater pollution prevention practices, support habitat improvements, and our citizen work on the creek. Recently, we landed a grant for nine school campuses to participate in our Clean Water Science Ambassador Program. The kids helped construct stormwater gardens, where stormwater was filtered through the soil so it didn't carry pollution to the creek. They also learned about creek ecology, water quality testing procedures, and stormwater management practices they can implement at their own homes to prevent water pollution."

"Have any of the students come up with special projects?" I asked.

"The kids at Parkview Elementary School, fifth graders, modified the activities they learned and shared them with younger kids at an all-school event in the park, which was amazing and showed what they had learned from their own perspectives. They really like getting in the creek to measure water depths and how fast an orange flows downstream to calculate stream flow." She dreamt of a day when they could share their activities and discoveries with the public and the City Council.

"I love our program," Timmarie concluded. "It's an opportunity for folks to start to think about the park and what they can do to improve water quality. Then, they can look in more depth into issues that concern them and borrow equipment so they can work on their own. We try to be advocates for good water quality locally and throughout the state."

Hope for the Trails

The Tuscan Formation popularly called Monkey Face silently stares down at hikers, dog walkers, and people who fish in Horseshoe Lake. Its perplexed expression makes me wonder if it is thinking, "What are you talking apes up to now?" The dusty, rock-covered trail to its top begins at the lake's eastern shore and rises gradually as it passes buckbrush, gray pines, and blue oaks. A few spots are steep and slippery, as we say in my hometown of Pittsburgh, Pennsylvania. Parents often bring excited kids on this adventure and hold their hands to lift them over the more challenging spots. The hike gives adventurers beautiful vistas of the Coast Range to the west and the park's rugged volcanic cliffs of the Tuscan Formation—the views are well worth the effort! The downward trek can be challenging—I am always grateful for my hiking stick.

"I have a hiking stick, too," a friendly six-year-old boy once told me.

"They are great. They keep you from falling down," I said.

"No, that's not it," he answered. "I have a band-aid, and my wound stings if I don't lean on my stick!"

Monkey Face's problem is that several side trails break away from the main one and lead hikers upslope so they can reach the peak quickly. People built these trails without the city's approval, and signs announce that the area they pass through is closed. Many guests ignore the warnings and chug uphill, scattering loose soil and rocks behind them. Hikers connect with the North Rim Trail from Monkey Face's top, but many of the trails are obscure.

Thad Walker grew up outside Asheville, North Carolina, where hikers can find ninety miles of trails into Pisgah National Forest and the Smoky Mountains. He came to Chico when his wife was hired to run the Adventures Outing group on the CSU Chico campus. "I'd never been here before, but I like the area and the park," he said. He soon came to appreciate the problem of unofficial trails that cross Bidwell Park.

Monkey Face.

"Historically, the park was managed as open space, and people could go where they pleased," he added. "If it is the middle of the rainy season, hikers can cause erosion. People don't want to walk in the middle of a trail in the mud. The path will grow from two to twenty feet wide in a short amount of time. And people want to get from Point A to Point B quickly. Some people just climb uphill for exercise. The number of park users has increased, and it is very easy to create a new trail."

Trail Restoration and Education

Thad considered starting a non-profit to promote trail improvement work. He decided instead to approach Chico Velo, a group that worked on bicycle trails and advocacy, to see if they would be interested in the issue. "I have a long history of trail advocacy, and they have staff and funds. Some of the trails were built for recreation," he said. "Some others are old roads that developed into trails and that lead to waterways. Water flows along them and picks up sediments that flow to the creek. A lot of our work focuses on stabilizing soil loss. We know how long soil takes to form; when it's gone, it's gone. All trail users have an impact—hikers, too."

Thad felt that people who had a chance to restore trails would understand the need for a well-balanced system in the park. He described how his group recruited volunteers to close and restore an unofficial trail. "Monkey Face is the thing to do for many people in the park," he commented. "Improving the trails will improve their experience and the health of the park." The crew placed native plant seeds and straw on the trail and placed straw wattles, barriers that would block erosion. A sign told hikers that this trail was now closed.

"We tell people why we are improving trails when they come for workdays," he commented. "They need to know what it takes to build and maintain trails. Experiential education is the most effective way. People want to step into a stewardship role. Our approach is to get people connected with trails. They will understand which trails are appropriate for bikes, horses, and hikers. They can share this information and go out and do trail maintenance themselves. We also work with other groups that focus on restoration. I am working on a project to develop an updated map of the trails in Bidwell Park. We also need better signs showing the trails."

"That's a huge issue, and Shane Romain shares your feelings," I said. "People just don't know where to go. But do you think dogs on the trails are a big issue? Dog owners let their furry friends wander and run free on Yahi Trail and other places where they are supposed to be on leashes. Kate and I once watched two free-running dogs snarl and leap at a Yahi Trail hiker who climbed onto a boulder. After their owner got the dogs under control and rushed away, the frightened hiker told us how another dog recently bit him in the park. And yes, you will find plastic bags filled with dog droppings in places where they wander."

"Absolutely," Thad said with a grin. "It's because of the increased number of dogs and people. Dog walkers are provided with dog bags for the waste, but they don't necessarily use them. They think there are no consequences for not following the rules. They sometimes just leave them and think the poop fairy will get them!

"People are passionate about their dogs, and there is only one dog park in Chico [DeGarmo Dog Park]," he continued. "If there were others, there would be less impact on the park."

"There needs to be some kind of rule enforcement and fines as well," I commented.

"I agree," Thad said. "When you do that, word spreads fast about the consequences. Fines are also a way to provide funding for the park."

"I think education is the best way, though," I said.

"Everyone should be able to bring up ideas for the park and go through the public input system. They need to understand the master plan for the park, and the impacts trails can have on archaeological sites, plants, and wildlife. We also need to use social media to spread information about the park—as much as I use the park to try to escape it!" he said, laughing. He reflected that mountain bikers are increasingly aware of the park's needs and that horseback riders are usually responsible for minimizing their impact.

"The park is one economic driver in our economy," he concluded. "Investing in the park is investing in the community. Understanding the past helps build the future."

Picnicking with PALS

A group of about seventy PALS volunteers gathered for their annual picnic at One Mile Recreation Area on a cool October 2019 afternoon. Shane praised his team's work, from trash pickup to restoration to serving as park ambassadors. We discussed our projects while munching on meat and vegetarian burgers, watermelon, potato salad, brownies, and other treats.

Aaron Logan is involved with a network of people interested in improving their lives and the world in a fun, community-based way. "We found that City of Chico has an Adopt-a-Site program. It seemed like something we could continuously focus on and see the progress we've made," Aaron said. "We walked through the park with Shane Romain and found this beautiful spot. Its beauty was being restrained by overgrowth. It seemed like a perfect spot to maintain so passers-by could see its beauty."

Kate and I worked with Aaron and his friends several times collecting trash around the site and removing an oak that fell during a storm, blocking the creek's flow. We also removed many invasive plants out of that spot.

"Himalayan blackberry and vinca are two big ones," Aaron. "Black walnut is a native plant, but it takes over a site. We removed blackberry that was growing up, and walnut branches that were hanging down!"

PALS member Linda coordinated the Ivy League, a project that removes English ivy from oaks and other trees. While the ivy is a beautiful plant whose presence makes Lower Park look like a rainforest, it is a significant problem. Linda commented, "The most important reason for removing the ivy is that it once it climbs up into the canopy, it prevents the leaves from getting sunshine. It can also damage the bark. Ivy can kill trees. Damage to oaks also hurts acorn woodpeckers, scrub jays, squirrels, and other animals that rely on them for food and shelter. We do not cut the wild grapes because the leaves are spread far enough apart to allow the leaves of the tree to get sunshine. The [California] wild grape [*Vitis californica*] is a local, native species. The English and Algerian ivy that we find in the park are non-native and invasive.

"We use hand saws and strong clippers to cut the ivy, which wraps around the trunks like choking tentacles," she added. "The work can be very tiring, and we need to keep our eyes open for poison oak! We would not remove all the ivy even if we had enough volunteers. Pulling the ivy off the bark can damage it. Essentially, we remove all the ivy at the base of the tree and about nine inches up just so we can see any we have missed. If we had enough volunteers, which we never will, we could pull out all the ivy by the roots. About a year after we cut the ivy from a tree, we have to come back and do it again."

Linda and her husband Doug took the annual training for PALS volunteers after they saw a notice in the *Chico Enterprise-Record*. "Some of the volunteers are Park Watch members, and some just found out about the Ivy League from various sources like walking through the park or Facebook. "I would guess that we've cleared about seventy-five percent of the trees in Lower Park that had ivy growing on them," Linda commented. "Many people who pass by ask what we are doing and tell us how grateful they are after they understand why the work is important."

The evening ended with Shane's praise of PALS volunteers who had been involved for five, ten years, or more. Then we played a trivia game where Shane asked people to answer questions about the park. I found that a lot of the dates escaped me, but when Shane asked the group to name some proposed projects that never happened, I answered, "An auto campground!" Shane rewarded me with a reusable grocery bag. When we talked at the picnic's end, Shane and I agreed that we need as many educational programs as possible. The park deserves dreamers—and it gets them!

Sycamore Pool at One Mile Recreation Area in autumn.

CHAPTER TEN

Children's Education in the Park

Preschoolers Hit the Trails

We environmental educators are an idealistic crew. We hope our work stimulates others to connect with their world, love it, and take responsibility toward healing it. I've worked in this field for several decades; my projects include extensive work with museums and other outdoor programs in the Bay Area and in Chico. I spent seven years developing and working on a place-based program at a culturally and economically diverse elementary school in Oakland. I used to run into one of my former students at neighborhood coffee shops during her college years. She told me she was considering becoming an environmental lawyer; maybe I influenced her! Bidwell Park's educators also hope hands-on education can encourage kids to protect this wondrous place.

Big Chico Creek roared through an oak-bordered meadow at Five Mile Recreation Area. Preschool children and their teachers gathered there one cool morning after days of pouring rain. Acorn woodpeckers emerged and pounded their food into tree trunks. One California quail perched on a shrub and called, "a-HA-ha!," telling its neighbors, "Here I am!"

"I saw a TV show about worms," a four-year-old boy with a shovel told me as he placed earthworm-filled soil in a cardboard box.

"What do you think about worms?" I asked him.

"Ehhhh…" he answered.

"Do you think they're interesting?" I continued.

"Kind of. They're slimy and squirmy, and they don't have bones. If they did, they couldn't squirm."

Other three- to five-year-olds arrived with their parents and prepared to spend four hours with Happy Acres Outdoor School. Scrub jays squawked from oaks that had dropped their leaves and looked like complicated spider webs. A group of girls sat with teacher Jocelyn Fitzgerald and wrapped twine around sticks they had found.

"These build hand-eye coordination," Jocelyn said. "Then they can spread out and build structures if they choose."

Several girls decided their twine sticks were magic wands. "We can make people do things they don't want to," one girl told me. "I can make them run away from us!"

"I used to be a lifeguard here and at One Mile," Brian Kehoe, the school's director, said. "It used to be there weren't so many trees here; this area had grass down to the creek. People can still swim here, but they stopped having lifeguards around 1990."

"Probably because of funding," I observed.

"Funding is everything," he agreed. "I've been teaching kids for eighteen years in a traditional kindergarten classroom. Then I took a year off, and now I do this.

"Kids are too tied to screens and media," he reflected. "Mentally, nature is what a three- to five-year-old needs—exploring, growing wonder. At this age, they don't separate themselves from nature; they are part of nature. We adults know we are in the park. They are the park! When they make ice cream from mud and sand, it's ice cream. Our staff just gets out of their way; we watch from afar and intervene if we need to. I wouldn't call it nature education; it's nature connection."

A girl interrupted us and said, "There's a puppy at my sister's school."

"A real puppy! Would you like one here?" Brian asked.

"Yeah!"

I wandered down to the creek with Brian, some of the kids, and Jocelyn. A boy drew in the sand with a stick while Jocelyn and other children found some raccoon tracks that looked like a baby's handprints. Deer tracks revealed two hooves that almost touched like crescent moons. Brian showed the young explorers a place where beavers had chewed on a cottonwood tree, leaving distinctive tooth marks.

I followed the staff and the children to an island, soaking my sneakers in the process. Some of the kids hung out by themselves; others talked with friends. "The children named this place 'The Rock Garden,'" Brian said. "They named other places 'Wizard Beach' and 'The Beaver Tree'—I don't know where they come up with the names!"

"They're defining the park for themselves," I noted. "That's great—many people don't have a relationship with this place."

"We want the kids to immerse themselves in imaginative play to the point where they don't know we exist," Brian commented. "I usually have my knife, and I whittle; that's how I disappear. They don't know I'm watching them. The idea of the forest school movement is that they work things out for themselves. That's the forest school ethos."

Three children approached Brian, holding a dead lizard on a leaf. "Poor little guy. It looks like he drowned," Brian observed. "But there are others here."

"Yeah," the kids agreed as they walked away to continue their explorations.

"I include science in my work with children," I said. "You can see science as a type of exploration and play, something that stimulates curiosity and wonder. We do experiments spontaneously so the kids connect with the things we are discovering.

"We classify rocks and fallen leaves and make groups of ones that are the same shape and color," I continued. "Other times, the young Galileos drop a feather, a stick, and a rock to notice which hits the ground first and last. Then we might find out which of these sink or float in a pond."

Brian agreed but said his program doesn't include scientific experiments. "We observe while kids do investigations without our guidance," he reflected. "There are pollywogs here in different stages of development. They will ask each other, 'Yours has legs. Mine doesn't. Is it a frog or a fish?' We like to let them figure it out.

"They've been here every day for two years," he added. "They see the river level go up and down, and they see trees both full and barren of leaves. They know the woodpeckers' life cycles. We watched beavers cut the trees, and they saw that the branches were gone the next day. They see the seasons change, and they know the sound of a hawk."

"What if they ask you something?" I asked.

"I like to show them things," he replied." A boy approached with a piece of "sea glass," a piece of broken, colored glass that the creek had tumbled, polished, and smoothed. "Can you hold it up to the light?" Brian asked.

The boy did this and declared, "I'm going to give it to my mom."

Brian said. "When these kids go to school, they will be curious. They know if you flip a rock over, something cool will be there. And as they grow into adulthood, they will know nature is a place they can go to; it will be there for them."

"And they will have a basis for making decisions when controversies about the park come up," I added.

Brian howled like a coyote at ten o'clock. The children howled back, and everyone returned to the meadow for Circle Time. Children could choose to participate, to watch from the group, to do something safe, or do independent activity. Most of us sat on a tarp, and I introduced myself to the curious preschoolers.

"He is writing a book about children playing in the park," Brian said. "Maybe he'll talk about you in the book; you'll be famous!"

"*YEAH!*" the kids cried as a group.

Brian and the other staff members led the children in a song: "*Good morning to the flowers, beasties, birds in the trees; good morning to you and me!*" We played a variation of "In and Out the Window," which began when children decided which animal to become. Each player changed into a bobcat, a jackrabbit, a fox, an opossum, an owl, or a snake, then ran back and forth beneath their friends' outstretched arms. Then they stood on one leg while Brian recited a poem about a great blue heron. They curled up to become seeds, lifted their arms to sprout like young plants, and drifted like leaves or feathers to the ground. Circle Time ended as the children gathered in a line, got down on their stomachs, and slithered like snakes as they hunted for snacks.

"I had to get a permit to do this," Brian said. "One lady with the Bidwell Park and Playground Commission asked me, 'What are you trying to do with them?'"

Brian answered, "We are growing new commissioners! They liked that!"

Explorers All

I volunteer with Jon Aull's education programs at Butte Creek Ecological Preserve, south of Chico, and at Big Chico Creek Ecological Reserve, which connects with Upper Bidwell Park and reaches into the Cascade foothills. We welcome third- to fifth-graders to these year-round habitats for black bears, mountain lions, and a huge range of birds. Our program focuses on fire ecology, difficulties salmon and migratory birds face in their journeys, the Maidu people's uses for native plants, and much more.

Jon has worked with these programs on California State Enterprises land for several years. He preceded this job with work as head naturalist at the Big Chico Creek

Big Chico Creek Nature Center.

Nature Center in Bidwell Park. Robert Dresden, who worked for the Butte County Office of Education before he followed Jon at the nature center, leads programs for the THRIVE home-school program in the park.

The nature center is near the World of Trees Nature Trail and Cedar Grove. Chico Area Recreation District, which coordinates sports and recreation in the park, manages the center. Pacific Chorus frogs springtime "ribits!" frequently ring from the pond near the older building. Redwoods create a setting where educators can gather with kids, and trails lead explorers to Big Chico Creek. Its older building is home to a screech owl, rabbits, a range of snakes, Hunter the red-tailed hawk, and John Bidwell the desert tortoise. All have been injured, orphaned, or rescued from irresponsible owners and could not survive in wild habitats.

The newer building includes a laboratory with walls covered with photographs and murals of the park and its wildlife. The staff considers Bidwell Park their classroom and presents educational programs to preschool, elementary school, and home-schooled children. They offer day camps during school vacations and nature-themed birthday parties.

Jon said, "I think one of the good things we did at the center was to build the big building. I coordinated all the exhibits and pictures that are in the lab and wrote the accompanying text to tell Bidwell Park's story. The photographers asked me where to get good shots.

"When I was there, all the rescued animals were native wildlife. My philosophy was I wanted to talk about animals in our backyard and their value in our ecosystems. We stressed things like why we don't kill rattlesnakes. John Bidwell, the desert tortoise, has been there for years. He isn't local, but he offers a chance for people to focus on endangered species."

"Did you have any surprising adventures with kids in the park?" I asked.

"The nature center is in a safe part of the park, near the center of town, but it sits right on the creek's riparian corridor. Once, I was sitting with sixty kids, and a bobcat wandered by! Another time, a mountain lion came to Cedar Grove. Fish and Wildlife officials darted it so it would be unconscious and moved it to a wilder area. Sometimes, people would run inside and yell, 'There's a mountain lion outside!' but it was probably a bobcat."

While the center does not accept animal donations from the public, guests once brought a ringtail, a usually reclusive relative of raccoons, in a carrying case. It escaped from its confinement and ran all over the center, causing chaos until the staff caught it. "People would often leave baby birds in boxes at the center's front door," Jon observed sadly.

"When I worked at the center, there was a sign that said, 'Bidwell Park Information Center.' I think it's still there," he continued. "We were always a shoestring operation, and the city stopped funding us around the time when I left. We never really had the funds. I had Upper Park as my classroom when I worked with the nature center. I did geology hikes, programs at vernal pools on Bidwell Ranch, hikes with the California Native Plant Society, and much more."

"Were your programs based on free exploration or were they more structured?" I asked.

"They were serving schools and teachers, so they were based on the California science standards," Jon said. "Some teachers would tell me that their visits were the only chance they had to cover science, and they would ask me to do the same program year after year so they could cover the standards. The camps were looser; they were more based on exploration."

How to Teach in the Park

"I included experiments to supplement many of my programs," I said. "If we had explored a stream or wetland, I'd drip water on waxed paper, and the kids would blow in it through straws. It stuck together, and we talked about how water is cohesive and has a skin where some insects can live. Then we dripped soap into it to see how pollution could break the cohesion."

Jon found it hard doing science activities with the large groups coming to his programs. "I basically had thirty kids and a teacher for an hour and a half," he commented. "We would observe landforms, plants, and animals, and I'd share information about the things we'd seen. Sometimes there would be parent helpers and sometimes there wouldn't be."

"An exception would be where we did water quality testing," Jon continued. "We did experiments to see if stream water was polluted, and we classified the insects and other invertebrates that lived in the water. But I liked the teachers to have the option of expanding into investigations and experiments later."

I asked, "Do you think it changes kids' attitudes to be in the park for an hour?"

"Absolutely," Jon said. "I used to ask kids, 'Who's ever been to Bidwell Park before?' It's amazing how many of them hadn't. If we want kids to become stewards of the land, they need to experience contact with it."

"I hiked in Bidwell Park for thirty-seven years," Robert Dresden told me when we met after my talk with Jon. He mentioned a childhood experience where his brother upset him by killing a snake. His work with the nature center included night hikes, geology treks, habitat explorations, life cycles of oaks, and more.

"A big part of my work with THRIVE is to help people feel comfortable outdoors," he continued. "Kids have a natural fluency with nature, a hanging out kind of fluency. They need to play. They explore the park, climb trees, and see mushrooms growing. I lead them where they need to go."

"Part of the fluency involves knowing we're going to walk," he added. "We walk single file. This can be new to many youngsters, who often find themselves in cars and are unfamiliar with exercise." At first, some children hiking on rugged, rocky terrain for the first time stumble. Robert says they needed to learn to hike carefully and develop skills and confidence to safely walk in the park and wild places.

"The park has more that can be covered than other environments," he continued. He played his recorder and told nature stories while kids explored the park's habitats. "That centers them and helps them explore consciously,"

"It's great that they see nature programs with elephants and tigers," Jon Aull commented on the day we talked. "And that they love orangutans. But we have amazing animals here. Kids don't know what's out there. When they hear about Monkey Face, they think monkeys are there, and when they hear about Alligator Hole, they think they'll find alligators.

"If you like local animals, you'll protect local places. Maybe it would be good if we could tell them which name the Mechoopda gave to Monkey Face."

"What did they call it?" I asked.

"I don't know," he admitted. "Maybe that knowledge was lost. I've heard there was a mountain they called 'Old Man,' maybe that was Monkey Face. I try to break down misconceptions about the Mechoopda. Kids are amazed that they used plants in the park for food and still do sometimes. 'I didn't think you could eat plants,' they say.

Making Education Concrete

"Many don't know what food is or where it comes from," I commented. "When you ask them where bread comes from, they say Safeway."

"I ask them, 'What do we eat that's grass?' Jon replied. "Rice and wheat, of course. There's an idea that the Maidu are strange and different. Kids don't understand that we use animal skins for clothes. I ask them, 'Do you use leather?' I try to convey that the Maidu have a sophisticated culture."

"David Ororo, who writes about mushroom identification and ecology, believes that the best way to connect people to a natural place is to help them understand they can use it to survive," I said. "He feels that people who gather and eat wild mushrooms will value the land more deeply than people who only come to look at them."

"I think that has its place," Jon replied, "but there's an impact there when people wander about. It's not so big with mushrooms; they are fruiting bodies that produce spores for a few days. Another will grow where one is picked."

"I get a lot from observing and photographing wild fungi," I said. "Besides, we don't want people trouncing all over the places where they grow."

Jon nodded and added, "Here we have brodiaea bulbs that can be eaten, but they won't grow back. People shouldn't dig for them. We can tell people to gather and eat the introduced stuff, like Himalayan blackberries, though. You got to reach people in a lot of ways. But stuff happens. I've heard about people who went out to see wild orchids, and soon the flowers were gone."

"How should people see the park then?" I asked,

"I've seen it getting crowded," he replied. "I'm an old curmudgeon; I don't like to see dogs off leash and all the erosion around Horseshoe Lake. There's no soil on the trails. I'm a mountain biker, but I do my biking in places where they have soil. I'm sad to see disrespect for the park.

"I still love the park; I live close to it. It's like our big national park," he continued. "We have old-growth oaks and sycamores in our backyard. I do my wildflower hike in the spring; it's like seeing old friends. And it's within a short walk or bike ride."

"Educators and writers have similar attitudes," I said. "We put information out there and hope it reaches someone. Then they can pass it on to their families and friends."

"That's what we do," Jon agreed. "Teachers have a purpose when they let the kids explore," Robert added. "But the park is an organic educator. All kinds of people can come and learn here. It's Chico's heart."

Nature-Based Skills

Jahniah Mitchell's given name is Joni, but she prefers the name she created. "My partner Matthew Knight and I started taking classes at the Tom Brown Junior's Tracker School in 2008," she told me over tea at downtown Chico's Upper Crust Bakery. "That program covered learning survival skills like building your own shelters, making fires, and tanning animal hides. We also learned about tracking animals, bird language, and local plants. We took classes off and on for several years and lived there as caretakers from 2010 to 2011."

"Where was this?" I asked.

"In New Jersey," she replied.

"I'm guessing it is in the Pine Barrens," I said, grinning. "That's the only wild place I know of in New Jersey."

"Yeah," she replied, laughing. "I worked as a counselor for the Children of the Earth Foundation in New Jersey during the summer of 2011; it was the first children's camp I worked at. When we moved back to Chico, it was culture shock. We didn't want to get nine to fives; we wanted to share what we had learned."

She and Matthew set up tables at festivals to share baskets, hides, bow drill kits for building fires, and other materials they had learned to use. They got a business license in 2012 and started offering workshops and programs for charter schools, beginning with Wildflower School. Their reputation spread through the home-school networks. Home-schooled children initially came for one hour a week in 2012.

These parents can now sign up for four to six hours. There are three groups based on the children's ages. Four- to seven-year-olds join the Forest Foxes, and seven- to eleven-year-olds form the Nature Ninja. The teachers call the oldest group, the twelve- to fourteen-year-olds, Woodland Scouts.

We both grinned as Chico's well-loved pedicab driver passed us on the tree-lined street, rapping along with a recorded song as his passengers clapped and cheered. As they moved down the street and the music faded, I said, "I think public-school children really need a program like this. They really don't get chances to explore nature as much as they need to."

"They need it terribly," Jahniah agreed. "We also teach public-school kids, either through field trips or at our spring break and summer break camps. Richard Louv, who wrote the book *Last Child in the Woods* (2008), says kids can identify many corporate logos, but they can't describe five local plants and animals. It's part of our mission that kids can name the life around them."

"How do you teach kids to connect with the park?" I asked.

"The main thing we teach is awareness," she replied. "With technology, kids are so focused they don't use their peripheral vision or other senses. We do a lot of sensory enhancement. They're constantly learning to use their ears and to walk very softly. We do a lot of blindfold activities, so the kids are forced to rely on their other senses."

"Brian and the Happy Acres program do a lot of free exploration," I said. "Do you feel that your program connects with theirs?" I asked.

"We hang out with Brian and talk, but we're not really connected. We support each other's work and vision. Brian is a wonderful asset to our community!" Jahniah replied. "We often get their students who have 'aged out' of the program. Our youngest group, the Forest Foxes, does free exploration because it is so crucial to their development at that age. But it's not totally free exploration."

Teaching Knowledge and Skills

"We have a goal and a hidden curriculum," she continued. "We guide the children through their explorations, and we use games, activities, and stories that we teach each day. They learn how to track local animals and how to identify plants that are useful. They gain basic survival skills like building shelters and making fires. We know where the animals live, and we take them to specific places for discoveries. When they find animal tracks, we ask them questions like, 'What do you notice about the tracks? How do they look?'"

"I do something real similar," I noted. "When I take kids birding, I give them charts that show birds that live in a place. When we see a bird, I say, 'What do you notice? Is it big or small? What do you notice about its beak?' until they can identify it from a picture. This helps them remember better than if I just tell them, 'That is an acorn woodpecker.'"

"Yes," Jahniah said. "Our kids also have journals where they can write or draw about what happened on a particular day."

"What about teaching through interactive games?" I asked.

"The kids love tail tag," she declared. "Everybody has a 'tail,' and they have to get each other's tails. It's all about hunting and being hunted. They have to be aware of what's happening."

Nature-based teachers agree that screen time can weaken children's sensory connection to the world. Jahniah publishes a description of the activities that's shared so parents can know about their children's experiences and discoveries. One "Story of the Day" in February 2019 described an opening circle where young children held a wool ball and tried to figure out what it was made from. "Some smelled it and guessed goat or sheep, while some guesses were more imaginative, like melted grass and dog fur," Jahniah wrote. "Wyatt (a teacher) tried to joke with them that it was an eagle pellet, but they weren't buying it. They're too sharp!"

Circle Time continued as the young explorers listened to a red-shouldered hawk's calls. Afterward, the children used a crushed rock mixed with water to temporarily paint themselves and a sycamore tree red. Jahniah described how they also used fallen trees as "perfect natural jungle gyms, with climbing, balance beams, and tunnels to climb through and explore. . . . We found some delicious miner's lettuce, which we picked up and savored together. I love seeing kids getting so excited about eating greens! Something about wild food really lights up their imaginations and enhances their feeling of connection to the land."

During one outing, the Nature Ninjas studied a stuffed squirrel and discussed whether it was a predator or herbivore. They looked at pictures of squirrel scat in a field guide to decide what kind of food these tree climbers ate. Many were surprised to learn that they were omnivores! Then they watched the rain-swollen creek and tossed oak galls into the current to understand its power and speed.

"We make sure they learn how to make ropes from plants; build a shelter that will keep them dry, safe, and warm; and how to make a fire." Jahniah said. "They work in teams and have to build a fire in five minutes using one match. It has to burn for five minutes, too. They learn about the three parts of a fire: oxygen, fuel, and heat. This helps them think about how forest fires start.

"They gather plants to make baskets," she continued. "The construction is a tactile experience that grounds the students in their surroundings. They also discover specific habitats where particular plants grow."

"Do you base this on Mechoopda culture?" I asked.

"No, we want the kids to respect that culture, but neither of us is Mechoopda," Jahniah replied. "We teach that the Mechoopda lived and still live here, but we come from a more general perspective."

"I've heard you rely on storytelling," I noted. "I've used stories to help kids deepen their imaginations and connections with the place where they live. I have a favorite from the Irish part of my background:

> A farmer ignored his wife's pleas to stay away from the faerie folk's forest on their land. He cut a tree and heard the faeries whisper about taking his wife during the night and replacing her with an enchanted wooden sculpture. He kept her in the bedroom while the faeries smashed furniture and plates, and all the farm animals panicked and wailed. The next day, the farmer agreed not to cut trees from that grove and promised to stay away from it.

"Kids learn from stories. They make up images instead of seeing them on a screen," Jahniah said. "We tell stories from a range of cultures and address the cultures they came from." The February 15, 2019, "Story of the Day" described a tale she shared with the Nature Ninjas. It told how her mentor, Tom Brown, and his brother watched squirrels build "nests" from sticks and leaves to stay warm in winter. They learned they could make shelters from these materials and that they didn't need tents or sleeping bags to survive a stormy night. The young naturalists built "debris huts" to protect stuffed animals, and the teachers poured water on these structures to test them. The children's creativity and determination helped all the critters stay dry!

"We meet in different parts of the park and focus on different ecosystems," Jahniah said. "I'm surprised when parents drop kids off and say, 'I've never been here before, and I've lived here for years!' We send a "Story of the Day"—what happened in a class. There can be follow-up at home. If a kid has a passion for the outdoors, but it's not at home, it can burst the kid's bubble. We always tell the parents, 'Have your kid show you where we went today and what we did there.'"

"Many people don't feel a connection to the park," I added.

"When we have kids for a long time, we focus on caretaking. If you can understand how things are connected in a place, you can see your connection. We want to get our own property, plant things, and build structures that won't be torn down. But land is expensive, and it won't be as beautiful as the park."

Bidwell Park is an environmental educator's dream. Through their efforts, they guide children to identify with it, to discover its surprises, and to share them with their families and friends. All these citizens can help guide the park through the uncertain days ahead.

CHAPTER ELEVEN

The Park Today and Tomorrow

Macbeth in Bidwell Park

I've never been scared in the nighttime woods, but Lower Bidwell Park gave a creepy performance as Scotland's wild country in Legacy Stages' 2019 production of *The Tragedy of Macbeth. A* great horned owl hooted as Banquo's ghost silently terrified Macbeth and again as Lady Macbeth tried to wash those damned spots from her hands. A guide led the audience of twenty-five from one scene to another on the creek's banks, and the autumn's chill mimicked the spookiness of bitter times.

John Croswaite, who played Macbeth, stood at the base of an oak and gave a riveting interpretation of the mad king's soliloquy: "Tomorrow, and tomorrow, and tomorrow." Macbeth came across as a decent fellow who was corrupted and maddened by his ambition. Lady Macbeth, also beautifully played by Jami Witt, pressured him to follow the path of political evil. Still, as his paranoia and guilt grew, his cruelty went farther than she had dreamt. This was a Macbeth one could both dread, pity, and understand in the politically chaotic days of October 2019.

The troupe used minimal props. The audience's flashlights and the cast's eerie orange lanterns provided the lighting. Legacy Stage approached the Bidwell Park and Playground Commission several months earlier and shared their plans for the performance. As far as Kate and I could tell, the theatre company cared for the park. The performance did not damage the places we visited, and no one left any trash.

I began to hope that respect and care for the land had replaced more damaging activities. Dennis Beardsley agreed with this thought in his email, "I believe the community's perception and expectations of Bidwell Park have evolved along with so many other social and environmental sensitivities over time. Since the 1980s, community expectations have definitely moved toward resource protection and not expanding development for recreational activities.

"In my mind, Middle and Lower Park are primarily recreational in character and need to be managed that way with proper maintenance and improvements," he added. He also commented on debates between conservationists and preservationists in relatively wild Upper Park. I will share his thoughts on the issue of drivers' access to remote areas via Upper Park Road shortly. This argument exploded in 2018, and some activists sided with conservationists who decided that cars should have a right to follow this route.

Another Traffic Fight

Hikers, joggers, swimmers, and cyclists follow unpaved, dusty Upper Park Road from parking lots near Horseshoe Lake to spots deep in Upper Park. They easily avoid potholes and rocks that jolt slow-moving cars. Oaks and sycamores separate Big Chico Creek on the road's southern side. Leaves that collect all the colors of autumn's rainbow collect here in October, and spring wildflowers on the road's north side become a silent fireworks display. Upper Park Road winds past the gray-brown volcanic cliffs, leading explorers toward Iron Canyon's basalt cliffs and dark mystery.

A gate blocks cars from using the road on Sundays and Mondays so Upper Park can recover from traffic impacts and hikers and cyclists can quietly enjoy the scenery. This barricade is also locked during times of wildfire danger and when winter storms cover the road with muddy puddles. On other days, drivers bringing families with children, senior citizens, and swimmers of all ages can go as far as the Salmon Hole swimming area. Another gate stops cars at this spot on all days to prevent damage and erosion along the steep, increasingly rough road. Many believe this policy helps prevent disturbances to plants and animals living in this undeveloped part of the park. However, others want the barrier removed so everyone can experience Upper Park's rugged country.

The road has caused arguments since its construction in 1939. "There was an early opposition to even building Upper Park Drive," Dave Nopel told me. "This would have been as early as the 1930s. It's not clear when it appeared. It went through an Indian mound. We don't even know where that was now!"

Many stated that Annie Bidwell's insistence that the park belongs to everyone meant that all park users, including senior citizens, children, and people with disabilities, had every right to visit the wilder areas. Others countered that heavy traffic disturbed wildlife near the road and created clouds of dust and fumes that coated leaves and choked hikers. They worried that Upper Park might become a party scene with piles of uncollected trash and that such overuse would disturb wildlife.

Locked gate at Upper Park Road near Horseshoe Lake.

Dennis Beardsley shared his thoughts about Upper Park's accessibility to people with disabilities and others who struggle to hike along the road. He compared this area to Lower Park, which is close to downtown Chico, reflecting, "Upper Park is an entirely different situation with literally no accessibility. There is a certain unspoken logic to keeping Upper Bidwell Park rough and basically unmanaged, as it limits public access with poor roads and lack of facilities. It disadvantages mobility and equal access to those who are differently abled. A paved pathway to Bear Hole with no vehicular access would go a long way to resolving many issues. Unfortunately, people did, and I assume still do, have an aversion and almost allergic reaction to the word 'paved,' which I think short circuits meaningful resolutions. Maybe things have changed over the last ten years. I would hope so."

These issues and arguments emerged strongly in 1995 when some commissioners and defenders of the park's wildness considered closing the ungated road at Diversion Dam and the idea of closing the whole road several days each week. Dissenters suspected preservationists wanted to stop car traffic along the road so the park could become an undeveloped nature preserve. They claimed that the Bidwell Park and Playground Commission wanted to close the road so it would not be maintained and would fall into disrepair, making Upper Park's wilder areas inaccessible to most people.

One speaker at the Commission's April 1995 meeting almost confirmed this attitude when he said that the best option was to keep the road in a poorly maintained state so only adventurous people who really wanted their cars to shake, rattle, and bounce would drive there. Others suggested using shuttles, buses, horse-drawn wagons, or pedicabs on the road while noting the city would have to charge passengers or to find a viable source of funding for these vehicles. Additional ideas included a kiosk on Upper Park Road that would hand out permits to drivers who wanted to visit swimming holes and a fee on cars that used the road to limit traffic.

During the late 1990s, community attention focused on people who used this area until very early morning hours on warm spring and summer evenings. Star gazers, who wanted to pursue their hobby in a spot with little interference from Chico's lights, were part of this group, along with nature enthusiasts who searched for nocturnal animals. Sadly, many other visitors left beer cans and other trash. Commissioners recommended that a gate be closed as night fell, noting that there appeared to be less trash in Upper Park when the road was blocked. This issue, like others relating to the road, simmered and sometimes boiled over for years.

The city tried to resolve the decades-old argument when it posted a questionnaire on its website in early 2018 seeking the public's thoughts about car travel on this road (Urseny 2018b). The survey's results indicated that most of the 3,000 participants supported full access for all auto traffic, allowing drivers to reach the more remote parts of Upper Park (*Chico News and Review* 2018). In spite of these findings, the Bidwell Park and Playground Commission's Conservation Committee recommended in August that the gates and restrictions would remain but that the road should be improved for emergency vehicles (Urseny 2018d).

Former Commission chair Elaina McReynolds-Baird reflected on the Commission's, saying, "There was a turnabout for emergency vehicles at the end of Upper Park Road. The Commission was concerned that if people could party up there, and someone was injured, it would be hard for emergency vehicles to get there and find parking. We agreed to give the cars continued access to fifty percent of the road, as far as Salmon Hole, but we wanted to keep studying the idea of cars going farther while looking closely at the condition of the road."

Former Commissioner Scott Grist added, "I completely disagree that any private vehicles should be allowed past Horseshoe Lake, let alone Salmon Hole. The dust created by traffic is a huge deterrent to people walking or riding bikes on that road and more vehicles deeper in the park will inevitably lead to more trash and misuse of the trails and swimming holes." The fact that traffic disturbed loose soil and silt, which flowed from tire tracks and damaged the stream during heavy storms, also remained a concern for many park defenders. It wasn't clear to the commissioners that citizens received information about this issue or the increasingly steep, rugged road before they participated in the survey.

In May 2019, Chico's Public Works Department received a $1 million grant from the State Water Resources Control Board to fund maintenance on Upper Park Road and to limit the amount of silt that flowed to Big Chico Creek. The Bidwell Park and Playground Commission applauded the grant at an October meeting but continued to recommend to the City Council that the road be open only to emergency vehicles above Salmon Hole (Urseny 2018d). Eric Gustafson of Chico's Public Works Department addressed a December 3 City Council meeting. He stated that most people did not know that the unpaved road's steepness increases dramatically beyond Salmon Hole. He mentioned a study by the Pacific Watershed Association that described how more than 450,000 drivers now use the road annually and that forty-three sites had experienced significant problems with erosion. Gustafson supported the Commission's position that the rough road above Salmon Hole be limited to emergency vehicles.

Surprisingly, no speakers disagreed with the idea that private car access stops at Salmon Hole. Speaking as a citizen, Elaina McReynolds-Baird described the city's economic plight, which had made road repairs difficult so far. Other speakers agreed that funds were inadequate and that there were not enough paid staff to keep the road open to all cars past Salmon Hole. One speaker recommended a trolley system to take seniors, children, and other visitors far into Upper Park.

The City Council stunned many people in December 2019 when they disagreed with the commissioners and voted to allow cars access to Upper Park Road five out of seven days. The decision was rather complex. Drivers could reach the far end of the road two days a week. The road would be closed to them for two days, and they could drive as far as Salmon Hole three days a week. This last policy changed the current regulation where cars must stop at Bear Hole, a point closer to the road's origin on Sundays and Mondays. The council decided the confusing schedule would be clarified in the future (Epley 2019b). Shane Romain commented, "The Upper Park Road is in environmental review. We hope to start work in fall 2021."

The Case of the Missing Oaks

Another controversy arose in March 2019 when a work crew of inmates from California's low-security Salt Creek Conservation Camp (Paskenta, CA) accidentally cut down thirty-one healthy valley oaks. The city pays the California Department of Forestry and Fire Protection (CAL FIRE) $200 daily to supervise this crew. This arrangement usually works well, but in this case, poor communication led to a gigantic mistake (Tuchinsky 2019).

Shane Romain described an old grove of introduced catalpa trees that grew next to the Chico Creek Nature Center. Western catalpas hail from a small area in the southeastern United States, but people brought them to many other parts of the United States and Canada. Their white, trumpet-shaped flowers adorned with purple and yellow spots make them a well-loved ornamental. Their big heart-shaped leaves and cigar-like seedpods also stand out. With no objective evidence to back their claims, some people believe that their bark contains chemicals that can cure malaria, whooping cough, and asthma (Lederer and Burr 2019).

The catalpas by the Nature Center died during the drought, leaving dry fuel that could have contributed to a major fire. "That area is fire-prone," Shane said. "There were no funds to remove them. They were also close to neighborhoods and Park View Elementary School.

"Once the work started, we discovered there were more catalpa trees than we realized," he continued. "There was miscommunication between our staff and the CAL FIRE staff. Oaks that were healthy were accidentally marked to be taken down." Field supervisors from the city were called away to review other projects, and the crew removed the mistakenly marked oaks and the dead catalpas.

While the community agreed that the mistake had risen from a lack of funds, sufficient staff, and poor communication, Chico remained divided and angry about the city's actions. In April, one tree expert told the Bidwell Park and Playground Commission that he believed thirty-one oaks, not twenty-seven, had been cut. Another stated that the mistake had cost the city $221,000 and would affect the area's ecological integrity for decades. City officials traced the mistake to the lack of staff members who can concentrate on Bidwell Park and other open spaces. Within weeks, the city announced that it would update the methods for marking trees, showing which ones should be cut or allowed to remain. The city would give the Bidwell Park and Playground Commission and the public a work plan before any trees were removed, and the City of Chico agreed to pay $13,000 to plant new native trees (Dougherty 2019; Epley 2019a; Urseny 2019b).

"In my opinion, the area by the nature center will be healthier than it was," Shane told me. "The dead trees were shading out new growth. There were new cedar seedlings growing there. They will now get sunlight and grow rapidly. If the area had caught on fire, it would have been catastrophic. That's part of the challenge of managing Bidwell Park. At the end of the day, everybody cares deeply about the park, and we're trying to do the best we can. Mistakes were made; it was unfortunate, but if the city had done nothing and the area had caught fire, it would have been catastrophic. I wish people would see we are all in the same boat."

Maaaaaaaaaa!

Sometimes, citizens find common ground around the park. Capra Environmental Services originally brought 500 to 800 goats into the park during the summer of 2019. They devoured yellow star thistle, Himalayan blackberries, and other invasive species and consumed undergrowth that could fuel hot fires. The goats cleared about an acre of ground each day and were then moved to another overgrown area. Goat watching became a favorite activity for grownups and kids (Sharaga 2018a; Urseny 2019d).

This was far from a new idea. In February 1976, the Bidwell Park and Playground Commission discussed allowing 160 head of cattle to graze in Upper Park to reduce the fuel load that could contribute to fires. Some botanists commented that this plan would only be successful if the animals overgrazed, meaning that they could harm native vegetation, and the Commission rejected the plan.

Kate and I frequently watched as the goats contentedly munched in an area where an electric fence kept walkers from hugging, petting, or scaring them. They climbed onto logs or stumps to reach the taller weeds. A couple of large guard dogs wandered among the goats, sometimes chasing those who dared to steal their dog food. These pooches wagged their tails at passing walkers, but people told us they would attack anyone who crossed the fence. A herdsman also kept watch and made sure no one

Goats and their guard dog in Lower Park.

tried to harass or snatch his animals. The goats have returned several times, and many people love that they feast on poison oak.

The Endless Invasive Plant Problem

It would be wonderful if the goats could solve the introduced plant problem overnight, but this ongoing issue will require intense attention and a strong vegetation management plan. Some invasive is a problem in all parts of the park. Olive trees grow dense branches and thick leaves, blocking light from other plants. With its toe-jabbing thorns, the puncture vine spreads quickly and is a hazard to barefoot kids and tires everywhere. Misnamed Himalayan blackberry, which hails from Europe, seizes land in all areas where it grows (Friends of Bidwell Park n.d.).

Some introduced plants are more specific to particular parts of the park. English and Algerian ivy cling to oaks in Lower and Middle Park. With its striking yellow blossom, Scotch broom takes over streamside areas in Middle Park. Upper Park is home to springtime tumbleweeds and land-seizing black mustard with its abundant yellow flowers (Friends of Bidwell Park n.d.).

These species and others exist in all three of the park's main sections. There's a desperate need for a detailed study showing the exact spots where they thrive and others where they can't be found. Invasive plants are often beautiful, and many park lovers don't understand how they harm native species by taking more of their share of space and water (Friends of Bidwell Park n.d.).

People's perspectives on vegetation management seem to hinge on whether they think the park should be a wildlife preserve or a place for human recreation. These disagreements seem more muted, and the positions less pure than in the past. Still, echoes of the old debates between conservationists and preservationists remain as allies try to work together.

Park Enthusiasts Sometimes Disagree

Lise Smith-Peters, a Bidwell Park and Playground Commissioner in 2019, and I planned to meet at the Tin Roof, a bakery and restaurant in downtown Chico. I arrived and found that the café had just closed for the day. After a flurry of cell phone calls, we connected at Burger and Brew Restaurant for explanations, apologies, and good laughs before discussing the park's health over beers.

Lise passionately defended the park's native plant communities and the animals that make them their homes. "We need to change the mind frame for managing the park," she said. "Officials are into maintenance, safety checks on swing sets, putting signs up, and opening and closing gates."

"It sounds like you are saying they focus more on equipment and buildings than ecology," I commented. "But these are important things for a public park in a town. There's a basic question: does the park exist so people can have recreation, or should it be more of a nature preserve?"

"It's both," Lise said, "but we need to create a mindset and funding for ecological habitat preservation. We love our park, but people need to know the differences between Lower, Middle, and Upper Park. They are not the same. We have sycamores, valley oaks, and other natives, but the park could become a trap full of invasive plants in fifty years. There's no planning; everything is done in a reactionary way. The ecological balance of the park is at stake, along with habitat for animals."

Lise sipped her Sierra Nevada wheat beer and reflected, "The Commission used to do their own investigations and write reports instead of being fed pabulum about conditions at Horseshoe Lake and other areas. We need to get back to that. Maybe sometimes the park even needs to be closed so we can take care of it."

"People would say that closing the park for studies and restoration would be the work of royalists and elitists who don't understand that Annie gave the park to everyone in Chico," I commented as I enjoyed my own German beer.

I laughed and agreed when Lise replied, "Well, maybe ecologists are people who don't want to drink beer by the creek, play disc golf, or put cigarettes out in the park in July. I want to say, 'Wake up, guys! This park is a resource; most cities don't have a place like it!'"

"People often stop and thank us for removing ivy from oaks," I said. "But some folks have told me that people call them killers when they remove star thistle."

Lise nodded and said, "Every four months, there will be a letter to the editor saying, 'They are removing the English Ivy!' But it is choking the oaks. What's wrong with removing it?"

Shane Romain's office sits in the same building where the city keeps the Bidwell Park and Playground Commission's minutes. Nearby Highway 32 takes travelers to the disc golf course, Big Chico Creek Ecological Reserve, and into the volcanic Cascade range. "A vegetation management plan must be based on best management practices and must recognize that each area must be managed differently," he reflected. "Lower Park is a high-use area that must be managed differently from Middle or Upper Park. Our current management plan is ten years old, and there has been so much growth of invasives in Lower Park, it is incredible."

He presented a slightly different perspective from Lise's when he commented, "Monitoring invasives is really about preserving safety—what's most beneficial to recreational park users. We need clear sightlines, clear trails so people can feel comfortable. Masses of invasives sometimes create situations where people do not feel safe. The park is overgrown; in 2013, many city staff were laid off. That was a huge blow we haven't recovered from. We were crippled for two years."

Former Commission chair Elaina McReynolds-Baird and I met for lunch in a popular downtown restaurant to discuss these issues. The line was so long, and Elaina needed to get back to her work as a development director for CSU Chico's summer programs, so we ran to a fine but less crowded Indian restaurant. We enjoyed curries with basmati rice and naan, and discussed the need for a detailed study of the park's vegetation.

Elaina agreed with Shane on the safety issue as she stated that one issue with overgrown invasives is that they make it difficult to find and monitor homeless campsites and to promote everyone, including the campers' safety. "Vegetation management is part of a larger issue. We have a transient, homeless population that lives in the park. One couple died there. A fire started in their over-vegetated campsite, killing them both."

"I support the idea that we need to reevaluate and update the vegetation plan with input from experts," she said. "We need to know which plants to remove and which to leave; which are natives and which are invasive. Also, we need to be clear about the problem of fuel for fires. The issue in Pulga, where the Camp Fire started [2018] was pine trees, which burn easily and at a high temperature. Here, we don't have as many pines; we have more oaks, which are slower to burn. We also have a prolific amount of ground vegetation. The goats, which eat ground vegetation, should be in the park permanently."

Lise also praised the goats but questioned some of the fire management practices. "I think there is an overemphasis on fuel. They are over-manicuring the park with tree cutting. I have files from Chico's fire chief saying there is not really a fire issue in Lower Park, it's more Upper Park."

She mentioned a practice of removing downed trees in parts of Lower Park. "Some of these downed oaks have been there for ten years, and they are chainsawing them in the guise of removing fuel. That's wrong. That's habitat they're destroying. Also, they say they are cutting trees to promote safety and make camps visible, but some of these areas don't even have encampments."

Former Commissioner Scott Grist commented, "I am a naturalist and an organic vegetable farmer in Chico. I joined the Bidwell Park and Playground Commission because I spend a lot of time in the parks and natural areas of Chico teaching wild edible and medicinal plants and other outdoor/wilderness survival skills. I love

Chico's natural areas, and I want to do all I can to advocate for their protection and restoration."

"What do you think about the need for a vegetation management plan?" I asked.

Grist answered: "It has been a slow process, but we are currently trying to update and implement a new vegetation management plan. We will be working with members of the local Mechoopda tribe and other professional plant/ecosystem experts to make plans to remove harmful invasive species and restore areas with the proper native species specific to those ecosystems.

"There has been so much human influence imposed on Bidwell Park that it is almost impossible to think of it as a nature preserve, but moving forward, we should be restoring native species and ecosystems while removing harmful invasive species. Obviously, we want the public to use and enjoy the park; it is the gem of Chico, but it might be good for the public to view the park as a preserve, giving the plants and animals who call it home the utmost respect while visiting."

Ali Meders-Knight of the Mechoopda Maidu tribe sipped her tea on the day we met at Blackbird Café and reflected that she and other members of the Mechoopda tribe have always known more about local native plants than city officials do. "You always had a sense of relating to the land," Ali said. "You don't have words in English for that reverence and paying attention. When you haven't had a burn in five years, you have plants that have been sitting there five, ten, twenty years. The reason the land was so beautiful when John Bidwell came through is the Maidu burned it.

"I spend a lot of time teaching children about traditional land management. When you let the park look like a jungle, people think it looks wild, beautiful, and natural. To me it's a hot mess; it needs to be cleaned.

Ali works hard to establish a program where the Mechoopda tribe can certify Chico State students, landowners, foresters, and others as being knowledgeable about traditional land management methods. She hopes for a trained task force composed of residents who will cut excessive growth and use fire as indigenous people did.

The park took a step forward in July 2020 when the city agreed on a draft of a vegetation management plan that might receive support from CAL FIRE. The proposal focuses on each ecosystem's needs in the park and other green spaces. It describes the use of prescribed burns, grazing goats, and other techniques to remove invasive plants that provide fuel for wildfires and includes Mechoopda land management techniques to support native plants' health.

These ideas have a chance to restore the park to a healthy state where native plants and animals can thrive.

Thoughts on the Park's Future

The Maidu have been in the northern Sacramento Valley since long before the pioneers arrived, and there's every reason to think they will stay and keep their deep connections with this land. "I think it would be in the city and county's interest to work with the Mechoopda tribe to develop a land management plan," Ali Meders-Knight commented. "It would include water management, fire-based management, and more. There could be a land management workforce to do large projects like burning and educating the public about why this is a safe practice."

"In my opinion, the biggest issue is that Chico and the world are changing," Shane Romain reflected. "Chico isn't the same as it was three years ago, five years ago, or thirty years ago. The park isn't being used in the same ways, especially since the Camp Fire. Use is increasing. Everyone loves the park and has an idea about how it should be managed. Bidwell Park is so ingrained in Chico's culture that any change will be political. We need to find new partnerships about how the park can be safe and healthy for the public to enjoy and [develop] a common view on the park's health.

"The park is Chico's crown jewel, but it has always been a low priority; it's understaffed and underfunded. It's frustrating how long things take. Some people are tired of waiting for work to be done. That's why rogue trails are being created. Volunteers are important, but there's no substitute for city oversight. We need signage about policies, information for the public, and a timely way of responding to maintenance needs. People are not cleaning up after dogs or picking up fishing line; dogs and wildlife are getting caught in it. The park was a gift from Annie Bidwell, but that was a long time ago, and she said it would be a thorn in the side of Chico if it weren't managed properly."

In 2021, the City Council developed a new policy toward the Bidwell Park and Playground Commission that may impact how the park is managed for years. Lise Smith-Peters and I discussed the situation over iced tea at a bakery-café in downtown Chico. "It was probably four years ago; the City Council changed the way Commission and other board members are chosen. Newly elected council members could appoint and approve of these people. This lasted for a year or two, then council voted to return to the original policy where the whole City Council could review applications and interview candidates for the Commission and city boards, and all council members had an equal vote." The council elected in November 2020 returned to the plan where only newly elected officials would decide about Commission and board members.

Neither Elaina nor Lise sit on the Commission any longer in late 2021, but both keep the strong love for the park they shared in earlier discussions. "John and Annie's vision is still apropos," Lise commented. "It's because of them that we have the park. We have an obligation to take care of it and focus on ecology. That's not happening. That's why we need things like the park-wide vegetation management plan. What would be cool would be for the city to see the value of the park, actively fundraise, and just make sure that ecology is included with maintenance. We also need the city to come up with an educational system. We need to educate city employees about which plant is a native and which is not. If I were rich, I'd donate to education. We need an additional education building."

"We need Park Ambassadors at the library," Shane Romain added. "We need people who can lead walks; our park ambassadors can't do it now. We also need more trail signage and junior rangers who can talk to people, but we don't have the resources."

Susan Mason of Friends of Bidwell Park added, "You have to keep educating people because there are new students every year, and new people moving into the area. Real education requires money. You don't want to just fill the park with signs— people don't read them!"

"When I was the park's Volunteer Coordinator, I tried to educate the youth at Chico State through talks," Lise Smith-Peters said. "I also used to talk to the Elks, Soroptimists, and others. An educational program has to be a four-pronged approach: press releases, talks, inviting people to the park, and social media, especially for young people. When I had people working in the park, I thought about educating people about the plants they worked with. They learned which are native, how Indians used them, and which are invasives. When crews do restoration work, we need to have a trained crew leader program where leaders can tell them, 'That's puncture vine; it needs to come out. That's elderberry; it is a native protected by federal law.'"

Lise continued: "Wes Dempsey was instrumental in collecting seeds to restore native plants in the park. For six years, I worked with Chico High School students to plant these species." She and Wes discussed each plant's needs, and she helped the students plant each type of seed under the best possible conditions.

Lise reiterated the importance of hands-on involvement, "The more you involve people, the more investment they will have in the park. A huge number of people who visit the park do nothing. We can tell them, 'You can take a mile run, but here's a trash bag. We don't have enough staff; we need your help.'"

Woody Elliott reflected, "You gotta get people sensitized to what natural resources are out there. People need to be sensitized to parks so they can vote for good management. Part of that is volunteerism, getting people to pull weeds and pick up trash. I've worked with state parks, so I'm an advocate for public use, but you got to do it in a concentrated way. Having people pile on top of each other in campgrounds, for example, is not always a very pleasant experience."

Ali Meders-Knight added, "There are issues like thousands of dogs in the park. That's why we need educational work. There is a sense of entitlement, but I try to educate people about indigenous land management and not accuse them of anything. I started doing it fifteen years ago; some of my students are in college now."

Ali promotes educational programs based on traditional ecological knowledge and strives to present Maidu perspectives on the park and other areas to everyone. "They don't realize that the land and the Maidu were here before the Bidwells and other Europeans arrived. We educate people about native peoples' ways of caring for the land. I have kids recognize forest garbage or plants that don't belong here," she said. "I also stress strategies like burning the land periodically to care for it."

Speaking as an environmental educator, I passionately agree about the need for public programs. As everyone says, the amount of misinformation and confusion about the park is astounding and painful. I remembered Monica and PJ, who I met at the 2018 Butte Environmental Council cleanup in the park. They were well-informed about the park but did not seem to completely understand the need for regulations.

"I like how there's not a lot of regulation and enforcement. People do the wrong things sometime, but you can be free, and not check-in or pay," Monica said.

"I go swimming at Bear Hole or Salmon Hole and hike in fall and winter. We saw otters one day when we were swimming, at 6:30 in the evening," PJ added. "One thing that's frustrating is they have the gate closed on Sunday and Monday. I understand its protection and fire suppression, but the swimming area at Bear Hole is far to hike."

I also thought of the 1974 letter to the editor of the *Chico News and Review* from a motorcyclist who couldn't understand why he and others couldn't use the park respectfully when no other place existed for them. "The older people who are in too much of a hurry to look twice for a motorcycle have made it too dangerous to ride on the streets . . .. Motorcycling is a sport, much as golfing, hunting, and fishing; when I step on a fishhook up in the park when I am swimming, I don't condemn fishing."

Monica and PJ, like other Chico citizens, are passionate about the park's needs. Park advocates need to think deeply about people who are not part of our social circles if we want to avoid repeating our thoughts only to our friends and to the detriment of not reaching anyone else. We will be frustrated, but we can make headway with some effort.

A Day with a PALS Volunteer

On a cool November morning a few days before Thanksgiving 2019, I walked through One Mile Recreation Area with Elaina McReynolds-Baird who was the Bidwell Park and Playground Commission chair. The valley oaks had lost most of their leaves, but some yellow autumn displays were still reflected in Sycamore Pool. "I've been a Park Ambassador for ten years. I wanted to do something about the environment, but there are people working around the environment who are passionate and hard to work with," Elaina laughed. "Park ambassadors were my people. I was drawn to this like a duck to water; you walk around and do things for the park."

As a PALS Park Ambassador, Elaina wears a yellow vest and name tag as she walks her route, picking up trash, and sharing information with people in the park. We talked about how information about restrictions was sometimes confusing. Elaina reflected, "There was a man who had tied a piñata to an oak branch when I was at One Mile with Shane Romain. Shane told the man, 'You can't tie a piñata to an oak branch, and it hurts the tree and violates a city code.' The man replied, 'Which code? I am having a children's party with eight, nine, or ten kids. What am I supposed to do?'

"Shane told him the code. He untied the piñata and came back and said, 'I am reading the code on my phone. It doesn't say you can't tie a piñata to a tree. What am I supposed to do?' Shane suggested he move the swings on a swing set to one side and hang the piñata there. It was a perfect solution, but the man was put out. It's hard; people live in apartments and want to do outdoor activities."

"That's where we need education about the park and regulations," I commented.

"Yes, we need more information about why smoking is prohibited," Elaina said.

We talked about Allison Gonzalez of the American Lung Association's Smoke-Free Parks, who did a presentation at the November 2019 PALS meeting. Bidwell Park is, in theory, a smoke-free facility, but many smokers continue to think it is their ashtray. Ms. Gonzalez mentioned that cigarette butts sometimes account for one-third of the litter in a park. They are not biodegradable and break down into small cellulose acetate particles that animals and toddlers might pick up and eat. Birds sometimes include this arsenic and lead-filled trash in their nests. Secondhand smoke is a real health threat, and kids who see people smoking anywhere, including in Bidwell Park, might decide it is a cool thing to do.

"There are no signs that explain the rules against smoking," Elaina said.

"We need education, but at some point, you do have to write tickets when people are continually ignoring the rules," I added. "That is what ended the use of ORVs in the hills."

"Yeah, and you never know what you will find. I was removing invasive plants; I put my hand in a bush and found a bag of pot. I gave it to the ranger," Elaina laughed.

"Do you ever find used hypodermic needles?" I asked.

"Yes," Elaina said. "One group found about fifty at a spot near Cedar Grove."

We came to a picnic site where someone had drawn an elaborate, colorful design on the table. Again, people must understand that this activity destroys city property. Fortunately, the artist used erasable colored chalk instead of wax, which is impossible to remove.

"Look, candy corn," Elaina sarcastically said, pointing to a pile of treats on the table. "What a great present for the animals!" The artistic picnickers also left a bunch of balloons tied with a ribbon and attached to a tree.

"I wonder if the picnic table artists really thought they were doing something that would make the park more beautiful," I asked as we placed their gifts in the trash.

"Maybe," Elaina said. "People are generally reasonable when I approach them about regulations. They just don't always know the rules." A man with two off-leash dogs passed us just then.

Elaina quietly told him that his dogs needed to be on leashes, but he walked on without responding. We passed another man with two unattached dogs a few minutes later. When Elaina mentioned the rule to him, he smiled, said, "Thank you," and continued on his way. Since PALS volunteers do not have the power to give tickets, there was nothing else we could do.

"Maybe he will think about it and bring a leash next time," I said.

"Hopefully," Elaina answered. "People are supposed to have a six-foot leash, but some have those expandable leashes. A woman was riding a bike when a dog shot out, and the woman flipped and wound up with $1,800 in medical expenses. People will always say their dog is under voice control, but my dog is never under voice control."

"No dog really is," I said.

We walked close to the creek along South Park Drive and watched a confrontation between acorn woodpeckers and a squirrel. A man who strolled with his two sons, who were probably eight and five years old, passed us. "Are you Park Watchers?" he asked as his kids laughed at the antics in the tree.

"Yes," Elaina told him. We told him about the procedure for applying to be a PALS volunteer, the training session each spring, and the work he could do.

"Can kids join?" he asked.

"You have to be eighteen," Elaina said.

"But there are cleanups where kids can help out," I said, mentioning the yearly BEC cleanup. He thanked us and walked on with his curious sons.

"People always thank me," Elaina smiled.

"They thank us for cleanups and removing ivy," I answered. "Sometimes we have to explain that we are helping oaks when we cut the ivy down. People from Friends of Bidwell Park tell me that when they are removing star thistle, people yell "Killer!" at them."

"No good deed goes unpunished," Elaina grinned. "Once on Make a Difference Day, people were removing ivy from a fence along the road that parallels South Park Drive. A neighbor came out and asked, 'What are you doing?'

"They explained all the reasons for removing ivy. 'Leave it!' she said. "I don't want to see the park!"

We grinned and waved at a four-year-old who walked with her smiling mom and said, "Look mummy, I want a yellow shirt too!"

"I have one more year as chair of the Bidwell Park and Playground Commission," Elaina sighed. "Sometimes I wonder what I've accomplished."

"You've kept meetings civil," I said. "That's an accomplishment."

"Yes, and I've volunteered," Elaina said. "We are enjoying this park today because of volunteers. My goal is to clean up the park. I carry my own bucket and gloves for trash. I use the Park Watch app to report on things like broken park benches and grills that are left full of ashes. Volunteers are critical to sustaining any resources in the city, especially the park, given that it is 3,670 square acres. We need education. We need to get more signs about park information, too, but people tear them down and graffiti them.

"The park is a legacy, but it can't be maintained with a minimal maintenance staff and a park administration that is stuck with rigid protocol," she continued. "I mean, they talk about how the park has no money, but they never go out on a limb to say, 'We really need this,' and fight for it. We're seeing with the oaks by the nature center disaster that when the park is stretched too thin, something is destroyed."

"What about a foundation that could provide funds?" I asked.

"We're talking about it, but someone will have to say, 'I will take the ball.'"

"I've also heard the idea that community people can propose and do fundraising projects for the park," I said.

"Yes!" Elaina agreed. "The concern is that the money raised would go into the general fund, and someone would say, 'It was collected for the park, but we need a new street lamp. The park's fund would have to be outside of the city's control."

The questions we discussed during that walk remained unresolved in July 2021. Elaina's term as chair of the Bidwell Park and Playground Commission ended, and she decided, for personal reasons, to maintain a status as a private citizen but to remain active with PALS. On July 9, 2021, we met for lunch at Om Foods, a Chico restaurant specializing in vegetarian and vegan meals but also serves fish.

Elaina enjoyed a fish dish while I tackled a large and delicious vegetarian burrito as we discussed the city's need for the park. "I want to focus on how a park contributes to a community. There are benefits to being in the park for children, older adults, and everyone. Despite the politics, the park will survive. But as goes the park, so goes the city!"

CHAPTER TWELVE

Concluding Thoughts

Does It Matter?

I began to write this chapter's rough draft on November 8, 2019, the first anniversary of the Camp Fire, California's deadliest wildfire. I have finally finished revising it in 2023 while COVID-19 is still with us. The pandemic closed countries and economies, and while social distancing, vaccinations, and other factors slowed the virus, confirmed cases and deaths remain. Climate change creates worldwide panic, especially in the areas where melting glaciers lead to shrinking freshwater supplies and where rising ocean levels threaten coastal settlements. Wildfires that many people connect with climate ravaged the western United States. California's biggest blazes flared during the summers and autumns of 2020 and 2021. Political and social unrest, violence, shortages, inflation, and Russia's invasion of Ukraine have recently dominated discussions. With all this in mind, is Bidwell Park still important?

The answer to that is an unequivocal *YES!*

"It's been proven through the history of this country and the world how important safe parks are," Shane Romain commented. "People can escape from the problems of the country."

Lise Smith-Peters agreed, saying, "The park has literally saved people in the pandemic year. It's literally one of the safest places you can be!"

Many people see the outdoors as a place where they can leave discomfort and uncertainty behind and find ways to restore themselves. This is especially true when a disease like COVID-19 makes indoor group activities dangerous. What will happen if people cannot find some peace in their lives and do not learn to approach divisive issues as thoughtfully as possible?

A growing body of data shows how contact with nature helps promote mental health in tense times. One unique study, "Visitors to Urban Greenspace Have Higher Sentiment and Lower Negativity on Twitter" indicated that time in an urban park with a decent tree cover reduces peoples' tension and anger. Researchers compared San Francisco residents who visited city plazas and urban parks where many trees grew with others who spent time in city spaces with few or no plants. They also monitored both groups' posts on Twitter. The people who visited the more nature-based parks posted positively-worded messages for as many as four hours; those who strolled through a more paved square shared more angry and tense messages (Micu 2019). A healthy attitude that lasts for four hours may not seem like much, but everything helps during these trying times.

Many more studies make this point. In 2016, the British Broadcasting Corporation reported on the Wildlife Trust's thirty-day nature challenge. Participants spent active time interacting and working with nature in one of many ways: they could feed birds, plant flowers for bees, or choose other activities. A survey after the month-long program showed that many people felt healthier and happier than before joining the project. The number of people who described their health as excellent increased by thirty percent (Coles 2016).

A study by the Barcelona Institute for Global Health indicated that adults with close experiences with nature as kids had better mental health than adults. Other studies show that outdoor experiences can lead to a sense of satisfaction and joy in one's life. They can reduce symptoms of heart and respiratory diseases and high blood pressure, ease tension, and relieve the symptoms of ADHD among children and adults. No one claims that contact with nature alone will solve all of humanity's problems, but it can help (Barcelona Institute for Mental Health 2019).

Many Chico residents visited Bidwell Park for comfort in November 2018. Kate and I came to the park on a cool afternoon, a few days after firefighters announced that the Camp Fire was contained. The air was as sharp as snow that day, but over 20,000 people had been displaced in just a few hours. The rain cleared the air of the toxic brown-gray haze so we could finally breathe and see the Coast Range on the far western side of the Sacramento Valley. Camouflaged killdeer called from Horseshoe Lake's shore, and a flock of red-winged blackbirds perched on a leafless oak, filling the place with their cacophony.

We walked toward the Yahi Trail and passed an acorn woodpecker that pounded its food into a telephone pole. Oaks above Upper Park Road had dropped uncountable leaves, while sycamores and willows still clung to theirs. Western Redbuds gave us a green and red psychedelic light show. A distant California quail called "chi-CA-go!!"

Rain gave Big Chico Creek back the thunderous voice it had lost during the summer's dry months. The day's drama peaked at Bear Hole, where bright autumn trees and shrubs flashed near the basalt's dark background. Here, the stream turned white as it crashed over the volcanic rocks. Somewhere, a Pacific Chorus frog called "ribit?" when we thought it should be hibernating. We found an orange-gilled fungus that clung to a space between a dead tree's branches. We couldn't identify it, but we were glad the park and everything that lived there still thrived.

State and national parks and other areas were closed for a while because many people refused to follow social distancing guidelines. We were grateful to be able to wander through Bidwell Park's wildflowers in areas that were large enough that hikers could stay away from each other. Most people we saw respected social distancing and many wore masks.

Kids Again

Children have an especially strong relationship with nature. Explorations in undeveloped areas challenge them intellectually and build problem-solving skills. Unstructured outdoor time, where kids choose their activities, develop their confidence, relieve stress and fatigue, and strengthen youngsters' imaginations and creativity. Adults who support children's care for a natural space help them create a sense of responsibility. Outdoor explorations offer young explorers many chances for physical exercise (Cohen 2023).

My ongoing experiences as an educator convinced me that puzzles, blocks, and playdough are great indoor activities, but nature floods children's senses. They smell bay laurel's sweet sting, feel the difference between squishy mud and rough gravel, see butterflies flit erratically into shadows, and compare scrub jays' calls with hawks'. Adults who know the difference between toxic and edible plants offer the youngsters native blackberries and other delights to taste.

All this stimulation helps children's imaginations rush like the creek. They pretend sticks are wands as they confront wicked wizards, that pebbles are bird eggs they need to protect, and that boulders are drums that give different tones when young musicians pound on them. They solve problems creatively by using sticks to make levers that will move rocks or decide which twig they can use to dig the deepest hole.

Today's children need fresh air and exercise. Bidwell Park gives them many options, including Caper Acres. Children have visited this beloved playground near Sycamore Pool since 1970, and adults can only enter it if they come with someone thirteen years old or younger. Kate and I joined our friend there, long-time community activist and Spanish conversation group coordinator, Ann Polivka and her grandsons, Rey and Cruz, on a warm October afternoon.

We passed through the gateway that looked like a castle's gate and found ourselves facing a large boat where kids can climb to the tops of slides. A girl laughed as she spun around on a small merry-go-round-like ride surrounded by wood chips in case she fell. Adventurers made their way to the peak of a model Swiss cheese and hid in its holes.

Kate accepted the boys' invitation to climb to the boat's top. She found a mounted metal tube, a pretend telescope that young ornithologists used to focus on birds. A simple chart of local species helped them decide if they were looking at an oak titmouse, a raven, or a very different bird.

"What do you want to do today, Grandma?" three-year-old Rey asked Ann.

"I want to watch the birds in the sky and feel the breeze on my skin. I want to watch you play and wipe your noses!" she laughed.

"The dinosaur on my shirt is nice," Rey told me. "I like to climb and jump here."

"I want to play with all the people," four-year-old Cruz added.

The area was full of young park lovers aged three to eleven. Some rode on a spinning tire swing. Others played on a seesaw. The new crooked houses, two brightly colored climbing structures that lean in different directions, fascinated Rey and Cruz. "They like the crooked houses," Ann said. "They don't have to have me with them, and they can get up high. Also, there are almost always kids. This is a mellow, fenced-in place where it's easy to keep an eye on them. I brought my kids here thirty years ago when they were small. I like the oak trees, and the kids like the mulberry bushes," Ann commented. The boys also love to swim at Sycamore Pool and at a spot near the Yahi Trail. As they grow, they may work with PALS or become park commissioners.

Bioregionalism in the Park

The late Peter Stephen Berg was a true San Francisco figure. He had been a civil rights activist in the South. After moving to San Francisco in the 1960s, Peter became involved with the San Francisco Mime Troupe and the Diggers, the more radical wing of the hippie community. He and his partner Judy Goldhaft founded the Planet Drum Foundation, a big player in the bioregional movement.

Peter saw bioregionalism as a locally-based cultural movement that strove to connect human settlements with their surroundings. Climate, soils, waterways, geology, plants, and animals impact the ways we live. Conscious citizens connect their towns and cities with the earth in healthy ways and work to preserve wilder places. Planet Drum Foundation promotes this idea worldwide, even connecting to an ecologically-based community project in Ecuador. Judy continues to share the perspective that natural scientists can combine with indigenous leaders and people from all cultures, educators, writers, artists, musicians, and local activists and officials to return cities and settlements to a healthy connection with their local place (Planet Drum Foundation n.d.).

I was lucky to present educational programs with Peter and Judy early in the early 2000s. We gathered with teachers, parents, scientists, and others in San Francisco city park, Glen Canyon Park, to discuss the city's connection with the Bay Area ecosystems. I shared some hands-on ecology activities, and we guided people along trails where we discovered cliffs made from layered chert, native willows, oaks, fungi, red-tailed hawks, rabbits, and deer.

Judy and Peter discussed San Francisco's history and culture and led us in a map-making activity. They encouraged participants to map their bioregion, including its climate, soils, landforms, and native species. Then, everyone included their favorite and least favorite human activities, from traffic and landfills to community gardens and bike/pedestrian paths. Everyone named their maps and kept them as a symbol of their growing connection with their local world.

Sadly, Peter left us in 2011. Poet and environmental activist Gary Snyder and actor Peter Coyote came to his memorial, along with Kate, me, and hundreds of others. Judy guided us on a walk through a city park, where we howled like coyotes as dusk grew. Suddenly, a red-tailed hawk circled us, and everyone called, "Hi Peter!" I think of him when I see a hawk circling Monkey Face. He would have loved this park and understood it connects Chico to the Cascade range and the Sacramento River watershed. I imagine him sharing the map-making activity at One Mile, Horseshoe Lake, or anywhere in the park. Maybe Judy will come to Chico and do this one day!

Environmental education and advocacy groups like Planet Drum Foundation seem especially necessary when many politicians strive to weaken environmental policies around clean air, healthy water, and endangered species. Bidwell Park could be an example of public land that is administered and cared for in a sane and healthy way. Such a move would place Chico firmly on the map and compare favorably with the fame the town received in the days when actors Errol Flynn and Olivia de Havilland spent time filming in the park as Robin Hood and Maid Marian.

Bidwell Park is, and will continue to be, a multiple-use area. Many hikers, birders, and photographers love its trails. Others love to ride horses or mountain bikes on appropriate trails, while picnickers, swimmers, baseball players, and golfers use more developed parts of the park. People will disagree about the needed policies, but I hope we can understand the park's uniqueness and work together to keep it healthy.

We're Not the Center of Things

Chico's park enthusiasts and preservationists who love wild places need to remember that this is Mechoopda Maidu land and that tribal members see it as part of their home and their cultural heritage. The tribe has a long-standing agreement with the city that allows members to harvest elderberry, sedge, and willow so they can make baskets and musical instruments; the Bidwell Park and Playground Commission re-stated this policy in May 2021. They have overseen excavation projects to make sure that traditional sites are protected. Many park officials and proponents work with the Mechoopda to include native practices, such as prescribed burns, as part of a vegetation management plan.

Still, some of the ways the land is used disturb the Mechoopda. Around the time of the park's centennial celebrations in 2005, tribal member Arlene Ward commented, "It's hard to talk about our cultural heritage when others are here to talk about disc golf" (Urseny 2005a). Many people I interviewed for this book agreed that the Mechoopda deserve and need to be represented on the Bidwell Park and Playground Commission if tribal representatives feel this is a wise idea that would meet their needs. Lise Smith-Peters and I reflected sadly during the summer of 2021 that it could be a while before the city adopts this policy.

We must also remember that other living things might be far more complicated than we want to believe. The primatologist Franz de Waal and others talk about how some apes appear to have a type of culture; they learn to make tools and pass their knowledge on to their offspring and neighbors. Researchers are now discovering tool use among many other species, not just us.

Elephants and other mammals seem to recognize themselves in mirrors. Dolphins have names that they use when they call to each other. Many species also have a sense of altruism; they work together to raise young animals, and some adopt orphans. Plants appear to communicate chemically, and some researchers are studying a type of slime mold that behaves like it can learn how to avoid obstacles. All of these discoveries come from serious, peer-reviewed research and not from fantasies or wishful thinking.

There is no way of knowing what, if anything, our animal neighbors in Bidwell Park are thinking or feeling. But we have highly intelligent ravens, American crows, and scrub jays. Black bears might be problem solvers, and raccoons are among the animal kingdom's prized tricksters. We could assume that they are not conscious of their surroundings and imagine that the park is "ours" to use any way we please.

However, we can assume that Bidwell Park is a mystery, full of unanswered questions, and a home for intelligent creatures with every right to thrive. This neighborly way of treating the park is a healthy choice; we can visit it with curiosity and wonder. Kids and adults can find it a place to build new intellectual and physical skills, connect with their senses and imaginations, and become friends with the world. The sense of wonder and astonishment we gain will help strengthen us to confront climate change, war, racism, poverty, and all the world's endless woes. Maybe we will keep on keeping on.

"One Does What One Can"

It rained one mid-May night in 2019. This is very unusual for Northern California, whose annual dry period sometimes begins by this time. Big Chico Creek roared louder than expected as we hiked the Yahi Trail. Several pipevine swallowtail chrysalises clung to the bottom of the railing that led from Upper Park Road down to the trail. Kate and I hadn't seen many of the butterflies this spring, and we were excited to discover how many caterpillars had survived.

Four of the little larvae crawled over the trail and showed their orange warning spots, their way of saying, "Don't eat me! You'll throw up!" We thought about moving them to a safe spot where no one would trample them but decided they were safe in the uncrowded park and probably knew where they were going.

A western fence lizard lay curled up on the trail. We thought it might be dead but decided that it had frozen to hide from us. A hidden spotted towhee called its rapid "beepbeepbeepbeepbeep!" and a California quail replied nasally from the shadows. Wildflower season had peaked; the tidy tips, buttercups, and goldfields were gone. Still, California buckeye trees clung to their creamy, candle-shaped blossoms. A few lupines dotted the ground, and patches of blue and pale creamy brodiaea covered patches on the hills. Bush sunflowers lined the sunny parts of the trail, and wild rose shrubs were beginning to share their pink blossoms.

● ● ● ● ● ● ● ● ● ● ● ● ● ● ● ● ● ●

I keep thinking of a story I heard many years ago at a peace conference:

A mystic was going out into the desert to pray and meditate when he met a little bird lying on its back with its legs in the air.

"What are you doing?" the mystic asked.

"Well, I heard the sky is going to fall, and I decided to come out here and hold it up," the bird answered.

The mystic laughed and said, "How can you, a little bird, hold the sky up with your tiny legs?"

The bird replied, "One does what one can."

• • • • • • • • • • • • • • • • • •

The park astonishes us every time we visit it.

To protect it, one does what one can.

Blue oak in Upper Park.

Afterword

An Update

My dad used to tell me the ancient Romans said, *tempus fugit*—time flies. Then he'd laugh and add, "tempus fidgets." Time has certainly flown smoothly since the last events I describe in this book took place, but these have also been fidgety, chaotic years too, with no end in sight. This is as true for Bidwell Park as for the rest of the world. Seasonal changes move in their smooth but always surprising ways; at the same time, many of the park's problems remain unresolved, leading to stress for the people who love it.

Hordes of wildflowers erupted in Bidwell Park during the spring of 2023. Tidy tips, goldfields, butter and eggs, and sunflowers crammed the jade hills with every possible variation of the color yellow. California buckeyes' and redbuds' blossoms flooded Yahi Trail with off-white and pink patches while manzanita's urn-shaped flowers became small, green fruits. Frying pan poppies and lupines covered Salmon Hole's basalt with yellow and blue fireworks displays.

Big Chico Creek roared with the winter's torrential rain. California quails howled "a-HA-ha!" and Pacific chorus frogs chanted "ribit-ribit-ribit!" People flowed down the trails like melting snow. They thrived on beauty but also surprises, such as hooded mergansers who swam along the creek and the occasional osprey circling Horseshoe Lake.

The park's steadiness and unexpected joys make it seem like a harmonious, problem-free place. Yet many citizens continue to worry about the park's condition and its future. They talk about climate change impacts on vegetation, the growing possibility of wildfires, and some visitors' irresponsibility. Some Chicoans attended a panel discussion sponsored by Ethnic Media Services in October 2022 (Hanson 2022). This San Francisco-based group connects media professionals from many cultural backgrounds with a range of advocates, officials, and others to share thoughts on vital issues of the day. Some concerned citizens discussed the park's needs with me. As always, the range of opinions runs the gamut. The comments I will share here often present perspectives more than facts, and some points of view are controversial, but they illustrate the wide-ranging debates that continue to swirl around the park.

Lack of News and Money

Chico's Park and Resource Manager Linda Herman stated that the park's multiple entrances make it challenging to determine how many people have visited it in recent years. At the same time, she and other officials believe that the number of visitors has grown because of Chico's increasing population, especially after the Camp Fire. Also, they note that many Californians flocked to parks for relief during the COVID-19 pandemic (Hanson 2022).

Park enthusiasts need information about the park's condition and needs. Sadly, there has been a vacuum around the media's attention to the park. Chris Johnson is the current chair of the volunteer group PALS. He reflected that funding for reporters who cover issues such as the park is increasingly scarce as newspaper subscriptions and circulation fall. Citizens sometimes rely on social media for news, but these sources are more prone to rumors than facts.

Former Park and Playgrounds commissioner Lise Smith-Peters commented, "I think that the park has never gotten the news coverage needed to keep people in the know about this amazing, unique resource that we are lucky to enjoy. I think, in general, the public understands the resource that the park is to Chico. I know they don't understand the resources and ecological knowledge needed to care for the Park properly.

"Bidwell Park gets attention from the public in the sense of using it for their recreation," Lise continued. "During COVID, the park was instrumental for improving mental health and increasing exercise. For decades, the park has been used and "loved" to death. It deserves the attention of our community members to help with the costs of maintaining and replacing infrastructure, and ultimately, paying for a staff member who is an ecologist/biologist to implement a vegetation management plan and restoration plans throughout the whole park."

The fact that many people do not hear about the park's needs may have always contributed to a lack of funds to support its upkeep. Tom Barrett, who served as a park commissioner for twelve years, said, "When I was on the Park Commission, every year we had to go up in front of the council with our budget. Every year, we were asked, 'What is more important: the park or police and fire services? We aren't going to fund the park over public safety.'"

The Parks Department had a budget of $1,770,000 through 2023; this was a slight increase from 2019–2020 and amounts to less than 1% of the city's $211,000,000 budget (Hanson 2022). "I don't know of any park of this size that doesn't charge fees or payment for parking," Shane Romain told me as we sat in his office on a warm April morning. "We only receive a small amount of money from the General Fund. Our infrastructure has aged—our bathrooms and irrigation system, for example. To keep the Jewel of Chico polished, we need funds. We look at grants, but they take time. We're going to implement parking fees in Upper Park. That money's earmarked to stay in the park to improve parking lots and roads. It will generate a significant amount of money. It will be collected at parking kiosks like the ones downtown where people use credit cards. They can also buy annual passes."

Chico's voters passed Proposition H, which increased the city's sales tax from 7.25% to 8.25% in the general election on November 8, 2022. Chico largely plans to use the money to support public safety and infrastructure (Downs 2023). The description of Measure H in the voters' handbook mentioned improvements to Bidwell Park, but Chris Johnson stated that no funds for the park were written into the actual ballot measure, and no law requires that the park be included. As a result, the promise of money for the park may not be met.

"City Council is still discussing how to distribute that money," Shane Romain commented. "Hopefully, some will be used to improve South Park Drive and Peterson Drive in the park."

Emergency Vehicles, Silt, and Cars

When it comes to the question of vehicles in the park, the controversies around Upper Park Road remain. Roadwork was completed from the Horseshoe Lake parking lot as far as the sign that listed rules for Upper Park. The road's disrepair and rugged condition is one reason for the repairs. New gravel covered rough patches that made driving on the road difficult (Weber 2022). Shane Romain told me. "There are rolling dips there. The fire department was concerned that they couldn't get engines up there. The main reason for the work is to allow emergency vehicles greater access into Upper Park." He also mentioned that sediment that would flow to the creek could be harmful to fish. "Drainage is important too. When we got torrential rains before, it eroded a lot of road surface and exposed a lot of rock. We got a grant to do road work and keep silt out of Big Chico Creek. It improves the road's quality as well."

Shane also commented that the gate that blocks drivers' access beyond Diversion Dam will eventually be moved up the road, allowing drivers to move farther into Upper Park. The City Council advised this policy in December 2019.

Dave Nopel and I met at a downtown café on a morning late in May. "I don't like to see incursions into Bidwell Park," Dave said. "There's no law enforcement up there. I've heard bicyclists don't like to ride on the gravel. I don't like to walk on it."

"There's some legitimacy to the need to fight fires and rescue people, "I commented. "Also, the fire department works on prescribed burns."

"I can appreciate the need to get emergency vehicles up there," Dave answered. "I saw where the city tried to get a big fire truck up there and couldn't do it, so they did have to fill in some of those dips in the road. But you and I both know what happens in Upper Park in summer. How do you stop people from trashing the place?"

Chris Johnson suggested that while the need to protect salmon and increase emergency vehicles' access was real, the city lacked an overall plan about how the improved road would affect the park. For example, with the improved roadway, drivers now easily reach speeds as high as fifty miles per hour or more, endangering hikers and wildlife. Rangers could enforce traffic laws, but since there are no such professionals in Upper Park, the city will need to rely on signs, which are ignored. Also, an increase in the number of swimmers at Salmon Hole (which is not easily accessible from the road) and other popular spots would make accidents more likely as more people attempt to climb into the canyon.

Tom Barrett stated in a letter to the editor of the *Chico News and Review,*

> The City of Chico destroyed it [Upper Park Road] for hiking to provide a better roadway for gas-powered vehicles. What was an accessible road/path for everyone has been covered in four to six inches of volcanic railroad ballast. It is a nightmare to walk on. . . . Upper Park Road is no longer accessible to casual hikers, strollers, (try pushing one through this stuff), wheelchairs (a failure to follow ADA requirements), narrow -tire bicycles, or horses (the ballast has very sharp edges and are not small stones. (Barrett 2023)

This range of opinions shows that the issues around Upper Park Road are contentious; hopefully, there can be discussions that resolve them.

Another Salmon Issue

The run-down Iron Canyon fish ladder, which dates from the 1940s, reentered the news in 2023. Fish ladders often decrease the distance salmon need to leap between pools as they migrate up a stream to reach their spawning ground where they mate and lay eggs. The 1906 San Francisco earthquake supposedly loosened boulders that damaged the Iron Canyon fish ladder, blocking the chinooks' path (Gebb 2023).

Salmon are considered a keystone species in California's streams and rivers; many predators, including back bears and raptors, prey on them (Gebb 2023). The Mechoopda, who have eaten salmon for millennia, consider them a deep part of their world. Of course, all hikers who are lucky enough to see these beautiful creatures are amazed!

The National Oceanic and Atmospheric Association (NOAA) will fund a collaborative effort to remove the ladder by representatives of Big Chico Creek Ecological Reserve, California Trout, the Mechoopda Tribe, Chico State's Interdisciplinary Wildland Management Master's Program, and other groups. The fish ladder's removal will allow salmon access to more than eight miles of their historic spawning grounds. Serious research and planning will begin during the summer of 2023 with construction planned for 2024. The Mechoopda will also work with an educational project to share knowledge about the fish's profound importance to their culture and the ecosystem (Gebb 2023).

"The size of the salmon run depends on what the water level in the creek is like," Shane Romain commented. "The past few winters, we've had very few, but during a good year, the numbers have been up to 300 plus. The fish prefer Butte Creek, which has fewer obstructions and deeper pools. Fish find more obstructions on Big Chico Creek."

Lise Smith-Peters said, "This idea has been floated for years. If they can install the fish ladder without tearing up the land surrounding Salmon Hole, that would be great. Fish ladders truly help with salmon's journey when natural situations have altered their access to the upper reaches of streams and creeks like with Big Chico Creek's Upper Park run."

Chris Johnson disagreed somewhat when he reflected that heavy equipment could damage wild habitat. He also commented that rules prohibited the moving and removal of natural objects from the park and wondered how the plan to remove boulders related to these regulations.

Tom Barrett also questioned the need for repairs to the fish ladder. "I'm all for restoring salmon, but when damage happens naturally, it's what's supposed to happen. I worked for the California Conservation Corps for years, and we had projects to open up creeks for the salmon; these creeks were closed by logging practices and not by natural events.

"Sure, salmon and lamprey have a role in the creek, but they can only get up the creek a short way before there is another stoppage point," Tom continued. "They should just remove the fish ladders, but their plan is to also break up all the big volcanic boulders that have fallen into the creek and 'make it better than nature could' so the fish can get past Iron Canyon. Then what? Every time a boulder falls in the creek, will they remove it to ensure passage for the fish for that entire mile?"

Invasive Plants and More

Vegetation management remains a big issue. Many citizens want the city to focus on the problem that hotter summers will kill many plants and fuel wildfires. "With climate change, our regulations are going to change," Shane Romain said. "Our oaks are aging out, coming to the end of their life spans. You can see how many we lose every year, and regeneration's not happening. They take a long time to grow. Invasive species are growing way too fast. Olive trees along the north side of Upper Park Road are increasing. We have to choose our battles—whether we will use manual removal, herbicides, or something else."

Park officials need to deal with ladder fuels, where dry branches that are lower on trees catch fire quickly and spread upward into the canopy. "In the past few years, we've reintroduced goals around fire fuel reduction. With climate change, our regulations are going to change," Shane Romain commented. "We are working with the fire department to reduce fuels like star thistle in the park. We can use prescribed burns and have fire breaks, spaces where embers can't spread and start fires easily."

Chico's Park and Natural Resources Manager Linda Herman said,

> We continue to use the California Conservation Corps and other workforces to help elevate trees and vegetation and to remove downed wood and invasive plants in the park and greenways. The park division is also working with Chico Fire and Big Chico Creek Ecological Reserve Fire Crew to use prescribed burning in Upper Park to help reduce fire risk. (Hanson 2022)

Chico State geography professor Mark Stemen told the Ethnic Media Services gathering, "The biggest problem we have with the trees right now that as the air warms, it can hold more moisture—so it's literally pulling the water out of the soil, out of the plants." He recommended that the city concentrate on planting and maintaining more drought-adapted plants in the park and in other habitats. Valley oaks, for example, have deep tap roots that can hold water relatively close to the soil's surface. Blue oaks' roots spread closer to the surface and can gather and hold water in their area (Hanson 2022).

Lise Smith-Peters added, "I have lots of thoughts on vegetation management as that is what I engaged with so much as a staff person, and I so enjoyed the study of Bidwell Park's flora. Goats, prescribed burns, responsible use of herbicides, and proper invasive weed removal are all tools in vegetation management. These tools should all be employed, but their use should be written into plans that identify the issues and solutions. Not all weeds are the same, and knowledge on what works to manage them takes education. You can make a weed situation much worse. Protection of native plants and the correct removal of invasive weeds would help balance out the park's vegetation to reduce fire risks and encourage native plant growth.

"When I served on the Park Commission, we reviewed and approved a vegetation and fuel management plan (that had a lot of boilerplate from plans of other parks in California, but without staff to apply for grant funding or donations, or having staff who have the knowledge to even implement the plan, it is a useless document. Again, another plan for the park that will sit on a shelf. You should see the library of plans."

The well-loved goats will remain a vital part of vegetation management. Shane Romain described a big problem with goats in Lower Park a decade ago. "There was no shepherd or guard dogs on duty. Dogs got into the enclosure and killed goats. Now Capra Environmental Services, our current goat-owning company, has guard dogs and a shepherd and does a great job!"

Dave Nopel commented, "I think goats are good. We oughta have our own herd. Whether there could be a place for them year-round, I don't know. They can be moved around. It's astounding to see how fast those berry bushes and other invasives can grow back."

Tom Barrett took a more critical perspective on this policy. He said, "Goats can be useful, but not the way the City is doing it. They don't eat ivy or periwinkle, which are major problems. They eat poison oak leaves and leave the branches, which will then branch out and increase growth from the goats' pruning. Second, [the City] waits until late in the season after all the weeds have set their seeds and the plants have stopped growing. If they did it earlier they might be able to control it by stopping growth. The goats eat some of the ground plants and spread them around. Vetch is heavy in all the places the goats have been because the goats spread their seeds around in balls of fertilizer."

Homeless Encampments in the Park

Long-standing disagreements about the situation peaked on April 8, 2000, when the City Council passed an emergency resolution telling police not to remove encampments from open spaces during the height of the COVID-19 health crisis.[1]

---

1   The issue of Chico's unhoused population remains unresolved and factious and will be mentioned briefly in terms of impacts to Bidwell Park. As a whole, this situation is very complex and falls outside this book's focus, but an appendix has been provided with a list of sources for people who want to learn more facts and perspectives.

Officials stated this was in response to a Centers for Disease Control policy that discouraged the eviction of campers since some could disperse the virus through the community. Also, it would be hard for unhoused people to connect with a healthcare provider if they were not living in a central location (Brown 2020).

One encampment in Lower Bidwell Park became a center of the controversy. Some Chico citizens felt that while the situation was unfortunate, many unhoused people would have nowhere to go if forced to leave the park. Others stated that camping was inappropriate and illegal in the park and that the camp led to too much trash, the presence of aggressive dogs, and other problems. Chico police evicted the campers on January 12, 2021, but the issues remain unresolved (Hanson 2021b).

The city issued seventy-two-hour eviction notices to campers in the Comanche Creek open space area on April 8, 2021 (Hanson 2021a). On April 11, Legal Services of California, representing eight unhoused people, sued the city to stop the evictions, claiming that while the COVID-19 pandemic had contributed to fewer shelter and housing options, the city treated homelessness as a crime (*Warren et al. v. City of Chico; City of Chico Police Department*).

The situation remained a very tense stalemate until January 14, 2022, when U.S. District Judge Morrison C. England signed an agreement between the city and the plaintiffs in the lawsuit. This settlement included an agreement from the city that social workers would assess each camper's situation and decide if the person could find another appropriate place to live. The city also agreed to build 177 pallet shelters with toilets, places to bathe, water, food, security staff, and other amenities at the former BMX (bike motorcross) site on the Silver Dollar Fairground south of downtown. The first resident moved into a shelter on April 18, 2022. A year later, residents talked about the benefits of living in a stable environment, but mentioned issues like summer heat on the site and shortage of cooking facilities. They looked forward to moving to more permanent settings (Layton 2022; Marsten 2022).

The presence of the pallet shelters allowed the city to close encampments again legally. Comanche Creek's campers had to move in early August 2022. They heard that the pallet shelters and the Torres Shelter were possible alternatives for them; however, some campers learned that the shelters were unavailable if they had spent a night on someone's couch while stationed at Comanche Creek (White and Devol 2022).

Eviction of encampments continued a year after the Comanche Creek campers were moved. At the same time, many people believed that more temporary spaces had become available. Some unhoused people avoided these facilities because they felt uncomfortable with rules and other conditions. Also, options for permanent housing had not increased as quickly as temporary shelters. Officials disagreed about possible policies. Some wanted to continue to evict encampments at the same time the city looked for shelter spaces. Others proposed managed campsites where unhoused people could live while they strove to improve their situations. All agreed that people who lived on the street needed to be treated with dignity and respect until solutions arrived.

Lise Smith-Peters commented, "Bottom line, being homeless is not against the law, and its cause is complex and for different reasons. I want Bidwell Park to be healthy and environmentally sound, so I don't think homeless encampments should be allowed to remain in the park as the resulting trash and hazardous materials are hard on the park's health. A federal judge has mandated our City to provide real shelter options to our homeless community, so hopefully, they do not have to resort to camping in the park and greenways."

Trail Work

Illegal trails in the park also remain a big concern. "There are people whose intentions might be good," Shane Romain said. "With a lack of rangers in Upper Park, it's hard to monitor that activity. They don't know how to do trail work and can both make trails more dangerous and increase erosion. The work is specialized—you don't just move dirt and rocks around and get good results. Bidwell Park is a big park, and the trail system has signs with poorly stated information. That might have contributed to people building rogue trails."

"Our best idea is to get the public on board about how people can volunteer to do trail repair," he continued. "Chico Velo does great work. I hope people might want to contribute to improving trail signage and that we can get a maintenance person dedicated to trails. There needs to be a person in Upper Park all the time."

"I have been heartbroken to see the bootleg trail work on Yahi Trail," Dave Nopel told me at a downtown café. "People have been going there late or early in the morning. They have power tools, probably battery-operated ones. They're cutting stuff ten feet up in the air and cutting vegetation back from the trail. Yahi's a beautiful trail. I don't have an answer as to why they are doing this. I think there are different ideas about what a mountain trail should look like."

Chris Johnson added that illegal cutting on the Yahi and Annie Bidwell trails has removed canopy sections. This has destroyed shaded microclimates, killing the organisms that thrived there, such as teardrop ferns. Hikers will also swelter more in summertime when shade will no longer protect them from sunlight. Also, piles of cut debris will act as fuel dumps, which will cause a fire to burn much hotter and kill trees and other organisms that might have survived otherwise. So far, Chris and the City have been unsuccessful in witnessing any of these folks at work.

Kate and I took a recent hike that confirmed what Chris and Dave described. Several plants, such as manzanita, had neat, regular cuts, indicating that they were damaged by people with power tools instead of a natural process. A fig tree that had shaded and cooled the trail for years had been cut. Some people infuriate me; I hope someone catches these people soon either in the act or with the use of trail cams.

The Park and the Community in 2023

Shane regretted having little time to develop PALS, the network that unites the park's volunteers. "My duties have changed significantly," he said. "I was tasked with supervising an encampment clean-up crew and our outreach engagement team. I'm finding a balance on all these moving parts. I will come back to PALS meetings when there is some normalcy. The meetings were geared to giving volunteers inside information. I want to have these again. I want to have a PALS appreciation event, too!"

Ali Meders-Knight of the Mechoopda tribe said, "Nobody's really touching and taking care of the land. The city doesn't have enough people at City Hall who have the information to move forward toward making the park something positive. It's been a while since we've had [elected] leadership that even understood ecology." Ali suggested that Chico seek grants to fund projects involving grassroots people in conservation and maintenance work, such as the project she works on at Verbena Fields. "If we could create those kinds of educational areas, especially low-income areas, I would like to measure the difference it makes. I think it's worth measuring and studying and getting money in because Chico's a great place to do it" (*also* Hanson 2022).

Tom Barrett commented, "My vision of the future of the park is to take management away from the city and put it into a non-profit Bidwell Park Foundation. The foundation would contract with the City to manage the park with City revenue and to be funded by donations. Another part of my vision is to have a Bidwell Park Conservation Corps (BPCC) and employ high school and college students in doing projects in the park. BPCC members would receive training on the natural history of the park and learn restoration practices. This would give them a part-time job, engage them with maintaining their park, and increase their pride of place."

"I hope the city and general population realize what an asset the park is to Chico and the region," Shane commented. "When the Camp Fire happened, and there were so many people displaced, the park was where many people came to get some peace. It was the same with COVID. A lot of people live here because of the park!"

"I don't think I've ever seen Chico grow so fast," Dave Nopel reflected. "Also, you and I have both seen big cultural changes over the past ten years. Our culture shows signs of faltering. Can we make changes in our behavior patterns? I've always been an optimist who thought we could make changes to avoid hurting ourselves and the world. I see that feeling dwindling, but I will try to hold on to that optimism.

"When I look at the park, it has weathered time so far. I think there are enough people here who love the park. You see them every day out there—walking, biking, riding horses, playing baseball—all of it. I think there are lots of people who'd rise up if the park were threatened by some city decision—we can hope."

"That's why I am writing this—to get attention back on the park," I said.

Lise Smith-Peters emailed me, "In the famous words of the Lorax, 'unless someone like you cares a whole lot, nothing is going to get better. It's not.' (Dr. Seuss 1971). Moreover, Bidwell Park is in the same situation unless the community demands more funding and investment for this amazing natural resource. I worry for the Park's sustainability and, ultimately, its health. The City of Chico must invest in more staff and in natural resource ecologists/environmental studies staff and trail crews. Trained and educated City staff and community members are the answer to preserving this amazing, beautiful resource that we all get so much enjoyment from."

• • • • • • • • • • • • • • • • • • •

Wildflowers still fill the park as the weather warms up in late spring 2023. Wild roses thrive along the Yahi Trail. Poppies are starting to fade, but the ones that remain glow brightly. More and more pipevine swallowtail butterflies fill the air, and I hear more California quails calling than before. The park is strong.

We must be strong, too.

Paul Belz, June 2023
Chico, California

An Upper Park trail.

Appendices

Bidwell Park History

Timeline

Bidwell Park Maps

Bidwell Park Rules & Regulations

Bidwell Park Volunteer Organizations

Mechoopda & Maidu Sources

Unhoused Sources & Resources

A Brief History of Bidwell Park
Phil Lydon • January 1997[1]

Background

John Bidwell first saw the Chico area in March 1843, by which time the place name, Chico Creek, was already in use. Under provisions of Mexican law, Arroyo Chico was granted by California Governor Manuel Micheltorena to William Dickey the following year.

In two separate purchases in 1849 and 1851, Bidwell acquired Rancho del Arroyo Chico, totaling more than 22,000 acres. He filed a claim for the land before the U.S. Lands Commission in 1852, and the claim was confirmed the next year. In further legal jockeying, the claim was confirmed by the U.S. District Court for the Northern District in 1855, and eventually by the U.S. Supreme Court. The title patent was signed by President James Buchanan in 1860.

Public lands surrounding the grant were surveyed in 1853-59 following the U.S. Act of March 3, 1853, which provided for a survey of public lands in California. This survey established the system of sections, townships, and ranges that appears on modern maps (exclusive of the Mexican land grants). But it was not until 1859 that a formal survey of the boundaries of Rancho del Arroyo Chico was made and committed to a map.

John Bidwell led a varied and eventful life, serving (among other things) as Chico Postmaster, member of the U.S. House of Representatives, and officer in the California militia. He married Annie Ellicott Kennedy in 1868. An ardent Prohibitionist, her influence appears in the no-alcohol provisions of the various Bidwell leases and grants. Bidwell died at age 81 in 1900, followed by Annie Bidwell in 1918 at 78 years of age.

Growth of the Park

On July 10, 1905, Annie Bidwell signed a grant deed donating 1,902.88 acres to the people of Chico for a public park. She said at the time that this grant followed the desire of her late husband, expressed for some time before his death. On May 11, 1911, she signed an indenture granting a further 301.76 acres of parkland mainly along the north side of Upper Park to become effective upon her death. Approximately 37 acres were added to the Park in October 1921. When the "Forestry Station" parcel (now the site of Chico Creek Nature Center and the oak grove) was purchased from the University of California by popular

---

1   Reprinted courtesy Woody Elliot, Michael Stauffer, Tom Barrett, and Lise Smith Peters of Friends of Bidwell Park under Creative Commons license (CC BY-NC-SA 4.0 DEED). It can also be found on the Friends of Bidwell Park webstite (http://friendsofbidwellpark.org/park-info/history/a-brief-history-of-bidwell-park/)

    Information for the statements made in this brief history came from the minutes of the Bidwell Park and Playground Commission (BPPC). various contracts, leases, and deeds to which the City was a party, several books, pamphlets, articles on one or both of the Bidwells, microfilms of various newspapers published in Chico, oral interviews, and a few other sources.

subscription. Another 20 acres, the "Kennedy Estate field" (now the walnut orchard on North Park Drive), were added in the 1930s or 1940s. The City added another 1,420 acres, 40 of which were U.S. Bureau of Land Management land, on May 16, 1995.

Reversionary Clause

Annie Bidwell's grants of parkland to the City contained several conditions, which, generalized and paraphrased, were no alcohol; land must be used as a public park; preserve the trees, shrubs, and vines; no hunting; and no public picnics on Sundays. If these conditions were "broken or disregarded," title to the parkland would revert to her heirs.

The no-alcohol provision was standard in all the Bidwell deeds, including those for investment property. Following a court decision holding that the reversionary rights are property, they were sold in 1934 to satisfy estate debts. The Title Insurance and Guaranty Co. of San Francisco purchased all the reversionary rights, which were sold as a single package. The company was interested in the investment properties, but, almost as an afterthought, thus also acquired the reversionary rights to Bidwell Park. The company deeded the Park rights, in which it was not interested, to the City by quitclaim in 1948.

Park Roads

Bidwell Park and Playground Commission (BPPC) minutes of July 1935 note that the new road through the "Upper Area" of Bidwell Park is to be graveled by SERA, the Depression-era predecessor of the WPA (Works Projects Administration). North Park Drive, considered controversial at the time of its construction, was built in 1939. The road that now forms the main access to Upper Park was rerouted in 1955 to pass between the golf course and the rifle range. At that time, it was called "the alternate canyon road," and did not have an asphalt surface; the principal road access was across the Five Mile area. As part of the construction of the Five Mile flood-control complex (1964-69), the "alternate" road became the main access route. In September 1993, the main road was rerouted near the golf course in order to allow modification of two holes of the course.

There is little information concerning the locations and condition of roads or trails predecessor to the roads described above.

Iron Canyon

Iron Canyon is the water-carved gash through black basaltic rock east of Bear Hole. The name was used in an article in the June 1888 issue of *Overland Monthly*, but when the name was first applied is not known. A mass of rock debris, said to have fallen about the time of the 1906 San Francisco earthquake, obstructed migration of salmon and steelhead further up Big Chico Creek. One falls in that section was 14 feet high. The State Department of Fish and Game in April 1957 offered to spend $25,000 clearing the fish barrier if the City agreed to install a fishway at Sycamore Pool. The City agreed, and the project, which included building 10 dams, was completed in June of the following year.

A Flume, a Dam, a Ditch

The Butte Flume and Lumber Company built a flume from Butte Meadows down Big Chico Creek in 1872-74. The flume crossed the creek several times, but, within the present boundaries of Bidwell Park, it remained on the southeast and south side of the canyon. Initially, the terminus of the flume was on high ground south of the creek (3/4 to 1 mile east of the Lindo Channel junction with Big Chico Creek). The settlement of Oakvale grew there; at its peak recording 108 votes in the 1877 election. Eventually the flume was extended farther west into Chico, and the settlement faded away.

The diversion dam on Big Chico Creek, just east of Bear Hole, and its ditch were intended to deliver water to the Park reservoir (now Horseshoe Lake) for use in the municipal golf course. BPPC minutes of August 1937 note that arrangements were being made for the diversion-dam site and that the ditch was under construction. During the following year, State approval to divert water from Big Chico Creek was obtained, but plans for the dam were still being discussed. In spring of 1940, the local National Guard unit complained about the rising water level in "the lake feeding the golf course," and the minutes note that the "conduit" leading from the creek to the golf reservoir is leaking. Was the diversion dam built by this time? Hard to say. On January 5, 1942, the State granted an extension of time (to December 1945) for completion and use of the diversion dam.

Talk of repairing the dam appears in the minutes of 1946 and annually thereafter for some years. There was even incautious talk of "permanent" repair (1947). In 1950, the Chico Rod & Gun Club asked and received permission to repair the dam and ditch, but a month later abandoned the idea because the project would be too big. Sporadic discussion of the dam and ditch continued to 1957 when a water-skiing group asked permission to lay 1.5 miles of 8-inch concrete pipe in the old ditch to bring water to the lake. In January 1959, the City filed an application with the State Water Rights Board to use creek water for the reservoir, an action possibly related to the water-skiing project. In 1967, the minutes note that unused concrete pipe from the project is surplus. That same year, a local hiking organization received permission to build a hiking trail partly along the old ditch, which by then was probably no longer in use for carrying either water or concrete pipe.

Day Camp, Archery Range, Yahi Trail

The old Day Camp and archery-range sites are situated about one-third mile east of the eastern high-power line in Upper Park. An archery range area was established by an archery club in 1946. Day Camp began when the director of the City's Recreation Department received permission to hold a five-week, summertime "day school" in conjunction with Chico State Teachers College, in the area of the archery range. The name "Camp Cha-Da-Ka" was attached to it. In 1953, another archery group asked to develop an archery range, opposite the Day Camp, and in 1957, they expanded it from 14 to 28 targets. In 1967, the group asked BPPC for financial aid in maintaining the range. The site gradually declined and was not used after about the early 1970s. In January 1967, a local hiking group received permission to build a 6-mile hiking trail, beginning at Day Camp and extending to near

Salmon Hole. The gasoline crunch of the early 1970s caused relocation of Day Camp to the Five Mile area in 1973 in order to reduce travel distances by buses and other vehicles.

Rifle Range, Golf Course, Horseshoe Lake

The **rifle range** near Horseshoe Lake actually was two rifle ranges. The older one was built in 1926 for "the local military company" (July 1926 minutes). The only visible evidence of it today is the concrete-lined target pit located in a small mound just northeast of an arm of Horseshoe Lake. The firing line was located more than 400 yards to the southwest.

For six years, the National Guard (Co. G, 184th Inf.) had an exclusive-use lease on the site. In subsequent years, the BPPC minutes reflect an increasing level of conflict over use of the range: the National Guard wanting exclusive use and local gun groups wanting a shared-use arrangement. A skeet shooting area was established in 1936, but a permanent site, also northeast of Horseshoe Lake, was not developed until 1948. Leases to local gun clubs during the 1940s and later commonly involved both the rifle and skeet ranges.

A second rifle range, for several years referred to as the "small-bore" range, was developed in 1950 just north of the gate that is used to close Upper Park during rainy weather. Sporadic use conflicts continued, and in 1958 the older, large-bore range was deactivated.

The remaining rifle range was used by both military and local gun groups into the 1960s. Concrete firing stands and a metal roof were built in the 1970s. Use of the rifle range and skeet area continued to decline, however, and their last use was in the late 1980s. The wooden building next to Horseshoe Lake, used as an indoor range, was built by a local gun group over a two-year period beginning in mid-1957.

A **pistol range**, constructed during 1953-54, was located south of the eastern 9-hole portion of the golf course. It was built for the Chico Police Department, but was also used by various military units and law-enforcement classes from Butte Junior College. Use declined in the 1970s and was eventually discontinued.

Chico's 9-hole Municipal **Golf Course** south of Horseshoe Lake was already established by the time first mention of it was made in the BPPC minutes (1921). A new golf-course clubhouse was built in 1925, and again in 1945 and 1952, with various repairs and modifications during the intervening years. The City turned over operation of the course to various private groups beginning in 1939. Nine more holes were constructed in an olive grove east of the old course during 1954-57. In 1993, two holes of the old course were modified, resulting in relocation of part of the road giving access to Upper Park.

In BPPC minutes and newspaper articles, **Horseshoe Lake** usually was called the Park lake, the Park reservoir, the golf-course reservoir, etc. "Horseshoe Lake" does not appear in the minutes until April 1961. In 1936, the WPA was considering building "a restraining dam near the golf links." Late the following year, the lake is called a "reservoir" in BPPC minutes, implying that the WPA dam was built by then. In 1939, reference appears to a dam, reservoir, and water-supply system for the golf course. In the late 1950s, a small spillway dam was constructed to better control runoff across the golf course.

The **Easter Cross** has been at its present site for a long time. A wooden cross was cut down by vandals and replaced by a local group in 1958. Ten years later, it was replaced by a steel cross made from a surplus light standard. Also in 1958, a local group built a dirt track east of the Easter Cross, for use in soapbox-derby contests. Increased erosion resulted in closure of the track in the 1970s.

Five Mile Area, Hooker Oak, Live Oak Grove, Riding Arena

The first **Five Mile** dam was built on Big Chico Creek around 1859 to supply water to Bidwell's flour mill. A sheep camp was located below the dam, and the shepherd's cabin was used as a dressing room by bathers who swam in the pool behind the dam. In 1887, John Bidwell built two roofless dressing rooms at the Five Mile pool, which were not replaced until 1922. In 1925, the BPPC adopted the name (proposed by the Chico Art Club), "Hooker Oak Swimming Pool," for the water behind the dam. From 1964 to mid-1969, the Five Mile area was closed to the public while the Big Chico Creek–Mud Creek flood-control project was under construction. A dam was built to replace the old structure, and picnic sites and a footbridge were built. The old road that passed into Upper Park along the north side of the present Five Mile picnic areas was cut by excavation of a diversion channel, so a new access road into Upper Park was built north of Lindo Channel.

The famous **Hooker Oak** tree was named after Sir Joseph Hooker, a renowned English botanist who examined it during a visit to the Bidwells in 1875. It was a valley oak (*Quercus lobata*) located at the north end of the parking lot that forms part of the Hooker Oak Recreation Area. Its spreading branches had reached a circumference of about 500 ft and its age was widely reported as 1,100 years when approximately the eastern half fell during the Columbus-Day storm of 1962. Ring counts of the largest branch to fall suggested an age of 400 years or less. Despite efforts to preserve it, the remainder of the tree fell in a windstorm in 1977.

The area around Hooker Oak, proposed in 1904 as a site for a U.S. Plant Introduction Station, was used for many years as a hayfield and prune orchard. In 1950, a Recreation Committee (formed in 1946) relocated a softball field at Chico High School to a spot just east of Hooker Oak. CARD developed the Hooker Oak area in 1957 and in the next year, began a 25-year lease from the City to operate it as a recreation area.

Live Oak Grove was large grove of trees is located between the Five Mile diversion channel and the Manzanita Avenue access road into Upper Park. A local midget-car racing group built a 250-ft-long track inside the Grove in 1955. Three years later, a motorcycle group received approval to build an oval racing track at the site. It was used only intermittently and, in 1966, the permit to use the track was rescinded. Before 1964, the access road into Upper Park passed through the southern part of the grove.

Beginning in 1953, local horse-riding groups approached BPPC seeking a place in the Park to build a **riding arena**. The present site, just west of Live Oak Grove, was selected by a riding club as early as 1958, but a temporary arena was not built for another 10 years. It fell into disuse during the 1970s, but the facilities have been rebuilt since then.

Freeway & Power Lines

Two high-voltage power lines cross Upper Park, one near the Easter Cross and the other about a third of a mile east of the east end of the golf course. The western line was built by the U.S. Bureau of Reclamation in 1944 and the eastern line by PG&E in 1964. Both crossed the Park, despite opposition from the BPPC, by virtue of condemnation actions. The freeway, first mentioned in BPPC minutes in 1956, was built in 1963-65. It had been opposed by formal resolution of the BPPC in 1958, and again, in response to a court action, in 1960.

Forestry Station and Kennedy Tract

(Portions of the next two paragraphs are based on tapes dictated by Janeece Webb in May 1992)

The Forestry Station tract of land includes the present-day sites of the old deer pen (near the corner of Forest Avenue and East 8th Street), Chico Creek Nature Center, and the "World of Trees" grove to its west. John Bidwell, who was interested in silviculture, donated about 37 acres to the State in 1888 for use as a forestry station. The State Forestry Board began experimental plantings of exotic (non-native) trees at the Chico Forestry Station, which eventually held many thousands of trees. In 1893, title was transferred by the State to the University of California, which continued the earlier forestry work and established the still-extant grove of Spanish Oak cork trees. The City purchased the site from the University in November 1921, with funds raised by popular subscription. In succeeding decades, it was used as a Park headquarters that included maintenance, storage, and an office and home used by the Park ranger or Park superintendent.

Just east of the present building of the Big Chico Creek Nature Center is a large wood barn, said to have been used for storage by John Bidwell. A small zoo was maintained near the barn from 1954 to 1958. The deer pens were already on the site having been started some years before. The small "rock house" adjacent to the Center on its south was constructed around 1980 and used as a museum and nature center. The Chico Creek Nature Center building was erected 10 years later. Public interest in a nature trail among plantings of the old forestry station first appears in the BPPC minutes of 1963 but the "World of Trees" nature trail was not established until 1976.

Approximately 20 acres at the present site of the walnut orchard along North Park Drive were owned by the Kennedys, relatives of Annie Bidwell. It became part of the Park before 1950, probably in the late 1930s or 1940s. The present-day walnut trees were planted in 1953.

One Mile Area

The dam that backs water for the "4th Street" swimming pool was built in 1923 and 1924. The next year, the BPPC agreed that the choice of a name for the 4th Street and Five Mile pools should be left to the Chico Art Club. The Club proposed and BPPC adopted "Sycamore" and "Hooker Oak" Swimming Pools as the formal names. The Sycamore Pool fish ladder was built in 1957 as part of an agreement by the State to clear an obstruction to fish migration in Iron Canyon. Caper Acres, built by volunteers and donated materials, was developed in the 1950s.

Proposals Made That Never Happened

Most of the types of use that took place in the Park left evidence of their existence. No trace remains, however, of an impressive array of uses that were proposed but, for one reason or another, never happened. A chronological list of some of these, taken from the BPPC minutes of 1918-1960, follows.

1918 An automobile campground near the Esplanade.

1918 A 20-acre fish hatchery.

1921 An aeroplane field near the golf course.

1926 Aeroplane field proposed again.

1932 Polo field in Upper Park.

1933 Winter-camp CCC building and site east of golf course.

1936 A stadium in Park; location not given.

1940 Campground for boys at upper end of Park.

1947 Improvements for 100-acre radar bombing site, plus 25-year lease.

1951 Develop unspecified area in Park for use of model-plane flying club.

1953 1.6 acres for fire station in Upper Park, plus 30-yr lease.

1955 Asphalt batch plant on 80 x 700 ft parcel in Lindo Channel north of Hooker Oak.

1955 & 1956 Automobile bridge over Big Chico Creek above Day Camp for private access south of Park.

1956 New large-bore rifle range for military group, with 10-year exclusive-use lease.

1959 Large dam on Big Chico Creek in Upper Park.

1959 Six "flying circles" in lower Park, each 140 ft across, for flying model planes.

Bidwell Park Timeline

A Partial List of Proposed and Actual Developments in Bidwell Park[2]

1918	20 acre fish hatchery proposed.
1920 (approx.)	Golf course put in – 9 holes.
1921	Forestry Station land added to Lower Park. Now the site of Cedar Grove, the Nature Center, and World of Trees.
1921,1926	Airplane field near golf course proposed.
1925	First clubhouse built at golf course.
1926	Company G, 184th Infantry gets permission to construct rifle range.
1932	Polo field proposed.
1933	CCC winter camp building east of the golf course proposed.
1934	Kennedy tract (walnut orchard) added to north side of Lower Park.
1937	*The Adventures Of Robin Hood*, starring Errol Flynn and Olivia De Havilland, was filmed in Lower Park.
1937 (and prior to)	Horseshoe Lake reservoir in existence.
1939	Petersen Memorial Drive built by CCC.
1940	Overnight campground proposed in northeastern end of park.
1941	Military camping okayed.
1942-45	Diversion Dam built (year uncertain).
1946	Archery area established by Glenn Archery Club.
1947	25-year lease and improvements on Radar bombing site proposed.
1949	Recreation District formed (CARD).
1950	Softball field moved to Hooker Oak area.
1950	Water control dams on Chico Creek proposed.
1951	Day Camp established by CARD and Chico Teachers College.

---

2   Reprinted courtesy Woody Elliot, Michael Stauffer, Tom Barrett, and Lise Smith Peters of Friends of Bidwell Park under Creative Commons license (CC BY-NC-SA 4.0 DEED). It can also be found on the Friends of Bidwell Park webstite (http://friendsofbidwellpark.org/park-info/history/a-brief-history-of-bidwell-park/)

1951	First mention of Easter Cross in BPPC minutes.
1953	CDF Fire Station (1.6 acres) proposed NW of Live Oak Grove (30 years).
1953	Horseback riding groups ask BPPC for arena site. Okayed, but no funds.
1953	Golf course expansion to 18 holes begins.
1953	Area near One Mile leased to CARD for Sycamore baseball field.
1953	Chief Evans asks for site for Police pistol range.
1953-54	Pistol range under construction.
1954	Campfire Girls dedicate Campfire Council Ring in Lower Park.
1954	Chico Rod & Gun Club construction begins.
1955	Local midget race car group builds 250' long track in Live Oak Grove.
1955	Proposal to expand Horseshoe Lake to 20 acres for "pleasure boating, water skiing, boat races, fishing for youngsters."
1955	Park land from Arcadian Ave. west to Warner St. is given to Chico State College
1955 & 56	Bridge requested for private property access above Day Camp.
1956	New rifle range requested for sole use of the National Guard, lease for 10 years
1957	Chico Rod & Gun Club construction completed.
1957-58	CARD develops Hooker Oak area
1958	$25,000 fish ladder built. 10 dams in 300' barrier.
1958	Motorcycle club asks to further develop Live Oak Grove area
1959	Dam on Chico Creek (upper park) proposed.
1960	Construction of Highway 99 freeway across Bidwell Park begins.
1963	PG&E claims it will cost $147,000 extra to bypass Bidwell Park with major power lines, plus $16,000/year. BPPC votes 3-1 to put lines elsewhere.
1964	PG&E power lines through upper park under construction.

1965	Sycamore Bypass diversion channel built.
1968	Chico Riding Club puts up arena.
1970	Five Mile Dam Recreation Area dedication.
1970	Caper Acres playground built.
1971	Footbridge at golf course replaced after old one washed out by high waters in 1970.
1972	Rod & Gun Club reports 77,300 targets used in 1971– possible cleanup of used skeet clay birds discussed.
1972	Extensive discussion and study of closing South Park Drive to cars.
1972	Rifle range shade structures built
1973	Upper Park to be closed from 11:30 pm to 30 minutes before sunrise to reduce vandalism.
1973	Trial period for dogs off leash in Lower and Upper Park starts.
1974	CARD proposes tennis court construction at Hooker Oak as part of renovation and improvement plan. BPPC opposed. City Council tentatively approves.
1974	Park Commission votes to stop issuing wood-cutting permits for Bidwell Park.
1974	Park Commission discusses instituting a city tree ordinance.
1974	Park Commission meeting minutes mention using sheep for weed control in park.
1974	Upper Park Road to be closed during wet weather at discretion of Park Superintendent.
1975	Park Commission discusses fire hazard in Park due to undergrowth.
1975	Banning of off-road vehicles on North Rim Trail discussed but no action taken.
1976	Bird sanctuary proposed for Lower Park by deer pen.
1976	Park Commission votes to close pistol range within 6 months.
1977	Bidwell Park site (by Mangrove Ave) proposed for new city/ county library.
1979	Roller skating to be allowed in Lower Park.

1979	Request to fly remote control planes in Horseshoe Lake area including creation of a takeoff/landing area.
1979	North Rim road to be closed to vehicles in the winter months.
1979	1300-acre arson fire in Upper Park.
1980	20-station Par Course approved for Lower Park.
1981	Upper Park controlled burns start, with 1/5 of area to be burned each year.
1981	Commission Minutes note that there is only one trash can in Upper Park, users are supposed to "Pack it out."
1982	Horse-drawn carriage tours proposed for Lower Park
1983	Golf Course leased to private concessionaire with Park Commission relinquishing control over golf course management.
1983	Bocci ball courts proposed for Hooker Oak area.
1983	1300 acorns planted along Upper Park Road on north side.
1983	Hwy 99 mural approved.
1983	Job title for Bidwell Park's two Community Service Officers is changed to Park Ranger.
1984	Park Department hires their first Urban Forester.
1984	Upper Park annual controlled burns stopped.
1985	Lost Park area surveyed and encroachments noted on maps.
1985	Tree nursery started in 1.2 acre Lower Park walnut orchard area.
1986	North Park Dr. to become one-way westbound, open 11 am-11 pm.
1987	Extensive discussion regarding use of park for military training.
1987	Discussion begins regarding feral cats in park.
1989	Chico Rod & Gun Club's rifle and trap shooting ranges close.
1989	Golf course expanded and Upper Park Road realigned.
1990	Shakespeare in the Park begins.
1990	Bidwell Park Master Management Plan (MMP) approved by City Council.

1991	Bidwell Park Wildfire Management Plan.
1992	1.5 mile "B" Trail built by volunteers from east end of Rim Trail to Middle Trail.
1992	0.4 mile Canyon Oak Trail (later renamed Maidu) built by volunteers from Middle Trail near Parking Area E to Rim Trail.
1992	Realignment of Upper Park Road and Golf Course using Mitigated Negative Declaration.
1993	Purchase of 40-acre BLM site on Hwy 32 (site of present disc golf courses).
1994	Chico General Plan approved. Bidwell Park, especially Upper Park, designated as a Resource Conservation Area (pp. 7-11).
1995	Acquisition of 1417 acres on south side of Big Chico Creek.
1997	Unofficial disc golf courses begin to develop on 40-acre Hwy 32 site.
1998	Annie Bidwell Trail proposed, to extend from Bidwell Mansion to end of Upper Park "within sight and sound of the creek."
1998-1999	Bloody Pin Trail rerouted and Guardians & Pine Trails built.
1999	1500 acre backfire covers north side of Upper Park between road and park boundary.
1999	Bidwell Park Trails Manual approved, described as a "work in progress."
1999	Existing disc golf course location approved by Park Commission and City Council, negotiations begin with Cal Trans regarding Hwy 32 access.
2000-2001	1.25 miles of Yahi Trail relocated and/or rebuilt.
2000-2002	Trail plan developed with 23 "Focus Areas", includes new creekside ABT pedestrian trail segments on the south side (1-1.5 miles?), new 1 mile segment of S. Rim trail, new trail from the N. Rim Trail starting at the power lines to Bear Hole, a new trail from the eastern end of Lower Trail to Bear Hole, a new trail from the Middle Trail to the potential Day Camp area bridge site, a new trail from the junction of the B Trail and Middle Trail to Parking Area U at the end of the road, reroute of east end of Upper Trail and several reroutes of Yahi Trail between Bear Hole and Parking Area P.

2001	Observatory built.
2002	Horseshoe Lake Fishing Pier built.
2002	GPS mapping of existing park trails and roads shows 40+ miles of official and frequently used unofficial trails and road on the north side and 28 miles on the south side.
2002	Bridges proposed above Day Camp and at the end of Upper Park Road.
2002	Boundary survey on south side shows that some park trails from disc golf area cross private property and may need to be rerouted.
2003	19-acre antimony, lead, copper and polycyclic aromatic hydrocarbons removal project planned for Horseshoe Lake and lead removal at former pistol range.
2003	Conceptual approval of observatory outdoor seating area & spotting pads, including realignment of the road to Parking Area C.
2003	Funding for update of Bidwell Park Master Management Plan and associated EIR approved by City Council.
2003	Conceptual approval of horse workout pen by Horse Arena.

Bidwell Park Maps

Because of size constraints, the following maps have been cropped to fit (reprinted here courtesy Chico's Park and Natural Resources Manager Linda Herman). However, complete color maps can be accessed and downloaded from the City of Chico at https://chico.ca.us/bidwell-park-maps or picked up at the Chico City Park Division office at 956 Fir Street in Chico.

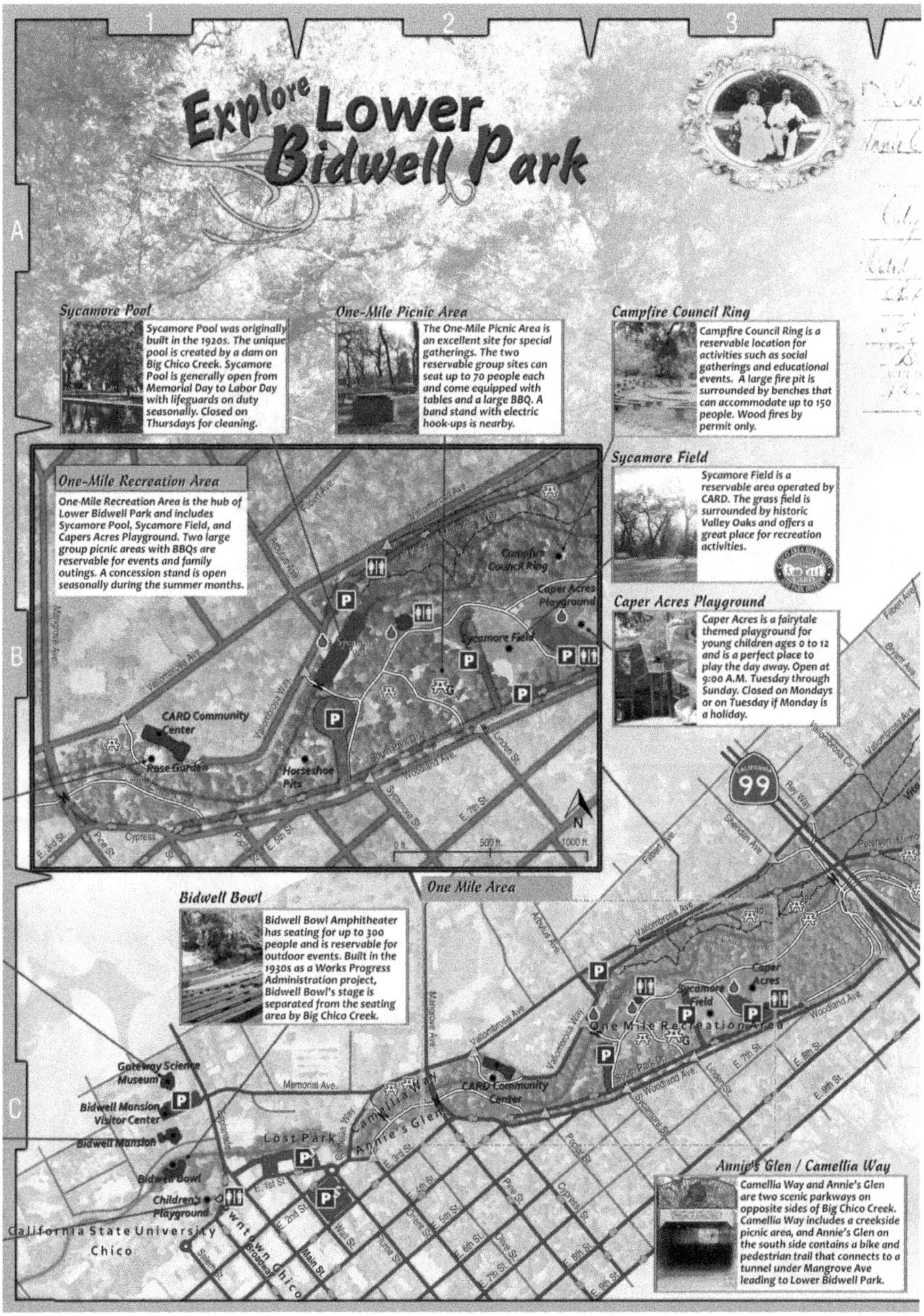

Explore Lower Bidwell Park
Sycamore Pool
Sycamore Pool was originally built in the 1920s. The unique pool is created by a dam on Big Chico Creek. Sycamore Pool is generally open from Memorial Day to Labor Day with lifeguards on duty seasonally. Closed on Thursdays for cleaning.
One-Mile Picnic Area
The One-Mile Picnic Area is an excellent site for special gatherings. The two reservable group sites can seat up to 70 people each and come equipped with tables and a large BBQ. A band stand with electric hook-ups is nearby.
Campfire Council Ring
Campfire Council Ring is a reservable location for activities such as social gatherings and educational events. A large fire pit is surrounded by benches that can accommodate up to 150 people. Wood fires by permit only.
One-Mile Recreation Area
One-Mile Recreation Area is the hub of Lower Bidwell Park and includes Sycamore Pool, Sycamore Field, and Capers Acres Playground. Two large group picnic areas with BBQs are reservable for events and family outings. A concession stand is open seasonally during the summer months.
Sycamore Field
Sycamore Field is a reservable area operated by CARD. The grass field is surrounded by historic Valley Oaks and offers a great place for recreation activities.
Caper Acres Playground
Caper Acres is a fairytale themed playground for young children ages 0 to 12 and is a perfect place to play the day away. Open at 9:00 A.M. Tuesday through Sunday. Closed on Mondays or on Tuesday if Monday is a holiday.
CARD Community Center
Rose Garden
Horseshoe Pits
Campfire Council Ring
Caper Acres Playground
Sycamore Field
Bidwell Bowl
Bidwell Bowl Amphitheater has seating for up to 300 people and is reservable for outdoor events. Built in the 1930s as a Works Progress Administration project, Bidwell Bowl's stage is separated from the seating area by Big Chico Creek.
One Mile Area
One Mile Recreation Area
Gateway Science Museum
Bidwell Mansion Visitor Center
Bidwell Mansion
Bidwell Bowl
Children's Playground
Lost Park
Camellia Way
Annie's Glen
CARD Community Center
California State University Chico
Downtown Chico
Annie's Glen / Camellia Way
Camellia Way and Annie's Glen are two scenic parkways on opposite sides of Big Chico Creek. Camellia Way includes a creekside picnic area, and Annie's Glen on the south side contains a bike and pedestrian trail that connects to a tunnel under Mangrove Ave leading to Lower Bidwell Park.
99

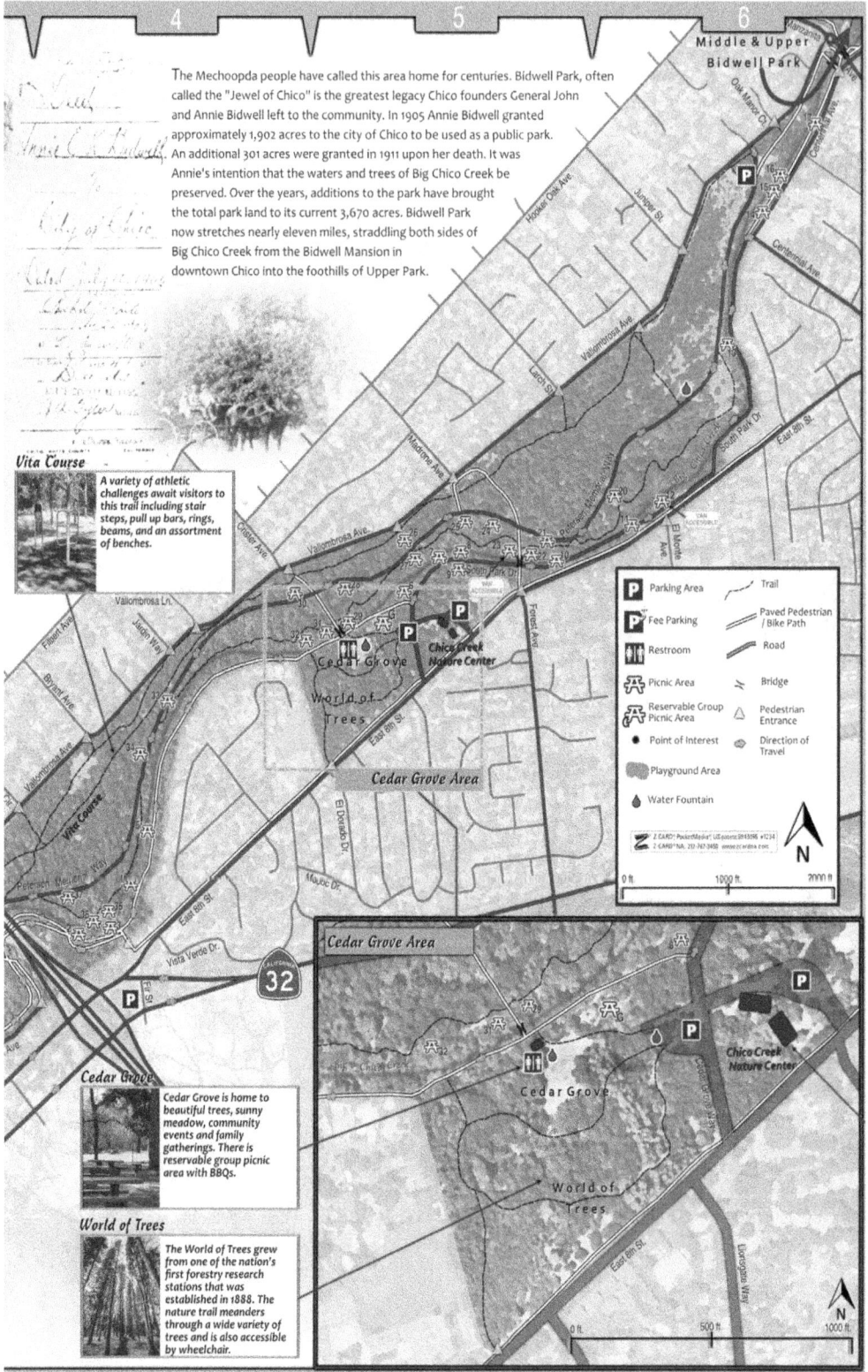

The Mechoopda people have called this area home for centuries. Bidwell Park, often called the "Jewel of Chico" is the greatest legacy Chico founders General John and Annie Bidwell left to the community. In 1905 Annie Bidwell granted approximately 1,902 acres to the city of Chico to be used as a public park. An additional 301 acres were granted in 1911 upon her death. It was Annie's intention that the waters and trees of Big Chico Creek be preserved. Over the years, additions to the park have brought the total park land to its current 3,670 acres. Bidwell Park now stretches nearly eleven miles, straddling both sides of Big Chico Creek from the Bidwell Mansion in downtown Chico into the foothills of Upper Park.

Middle & Upper Bidwell Park

Vita Course

A variety of athletic challenges await visitors to this trail including stair steps, pull up bars, rings, beams, and an assortment of benches.

Cedar Grove

World of Trees

Chico Creek Nature Center

Cedar Grove Area

P	Parking Area	Trail
P	Fee Parking	Paved Pedestrian / Bike Path
	Restroom	Road
	Picnic Area	Bridge
	Reservable Group Picnic Area	Pedestrian Entrance
•	Point of Interest	Direction of Travel
	Playground Area	
	Water Fountain	

N

0 ft   1000 ft   2000 ft

Cedar Grove Area

Chico Creek Nature Center

Cedar Grove

World of Trees

Cedar Grove

Cedar Grove is home to beautiful trees, sunny meadow, community events and family gatherings. There is reservable group picnic area with BBQs.

World of Trees

The World of Trees grew from one of the nation's first forestry research stations that was established in 1888. The nature trail meanders through a wide variety of trees and is also accessible by wheelchair.

N

0 ft   500 ft   1000 ft

Regional Map

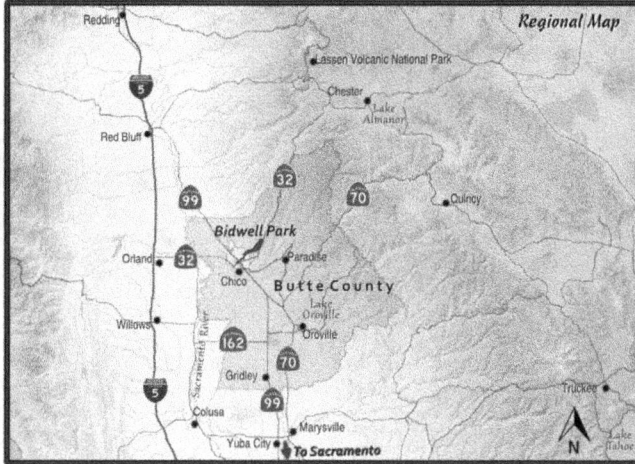

"We thank Annie and John Bidwell for having the foresight and generosity to give the park to our community, to Chico, for all to appreciate its beauty and splendor. And we feel the responsibility to carry on that vision, to protect this special place, to give it the tender loving care it deserves and to share it with the community ... we want to protect it for future generations to enjoy ... and grow in, and we want to share it with the wildlife whose home it is."

From the
Spirit of Bidwell Park

CARD Community Center

The main office has facilities for recreational programs and reservable multi-purpose rooms. The Creekside Rose Garden is reservable for special events. More information at chicorec.com or (530) 895-4711.

Gateway Science Museum

Gateway Science Museum is operated by CSU, Chico and inspires the exploration of science and natural history in this region and beyond. More information at csuchico.edu/gateway or (530) 898-4121.

Bidwell Mansion State Historic Park

Bidwell Mansion, the home of John and Annie Bidwell, was completed in 1868. Tours of the mansion and a visitor center are features. More information at www.parks.ca.gov or (530) 895-6144.

Children's Playground

Children's Playground was donated to the City of Chico in 1911 by Annie Bidwell. The scenic park area rests at the corner of CSU, Chico and Downtown Chico. There is a children's playground, large grassy area, and practice disc-golf baskets.

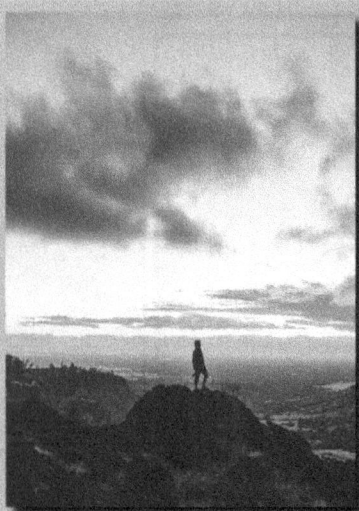

Bidwell Park is near the intersection of three geologic regions: The Sierra Nevada Mountains to the east and south, the Cascade Range to the north, and the Sacramento Valley to the west. There's just as much geologic diversity underfoot, thanks to ancient volcanic activity. The deepest layer of rock, the gray sandstone of the Chico Formation, is over 65 million years old and remains mostly hidden from view except for deep within Big Chico Creek Canyon. Layered on top is the dark basalt of the Lovejoy Formation which spread over the area as quick-moving lava about 20 million years ago. Large boulders of basalt rock line and lie within Big Chico Creek from Bear Hole to Brown's Hole. The top and most visible layer of rock is the 3 million-year-old Tuscan Formation, which forms the striking cliffs of Upper Bidwell Park. Rocks in this formation are the result of mud flows (lahars) from extinct volcanoes near current-day Lassen Peak.

Bidwell Park is "divided" by Manzanita Avenue. West of Manzanita Avenue is Lower Park. From Manzanita Avenue to Horseshoe Lake is considered Middle Park. The area upstream and uphill of Horseshoe Lake is Upper Park. Middle Park includes many community parks, recreation areas, and facilities steeped in history. Upper Park is a wonderful place to spend the day with its spectacular vistas, refreshing swimming holes, and miles of trails for hikers, mountain bikers, and equestrians of all skill levels.

Bidwell Park is home to a variety of important and sensitive natural resources in its diverse habitats, including native plant communities and wildlife. Several special-status species occur in its diverse habitats. The Park provides nesting and foraging habitat for many species of raptors. Big Chico Creek provides spawning and rearing habitat for spring-run Chinook salmon, and is home to five resident species of native, fish, many aquatic invertebrates, and amphibians. Big Chico Creek and its tributaries also serve as an important wildlife corridor, linking the habitats of the foothills with those of the Sacramento River.

Horseshoe Lake

Horseshoe Lake is a popular launching point for hikes further into Upper Park. Kids and adults can fish from the ADA-accessible fishing pier and trail. 14 and over - catch and release. Under 14 - catch and keep.

Chico Community Observatory

Chico Community Observatory opens at sunset on Friday, Saturday, and Sunday nights, weather permitting. Volunteer-led programs help open the night sky to the public.
More information at fb.com/ChicoCommunityObservatory or (530) 487-4071.

Bidwell Park Municipal Golf Course

Bidwell Park Municipal Golf Course is an 18-hole, par 72 course. The tree-lined course offers beautiful views, golfing for any skill level, and the Bidwell Bar & Grill. More information at www.golfbidwellpark.com or (530) 891-8417.

Wildwood Park

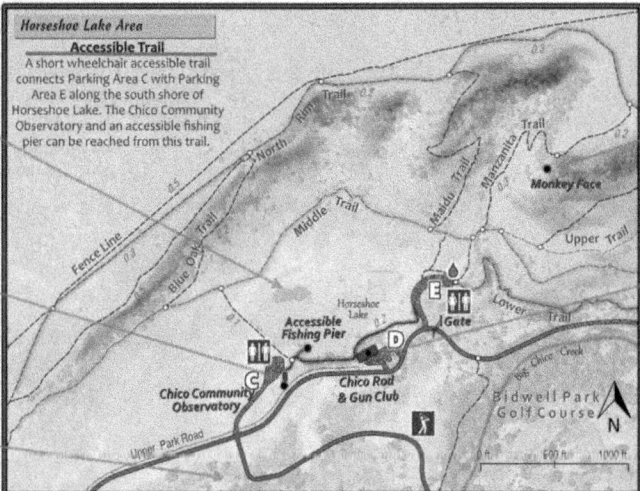

Wildwood Park is at the entry to Upper & Middle Bidwell Park. There are reservable picnic areas, sports fields, and playgrounds for multiple age groups. Operated by CARD More information at chicorec.com or (530) 895-4711.

Sherwood Forest Disc-Golf Course

Sherwood Forest is a 9-hole disc-golf course built for beginners. The course took on a Robin Hood theme to honor the 1938 film "The Adventures of Robin Hood" that was filmed nearby. Operated by CARD. More information at chicorec.com or (530) 895-4711.

Hooker Oak Park

Hooker Oak Park is 35-acres featuring several ballfields, a basketball court, two playgrounds, and reservable picnic areas. Former site of the historic "Hooker Oak Tree". Operated by CARD. More information at chicorec.com or (530) 895-4711.

Horseshoe Lake Area
Accessible Trail
A short wheelchair accessible trail connects Parking Area C with Parking Area E along the south shore of Horseshoe Lake. The Chico Community Observatory and an accessible fishing pier can be reached from this trail.

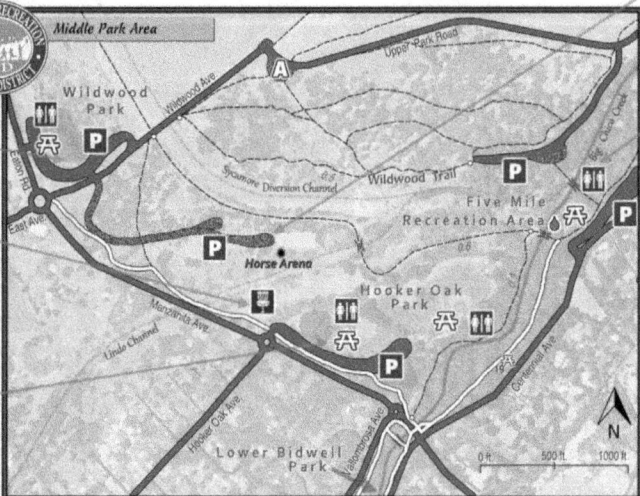

Middle Park Area

Explore Upper Bidwell Park

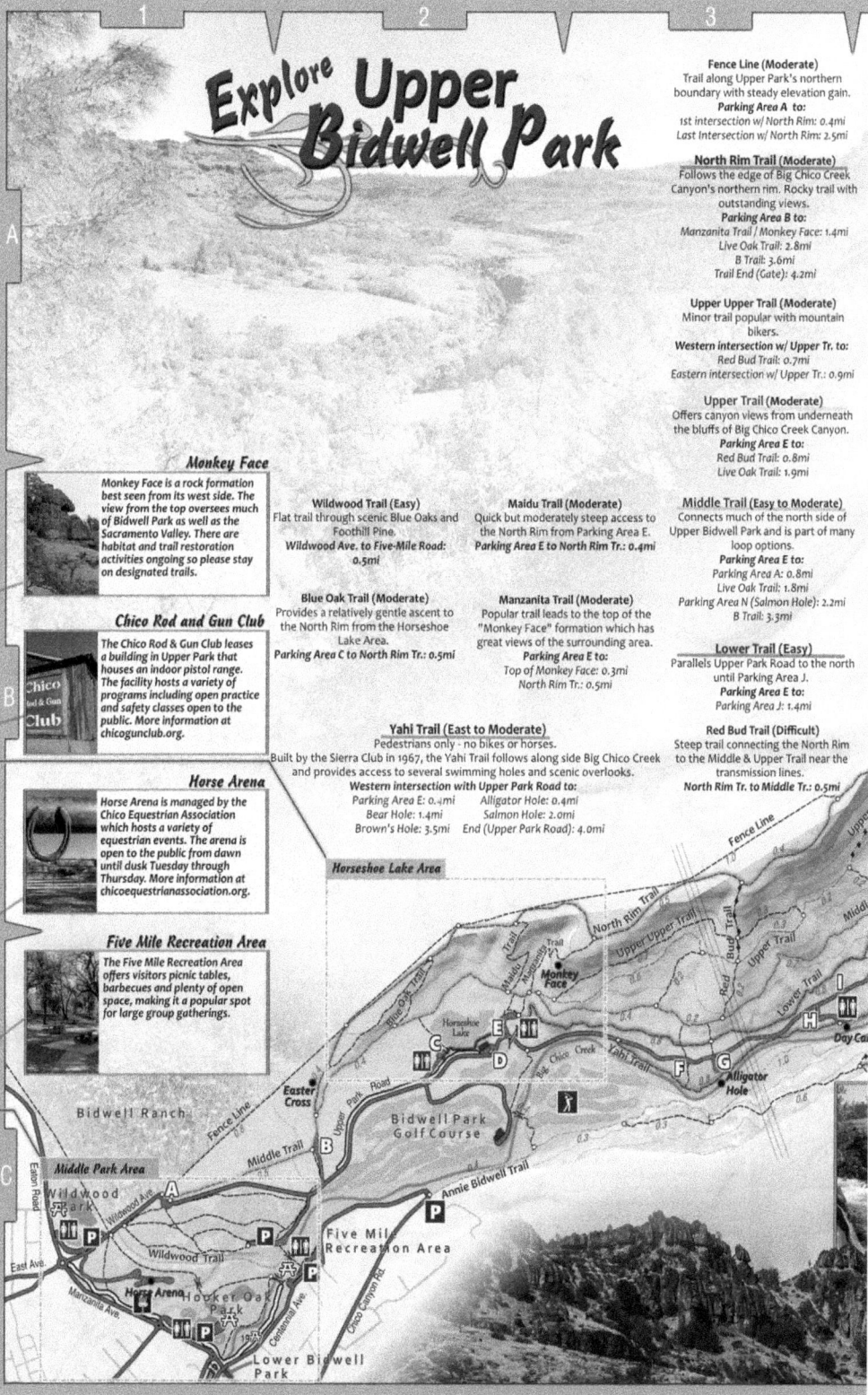

Fence Line (Moderate)
Trail along Upper Park's northern boundary with steady elevation gain.
Parking Area A to:
1st intersection w/ North Rim: 0.4mi
Last Intersection w/ North Rim: 2.5mi

North Rim Trail (Moderate)
Follows the edge of Big Chico Creek Canyon's northern rim. Rocky trail with outstanding views.
Parking Area B to:
Manzanita Trail / Monkey Face: 1.4mi
Live Oak Trail: 2.8mi
B Trail: 3.6mi
Trail End (Gate): 4.2mi

Upper Upper Trail (Moderate)
Minor trail popular with mountain bikers.
Western intersection w/ Upper Tr. to:
Red Bud Trail: 0.7mi
Eastern intersection w/ Upper Tr.: 0.9mi

Upper Trail (Moderate)
Offers canyon views from underneath the bluffs of Big Chico Creek Canyon.
Parking Area E to:
Red Bud Trail: 0.8mi
Live Oak Trail: 1.9mi

Monkey Face

Monkey Face is a rock formation best seen from its west side. The view from the top oversees much of Bidwell Park as well as the Sacramento Valley. There are habitat and trail restoration activities ongoing so please stay on designated trails.

Chico Rod and Gun Club

The Chico Rod & Gun Club leases a building in Upper Park that houses an indoor pistol range. The facility hosts a variety of programs including open practice and safety classes open to the public. More information at chicogunclub.org.

Horse Arena

Horse Arena is managed by the Chico Equestrian Association which hosts a variety of equestrian events. The arena is open to the public from dawn until dusk Tuesday through Thursday. More information at chicoequestrianassociation.org.

Five Mile Recreation Area

The Five Mile Recreation Area offers visitors picnic tables, barbecues and plenty of open space, making it a popular spot for large group gatherings.

Wildwood Trail (Easy)
Flat trail through scenic Blue Oaks and Foothill Pine.
Wildwood Ave. to Five-Mile Road:
0.5mi

Blue Oak Trail (Moderate)
Provides a relatively gentle ascent to the North Rim from the Horseshoe Lake Area.
Parking Area C to North Rim Tr.: 0.5mi

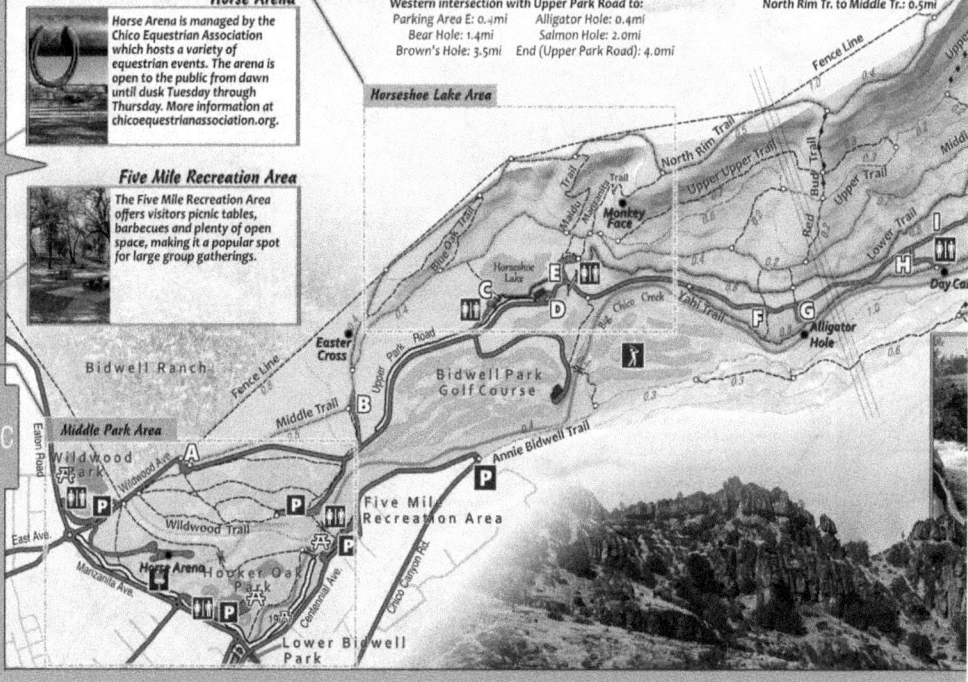

Maidu Trail (Moderate)
Quick but moderately steep access to the North Rim from Parking Area E.
Parking Area E to North Rim Tr.: 0.4mi

Manzanita Trail (Moderate)
Popular trail leads to the top of the "Monkey Face" formation which has great views of the surrounding area.
Parking Area E to:
Top of Monkey Face: 0.3mi
North Rim Tr.: 0.5mi

Middle Trail (Easy to Moderate)
Connects much of the north side of Upper Bidwell Park and is part of many loop options.
Parking Area E to:
Parking Area A: 0.8mi
Live Oak Trail: 1.8mi
Parking Area N (Salmon Hole): 2.2mi
B Trail: 3.3mi

Lower Trail (Easy)
Parallels Upper Park Road to the north until Parking Area J.
Parking Area E to:
Parking Area J: 1.4mi

Red Bud Trail (Difficult)
Steep trail connecting the North Rim to the Middle & Upper Trail near the transmission lines.
North Rim Tr. to Middle Tr.: 0.5mi

Yahi Trail (East to Moderate)
Pedestrians only - no bikes or horses.
Built by the Sierra Club in 1967, the Yahi Trail follows along side Big Chico Creek and provides access to several swimming holes and scenic overlooks.
Western intersection with Upper Park Road to:
Parking Area E: 0.4mi   Alligator Hole: 0.4mi
Bear Hole: 1.4mi   Salmon Hole: 2.0mi
Brown's Hole: 3.5mi   End (Upper Park Road): 4.0mi

Map labels: Horseshoe Lake Area, Monkey Face, North Rim Trail, Upper Upper Trail, Red Bud Trail, Upper Trail, Fence Line, Lower Trail, Middle Trail, Manzanita Trail, Blue Oak Trail, Horseshoe Lake, Big Chico Creek, Yahi Trail, Alligator Hole, Day Camp, Bidwell Ranch, Easter Cross, Fence Line, Bidwell Park Golf Course, Annie Bidwell Trail, Middle Park Area, Wildwood Park, Middle Trail, East Ave., Eaton Road, Wildwood Ave., Wildwood Trail, Horse Arena, Hooker Oak Park, Manzanita Ave., Centennial Ave., Chico Canyon Rd., Five Mile Recreation Area, Lower Bidwell Park

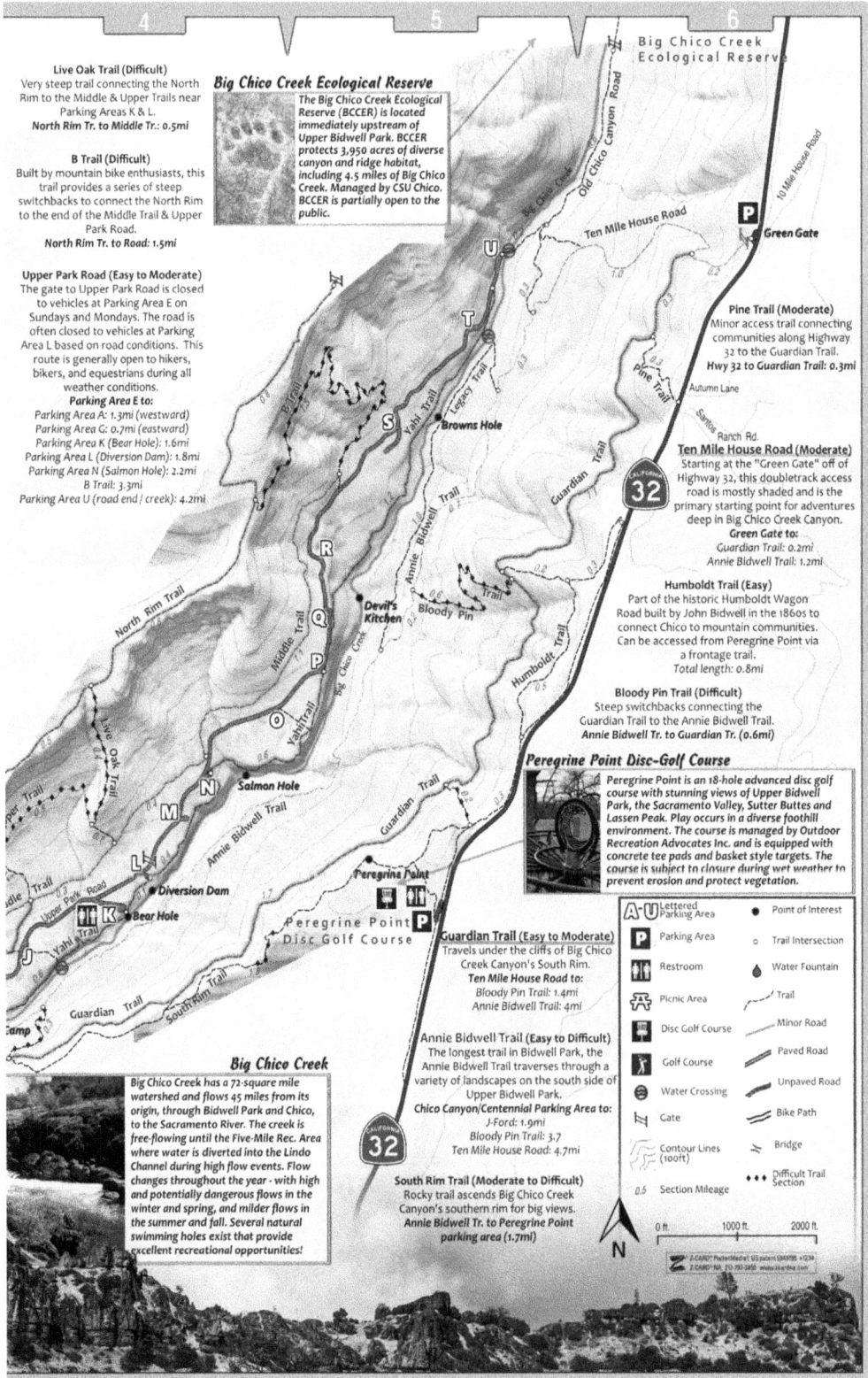

4 **5** **6**

Big Chico Creek
Ecological Reserve

Live Oak Trail (Difficult)
Very steep trail connecting the North
Rim to the Middle & Upper Trails near
Parking Areas K & L.
North Rim Tr. to Middle Tr.: 0.5mi

Big Chico Creek Ecological Reserve

The Big Chico Creek Ecological
Reserve (BCCER) is located
immediately upstream of
Upper Bidwell Park. BCCER
protects 3,950 acres of diverse
canyon and ridge habitat,
including 4.5 miles of Big Chico
Creek. Managed by CSU Chico.
BCCER is partially open to the
public.

B Trail (Difficult)
Built by mountain bike enthusiasts, this
trail provides a series of steep
switchbacks to connect the North Rim
to the end of the Middle Trail & Upper
Park Road.
North Rim Tr. to Road: 1.5mi

Upper Park Road (Easy to Moderate)
The gate to Upper Park Road is closed
to vehicles at Parking Area E on
Sundays and Mondays. The road is
often closed to vehicles at Parking
Area L based on road conditions. This
route is generally open to hikers,
bikers, and equestrians during all
weather conditions.
Parking Area E to:
Parking Area A: 1.3mi (westward)
Parking Area G: 0.7mi (eastward)
Parking Area K (Bear Hole): 1.6mi
Parking Area L (Diversion Dam): 1.8mi
Parking Area N (Salmon Hole): 2.2mi
B Trail: 3.3mi
Parking Area U (road end / creek): 4.2mi

Green Gate

Pine Trail (Moderate)
Minor access trail connecting
communities along Highway
32 to the Guardian Trail.
Hwy 32 to Guardian Trail: 0.3mi

Autumn Lane

Santos Ranch Rd.

Ten Mile House Road (Moderate)
Starting at the "Green Gate" off of
Highway 32, this doubletrack access
road is mostly shaded and is the
primary starting point for adventures
deep in Big Chico Creek Canyon.
Green Gate to:
Guardian Trail: 0.2mi
Annie Bidwell Trail: 1.2mi

Humboldt Trail (Easy)
Part of the historic Humboldt Wagon
Road built by John Bidwell in the 1860s to
connect Chico to mountain communities.
Can be accessed from Peregrine Point via
a frontage trail.
Total length: 0.8mi

Browns Hole

Devil's
Kitchen

Bloody Pin

Bloody Pin Trail (Difficult)
Steep switchbacks connecting the
Guardian Trail to the Annie Bidwell Trail.
Annie Bidwell Tr. to Guardian Tr. (0.6mi)

Peregrine Point Disc-Golf Course

Peregrine Point is an 18-hole advanced disc golf
course with stunning views of Upper Bidwell
Park, the Sacramento Valley, Sutter Buttes and
Lassen Peak. Play occurs in a diverse foothill
environment. The course is managed by Outdoor
Recreation Advocates Inc. and is equipped with
concrete tee pads and basket style targets. The
course is subject to closure during wet weather to
prevent erosion and protect vegetation.

Salmon Hole

Diversion Dam

Bear Hole

Peregrine Point

Peregrine Point
Disc Golf Course

Camp

Guardian Trail (Easy to Moderate)
Travels under the cliffs of Big Chico
Creek Canyon's South Rim.
Ten Mile House Road to:
Bloody Pin Trail: 1.4mi
Annie Bidwell Trail: 4mi

Annie Bidwell Trail (Easy to Difficult)
The longest trail in Bidwell Park, the
Annie Bidwell Trail traverses through a
variety of landscapes on the south side of
Upper Bidwell Park.
Chico Canyon/Centennial Parking Area to:
J-Ford: 1.9mi
Bloody Pin Trail: 3.7
Ten Mile House Road: 4.7mi

South Rim Trail (Moderate to Difficult)
Rocky trail ascends Big Chico Creek
Canyon's southern rim for big views.
*Annie Bidwell Tr. to Peregrine Point
parking area (1.7mi)*

Big Chico Creek

Big Chico Creek has a 72-square mile
watershed and flows 45 miles from its
origin, through Bidwell Park and Chico,
to the Sacramento River. The creek is
free-flowing until the Five-Mile Rec. Area
where water is diverted into the Lindo
Channel during high flow events. Flow
changes throughout the year - with high
and potentially dangerous flows in the
winter and spring, and milder flows in
the summer and fall. Several natural
swimming holes exist that provide
excellent recreational opportunities!

A-**U** Lettered Parking Area		● Point of Interest
P Parking Area		○ Trail Intersection
Restroom		Water Fountain
Picnic Area		Trail
Disc Golf Course		Minor Road
Golf Course		Paved Road
Water Crossing		Unpaved Road
Gate		Bike Path
Contour Lines (100ft)		Bridge
0.5 Section Mileage		♦♦♦ Difficult Trail Section

0 ft.   1000 ft.   2000 ft.

N

Bidwell Park Regulations & Advisements

Bidwell Park is full of fun and adventure! Help keep the park safe & beautiful. Please be familiar with the following important information.

Hours & Access:
Bidwell Park is open to the public from 5 AM to 11PM daily unless otherwise posted. Vehicle access varies based on season, location, and wet weather. For detailed vehicle access info and gate schedules visit www.chico.ca.us (Bidwell Park on drop-down menu) or call (530) 896-7800.

Be prepared!
Be sure to have everything you need to stay safe and comfortable including water, sun protection, and appropriate clothes & shoes. Watch for hazards! You may also encounter poison oak, ticks, rattlesnakes, large wildlife, swift water, or steep drop-offs. Avoid danger by staying on designated trails and explore with a friend.

Prohibited in Bidwell Park:
- Alcohol
- Glass
- All Smoking & Vaping
- Camping
- Campfires and BBQs outside of designated areas
- Excessive Noise
- Harming or removal of wildlife, vegetation, rocks, artifacts, etc.

Trail Safety & Etiquette:
Please stay on designated trails and roads for safety and to prevent resource damage. Tread lightly! During wet conditions, trails are closed to bicycles and horses to reduce erosion. Upper Park Road is open for bike and equestrian use during wet conditions.

Trail safety and courtesy are Bidwell Park standards. Please yield to other users as appropriate.

TRAIL COURTESY
YIELD TO

Bicycles must observe all California vehicular codes including one-way streets. Bicycle riding is not allowed in Caper Acres, on the Sycamore Pool deck, and on the Yahi Trail. Bike helmets must be worn at all time on unpaved roads and trails.

Motorized vehicles are only allowed on designated roads and in established parking areas.

Horses must cross at designated creek crossings and are not allowed in the One-Mile or Five-Mile-Recreation Areas

Dogs:
Lower Park. Dogs may be off leash from 5:30 AM until 8:30 AM and must remain under voice control. Dogs must be on leash at all other times.

Upper Park. Dogs may be off leash on the north side of Upper Park Road and must remain under voice control. Dogs must be on leash in all areas on and south of Upper Park Road.

Dogs are prohibited from harassing or harming wildlife or people.

Swimming Areas: Dogs are not allowed in Sycamore Pool, on the pool deck, or the surrounding grass area in Lower Park. Dogs are also not allowed in any other named swimming hole in Bidwell Park.

Fishing:
Fishing is subject to current CA Fish & Wildlife Code. Fishing is prohibited from any bridge over Big Chico Creek or the bank of any swimming pool or named swimming area in Bidwell Park.

Horseshoe Lake is catch & release for ages 14 and over. Under 14 is catch and keep. Persons over 14 must have a valid fishing license.

For detailed information on all City of Chico Bidwell Park regulations, contact the City of Chico Parks Department:

Phone: 530-896-7800
Road & Trail Conditions Hotline: 530-896-7899
Email: parkinfo@chicoca.gov
Website: www.chico.ca.us
Facebook: www.fb.com/cityofchicoparks

Welcome to Bidwell Park

Please help us keep the Park safe & beautiful for everyone by observing the following regulations

CITY OF CHICO
INC 1872

Alcohol	Alcohol is not permitted in any City Park or Playground.
Glass	No glass beverage containers allowed in any City Park or Playground.
Dogs	Dogs may be off leash from 5:30 AM until 8:30 AM in Lower Park -- All other times **dogs must be on a leash**. Along the north side of Upper Park Road, dogs may be "off leash" anytime. While *"off leash"*, dogs must remain under control via master's voice. Dogs are not allowed in One-Mile or Five-Mile swimming areas, or designated swimming holes in Upper Park.
Bicycles	Bicycles must observe all California vehicular codes including one way streets. Riders are expected to be courteous and yield to equestrian and pedestrian traffic. Helmets must be worn at all times in Upper Park except when on pavement. Bicycle riding is not allowed in Caper Acres or on the pool deck. Safe and courteous riding is the Park standard.
Horses	Horses must stay on designated trails. Horses are not allowed in One-Mile or Five-Mile Recreation Areas. Horses must cross the creek at designated crossings.
Trails	Please stay on designated trails and roads. Due to erosion issues, trails in Upper Bidwell Park are closed to bicycles and horses during wet conditions.
Fishing	Check California Fish and Game Regulations for fishing in Big Chico Creek. Horseshoe Lake: age 14 and over, catch and release; under age 14, catch and keep.
Camping	No overnight camping allowed. Bidwell Park is a "day use park" only.
Campfires	No campfires allowed. You must have a permit to use the council campfire ring. Portable BBQ's may only be used next to existing BBQ's in Lower Park and at the 5 Mile Recreation Area.
Noise	No loud or unusual noises are allowed, including: radios and head sets that can be heard over 50' away.
Vegetation	No person shall destroy, injure, cut, or take any natural condition of the landscape, including, but not limited to, flowers, shrubbery, plants, vines, trees, grass, wood, or rocks, in or from any city park or playground.
Swimming	While in the One-Mile swim area compliance with lifeguards is required for public safety. Lifeguards are on duty from Memorial Day through Labor Day.
Vehicles	Vehicle use is permitted on designated roads and in established parking areas. Please obey posted signs and speed limits.
Gate Closures	Upper Park gate at parking area E is closed on Sundays and Mondays and during seasonal wet periods. Gates can be closed for approved special events.
Park Closures	Lower park is closed from 12:00 am (midnight) until 5:00 am every day, unless directly and actively proceeding to a destination outside of the park. Upper Park is closed between the hours of 11:00 pm and 60 minutes before sunrise every day, unless posted otherwise.
Smoking	No smoking in Upper Park from May 1st - November 1st.

Bidwell Park Volunteer Organizations

Butte Environmental Council
313 Walnut Street, Suite 140
Chico, CA 95928
530-891-6424 • https://www.becnet.org/

> BEC is a long-standing environmental organization in Chico. It coordinates annual cleanups of Big Chico Creek and other waterways. These activists also plant trees and remove invasive species in Bidwell Park and in other areas.

Chico Velo
125 W 3rd St. Suite 210
Chico, CA 95928
530-343-8356 • https://www.chicovelo.org/

> Velo focuses on trail maintenance and works to educate volunteers about the appropriate use of trails in Bidwell Park. The group also advocates for bicyclists in Chico.

The Ivy League
530-896-7800 • email: parkinfo@chicoca.gov • https://chico.ca.us/volunteer-program

> These volunteers remove invasive ivy from trees in Bidwell Park. You can contact the Ivy League through PALS (Partners, Ambassadors, Leaders, and Stewards)

PALS (Partners, Ambassadors, Leaders, and Stewards)
530-896-7800 • email: parkinfo@chicoca.gov • https://chico.ca.us/volunteer-program

> This is a City of Chico sponsored umbrella group that coordinates a range of volunteer opportunities in Bidwell Park and other greenspaces in Chico. The possibilities include trash removal, educational and supportive interactions with park visitors, removal of invasive plants, and more.

The Stream Team
http://www.thestreamteam.org/

> This group, which is affiliated with PALS recruits and trains citizen scientists who test Big Chico Creek's water quality in Bidwell Park, as well as at spots upstream and downstream from the park.

More volunteer groups and activities can be found at the Friends of Bidwell Park's "How You Can Help Bidwell Park" webpage: http://friendsofbidwellpark.org/how-you-can-help-bidwell-park/

Mechoopda & Maidu Sources[1]

Mechoopda Indian Tribe of Chico Rancheria
(https://www.mechoopda-nsn.gov/)

Important Treatises on Maidu Language and Culture

Dixon, R.B.

1905   The Northern Maidu. *American Museum of Natural History, Bulletins* 17(3):119-346. New York.

R. B. Dixon's *The Northern Maidu* is a comprehensive and standard work on the social, political, and economic lifeways of the Valley Maidu, and may be considered alongside Kroeber (1925) as the region's most important reference works.

Heizer, R. F. and, T. R. Hester

1970   Names and Locations of Some Ethnographic Patwin and Maidu Indian Villages. *Contributions of the University of California Archaeological Research Facility, Papers on California Ethnography* 9(5):79-118.

Heizer's and Hester's "Names and Locations of Some Ethnographic Patwin and Maidu Villages" combed the journals of Arguéllo and Ordaz, and other early contact sources as well as the rich ethnographic field notes compiled by C. Hart Merriam, A. L. Kroeber to come up with a comprehensive compilation of Maidu village and place names on the Sacramento River corridor and along major streams in the Chico area.

Kroeber, A. L.

1925   *Handbook of Indians of California.* Bureau of American Ethnology, Bulletin 78. Washington, D.C.

1932   The Patwin and Their Neighbors. In *Publications in American Archaeology and Ethnology,* Vol. 29:4. University of California Press.

A. L. Kroeber's 1925 chapter on the Valley Maidu in his seminal opus, *Handbook of the Indians of California,* represents one of the most important primary reference works on Valley Maidu place names and land use. His 1932 chapter on the Maidu in *The Patwin and Their Neighbors* provides one of the most detailed and context-rich statements on the Kuksu Cult, the core spiritual and dance cycle tradition around which many Maidu social practices were organized.

Merriam, C. H.

1967   *Ethnographic Notes on California Indian Tribes III: Ethnological Notes on Central California Indian Tribes,* compiled and edited by R. F. Heizer, University of California Archaeological Survey, No 68, Parts 1–3. University of California Archaeological Research Facility, UC Berkeley.

---

1   Special thanks to Gregory White, Ph.D., for providing this list of Maidu sources.

1974   *Boundary Descriptions of California Indian Stocks and Tribes.* University of California Archaeological Research Facility, UC Berkeley.

1977   *Ethnogeographic and Ethnosynonymic Data from Northern California Tribes.* Assembled and edited by R. F. Heizer. Archaeological Research Facility, Department of Anthropology, University of California, Berkeley.

Merriam's *Boundary Descriptions of California Indian Stocks and Tribes* provides an inventory of Maidu sub-tribal groups and their traditional territories and boundaries based on Merriam's interviews with Valley Maidu elders in the early part of the twentieth century. His *Ethnogeographic and Ethnosynonymic Data from Northern California Tribes* consists of an edited collection of Merriam's extensive field notes and manuscripts on Northern California tribes including the Valley Maidu compiled during field studies between 1910 and 1935.

Powers, S.

1976   *Tribes of California. In Contributions to North American Ethnology,* Volume III, 1877, J. W. Powell, ed. Reprinted in Reprinted 1976, University of California Press, edited and assembled by R. F. Heizer. Berkeley, California.

Powers's works on California tribes (including the Maidu) have been published several times over the years, and the most readily accessible version is the 1976 compilation of articles published under the title *The Northern California Indians: A Reprinting of 19 Articles on California Indians Originally Published 1872-1877,* which contains a section on a visit Powers made to Chico in 1871–1872 when he consulted with knowledgeable Valley Maidu individuals.

Riddell, F.A.

1978   Maidu and Konkow. In *Handbook of North American Indians Vol. 8.* Smithsonian Institution, Washington D.C. R.F. Heizer, volume editor. pp. 370-386.

F. A. Riddell's *Maidu and Konkow* (Riddell 1978) provides a thorough summary of ethnographic information on valley and hill Maidu groups. The Volume 8 Handbook is a must-have for any well-stocked bookshelf.

Wilson, N. and A. Towne

1979   *Selected Bibliography of Maidu Ethnography and Archaeology.* California Department of Parks and Recreation. Sacramento.

Wilson's and Towne's *Selected Bibliography of Maidu Ethnography and Archaeology* is a unique, annotated inventory of published and unpublished source materials on the ethnography, ethnohistory, and archaeology of the Maidu people.

Local Vignettes on Maidu Life

Bidwell, A. K.

1896   The Mechoopda. *Overland Monthly, 27,* 2nd Series (February 1896):204–210.

Hill, D.

1978   *The Indians of Chico Rancheria.* California Department of Parks and Recreation. Sacramento, California.

Spenser, D. L.

1902   Notes on the Maidu Indians of Butte County. Originally published in *Journal of American Folklore, 21:242–245,* reprinted in R. F. Heizer (ed.) *Reprints of Various Papers on California Archaeology, Ethnology, and Indian History,* Archaeological Research Facility, U. C. Berkeley, 1973, pp. 51–53.

Nineteenth Century Illustrations of Maidu in Traditional Garb and Settings

Blackburn, T. C.

2006   *An Artist's Portfolio: The California Sketches of Henry B. Brown, 1851-1852.* Malki Press. Banning, California.

Kroeber, T. A. Elsasser, and R. F. Heizer

1977   *Drawn From Life: California Indians in Pen and Brush.* Ballena Press. Soccorro, New Mexico.

Evidence and Analysis of Genocide and Racial Injustice Suffered by Sacramento Valley Natives

Anderson, G. C.

2014   *Ethnic Cleansing and the Indian: The Crime That Should Haunt America.* University of Oklahoma Press. Norman.

Cook, S. F.

1943   The American Invasion, 1848–1870. *University of California Publications in Ibero-Americana 23. University of California, Berkeley.*

1955   The Epidemic of 1830-1833 in California and Oregon. *University of California Publications in American Archaeology and Ethnology* 43(3). University of California Press. Berkeley.

Heizer, R. F.

1974   *The Destruction of the California Indians: A Collection of Documents from the Period 1847 to 1865 in which are Described Some of the Things That Happened to Some of the Indians of California.* University of Nebraska Press. Lincoln and London..

Heizer, R. F. and A. J. Almquist

1971   *The Other Californians: Prejudice and Discrimination Under Spain, Mexico, and the United States to 1920.* University of California Press. Berkeley.

Hurtado, A. L.

1999   *Intimate Frontiers: Sex, Gender, and Culture in Old California.* University of New Mexico Press. Albuquerque.

1988   *Indian Survival on the California Frontier.* Yale University Press. New Haven.

Madley, B.

2014   "Unholy Traffic in Human Blood and Souls": Systems of California Indian Servitude under U.S. Rule. *Pacific Historical Review 83(4):626–667.*

2016   *An American Genocide: The United States and the California Indian Catastrophe, 1840–1873.* Yale University Press. New Haven.

Magliari, M. F.

2012   Free State Slavery: Bound Indian Labor and Slave Trafficking in California's Sacramento Valley, 1850–1864. *Pacific Historical Review 81(2):155-192.*

Rawls, J. J.

1976   Gold Diggers: Indian Miners in the California Gold Rush. *California Historical Society Quarterly 55(1):28–45.*

1984   *Indians of California: The Changing Image.* University of Oklahoma Press. Norman, Oklahoma.

Smith, S. L.

2013   *Freedom's Frontier: California and the Struggle over Unfree Labor, Emancipation, and Reconstruction.* University of North Carolina Press. Chapel Hill.

Street, R. S.

2004   *Beasts of the Field: A Narrative History of California Farmworkers, 1769–1913.* Stanford University Press. Stanford.

Unhoused Sources & Resources

- Chico Housing Action Team (https://www.chicohousingactionteam.net/)

- The Jesus Center, shelter (https://www.jesuscenter.org/)

- North State Shelter Team, an advocacy group (https://www.facebook.com/NSSTchico/)

- Safe Space, a winter shelter (https://www.safespacechico.org/)

- Torres Shelter, a shelter (https://truenorthbutte.org/emergency-shelter)

Articles

Hanson, Natalie. 2020, April 9. "Sheltering the Homeless Gets Funding: City Scrutiny Under Coronavirus Order." *Chico Enterprise-Record*.

Hanson, Natalie. 2021, May 7. "Business Owners Share Concerns for Impacts of Homelessness." *Chico Enterprise-Record*.

Olenyn, Jerry. 2021, January 13. "6.3 Tons of Trash Removed in Tuesday's Bidwell Park Eviction." KRCR. https://krcrtv.com/news/local/65-tons-of-trash-and-debris-removed-in-tuesdays-bidwell-park-eviction

Quevedo, Kerry. "Homelessness in Chico." Engaged Chico. https://chico.ca.granicusideas.com/ideas/homelessness-in-chico

Weber, Michael. 2023, September 28. "Year After Comanche Creek Cleared, Chico Continues to Evict Homeless Camps." *Chico Enterprise-Record*.

Weber, Michael. 2022, May 18. "Butte County Point – In-Time counts 1006 People Experiencing Homelessness." *Chico Enterprise-Record*.

Webster, Paul. 2021, December 10. "Findings and Desired Outcomes of Community Input Regarding Homelessness and Its Impacts in Chico." Policy Commons. https://policycommons.net/artifacts/2459464/findings-and-desired-outcomes-of-community-input-regarding-homelessness-and-its-impacts-in-chico/3481261/

Sources

Interviewees

Bidwell Park and Playground Commission Minutes

Websites

Bibliography

SOURCES

Interviewees

Aull, Jon (coordinator, Ecological Reserves Outdoor Education) interviewed December 21, 2019.

Barrett, Tom (park advocate) interviewed July 2017; May 20, 2023.

Beardsley, Dennis (former Bidwell Park director) email July 9 & 19, 2019.

Bruin, Michael (volunteer, Stream Team) interviewed June 8, 2019.

Burr, Carol, Ph.D. (artist and park advocate) interviewed June 27, 2019.

Dempsey, Phyllis (park advocate) interviewed July 23, 2018; July 30, 2019.

Dempsey, Wesley, Ph.D. (biologist) interviewed November 2 & 29, 2017; February 8, 2018; June 5, 2018; October 24, 2018; June 5 & 30, 2019; July 20, 2019.

Dresden, Robert (environmental educator) email June 15, 2021.

Dressler, Anton (volunteer, Stream Team) interviewed June 8, 2019.

Elliott, Woody (park advocate) interviewed July 2017; August 2017.

Fitzgerald, Jocelyn (teacher, Happy Acres Outdoor School) interviewed February 18, 2019.

Grist, Scott (former Bidwell Park and Playground Commissioner) email December 9, 2019.

Hammil, Timmarie (aquatic biologist and Stream Team volunteer) interviewed June 8, 2019.

Happy Acres Forest Outdoor children, interviewed February 18, 2019.

Johnson, Chris (2023 PALS chair) interviewed June 2, 2023.

Kehoe, Brian (director, Happy Acres Outdoor School) interviewed February 18, 2019.

Lederer, Roger, Ph.D. (ornithologist) email November 30, 2020; interviewed June 7, 2018; June 27, 2019.

Leek, Nancy (librarian) email July 31, 2020.

Linda (volunteer, Ivy League) email September 5, 2021.

Logan, Aaron (volunteer, Social Stewards) interviewed September 26, 2018.

Lopez, Noel (ranger, Bidwell Mansion State Park) interviewed April 4, 2018.

Mason, Susan (park advocate) interviewed July 31, 2017; November 29, 2017.

McReynolds-Baird, Elaina (former Bidwell Park and Playground Commissioner) March 20, 2019; November 24, 2019; September 29, 2020; July 9, 2021.

Meders-Knight, Ali (educator and activist) interviewed June 20, 2018.

Merz, John (park advocate) interviewed June 5, 2018; February 19 & 20, 2019.

Mitchell, Jahniah (co-Director, Earthbound Skills) email July 7, 2019; interviewed March 28, 2019.

Monica and P.J. (park cleanup volunteers) interviewed September 26, 2018.

Nopel, Betty (park advocate) interviewed February 19, 2019.

Nopel, Dave (Chico historian) interviewed August 2017; December 3, 2017; June 7, 2018; July 23, 2018; November 6, 2018; February 19, 2019; July 23, 2019; May 30, 2023.

Polivka, Ann (park enthusiast) and grandsons, interviewed October 8, 2019.

Romain, Shane (coordinator, Park Services) interviewed July 2017; August 2017; March 27, 2019; April 14, 2023.

Smith-Peters, Lise (former Bidwell Park and Playground Commissioner) interviewed July 2017; November 6, 2018; April 2019; April 2020; October 20, 2020; July 25 & 26, 2021; June 2, 2023.

Walker, Thad (volunteer, Chico Velo) interviewed June 18, 2019.

Withuhn, Charles (housing advocate) email May 26, 2021; interviewed October 7, 2019.

Wolf, Cindy (writer) email December 13, 2020; January 13 & 22, 2021.

Ziad, Jane (writer) email December 7, 2020.

Bidwell Park and Playground Commission Minutes

BPPC Minutes, 1918-1939

BPPC Minutes, 1918-1939

BPPC Minutes, 1939-1954

BPPC Minutes, 1954-1962

BPPC Minutes, 1962-1969

BPPC Minutes, April 1975-Feb 1983

BPPC Minutes, April 1996

BPPC Minutes, April 2019

BPPC Minutes, Feb1988-Dec1991

BPPC Minutes, January 1970-March 1975

BPPC Minutes, January 1992-January 1993

BPPC Minutes, January 1993-January 1994

BPPC Minutes, January 1994-March 1995

BPPC Minutes, January-February 2018

BPPC Minutes, March 1983-January 1988

BPPC Minutes, March 1995

BPPC Minutes, March 2019

Bidwell Park and Playground Commission minutes are available at the Chico Area Parks Department, 965 Fir Street. Minutes for city meetings from 2008 to the present are available online: http://chico-ca.granicus.com/ViewPublisher.php?view_id=2

Websites

Butte Environmental Council (BEC): https://www.becnet.org.

Chico Area Recreation and Park District (CARD): https://www.chicorec.com/

Chico Cat Coalition: http://chicocatcoalition.org

Chico Community Observatory: https://chico.ca.us/amenities/star-gazing

Chico Nature Center: https://www.chicorec.com/chico-creek-nature-center

Chico Outsiders: http://chico-outsiders.org/

Chico Peace and Justice Center: http://www.chicopeace.org/about/

Chico State Enterprises: https://www.csuchico.edu/cse/

Chico Velo: https://www.chicovelo.org/

Earthbound Skills: https://www.earthboundskills.com/

Engaged Chico: https://chico-ca.granicusideas.com/ideas/homelessness-in-chico.

Friends of Bidwell Park: https://friendsofbidwellpark.org

Hooked on Fishing: https://www.facebook.com/chicoHOFNOD/

Mechoopda Maidu Tribal: http://mechoopda-nsn.gov/home/

PALS (Partners, Ambassadors, Leaders & Stewards): https://chico.ca.us/volunteer-program

Paws of Oroville Society: https://pawsoforoville.org/

Planet Drum Foundation: https://planetdrum.org

Restore Hetch Hetchy: https://hetchhetchy.org/

Social Stewards Chico: https://www.facebook.com/socialstewardschico/

The Stream Team: http://www.thestreamteam.org/

THRIVE: www.thrive-enrichment.com

Bibliography

Abbott, Randy. 2005. "Disc Golf and the Future of Bidwell Park." *Friends of Bidwell Park.* http://friendsofbidwellpark.org/issues/disc-golf/disc-golf-and-the-future-of-bidwell-park/

Alley Cat Allies. 2010, October 18. "Alley Cat Allies Response to PETA: Feral Cats Deserve to Live." https://www.alleycat.org/alley-cat-allies-response-to-peta-feral-cats-deserve-to-live

Alworth, Roger. 1979. "To Some, Hooker Oak Still Controversial." *Chico Enterprise-Record.* May 23, 1979.

Andrews, Jean. 1977a. "Community's Reaction to Tree's Demise: It's like Losing an Old Friend." *Chico Enterprise-Record.* May 2, 1977.

Andrews, Jean. 1977b. "Protection of Fallen Hooker Oak Is Charged to Park Commission." *Chico Enterprise-Record.* May 4, 1977.

Arora, David. 1986. *Mushrooms Demystified: A Comprehensive Guide to the Fleshy* Fungi (2nd edition). Berkeley, CA: Ten Speed Press.

Aylworth, Roger. 1988. "Bidwell Park Ranger: Park and Playground Commission Looking at Revising Role." *Chico Enterprise-Record.* September 4, 1988.

Azbill, Henry. 1966, January 11. "Some Aspects of Mechoopda Indian Culture on John Bidwell's Rancho del Arroyo." Interviewed by Jim Neider, Association for Northern California Records and Research (ANCRR), California State University, Chico, Oral History Program/Northeastern California Program.

Azbill, Henry. 1985. *You Have to Know Who You Are.* Mechoopda Indian Tribe.

Baldwin, Chris. 2003. "Fork in the Trail." *Chico News and Review.* October 23, 2003.

Barcelona Institute for Mental Health. 2019, May 21. "Daily Contact with Nature During Childhood Could Lead to Better Mental Health in Adulthood." *Science Daily.* https://www.sciencedaily.com/releases/2019/05/190521193735.htm

Barrett, Tom. 2023. "Letter to the Editor: Road Less Travelable." *Chico News and Review.* May 4, 2023.

Bash, Rachel. 2015. "Park Watchers." *Chico News and Review.* February 26, 2015.

Behlmer, Rudy, ed. 1979. *The Adventures of Robin Hood.* Wisconsin Center for Film and Theatre Research. Madison: University of Wisconsin Press.

Bidwell, Annie. 1905. "Annie Bidwell Deed." *City of Chico.* https://www.ci.chico.ca.us/sites/main/files/file-attachments/aanniebidwelldeed.pdf?1578446238

Bidwell Park and Playground Commission. 2013. "Agenda Item: Consideration and Input on the Sale of Alcohol at the Bidwell Golf Club." *Policy Advisory Committee.* https://chico.ca.us/sites/main/files/file-attachments/pac_agendaandreports_13_0919.pdf?1574405294

Bidwell Park Golf Course. 1982. "Mission Statement." https://www.golfbidwellpark.com/contact/bidwell-park-golf-club

Big Chico Creek Watershed Alliance. "Watershed History." In *Big Chico Creek Watershed Project.* https://www.csuchico.edu/bccer/_assets/documents/bigchicocreekwatershed-ecr.pdf

Bizjak, Tony. 2019. "Chico's Post Camp Fire World: Car Crashes, Frayed Nerves, and Bare-Knuckled Politics." *Sacramento Bee.* June 5, 2019.

Boelens Joanne. 2010. "Park is Big Enough for a Cross." *Chico Enterprise-Record.* October 22, 2010.

Born, Carolyn. 1975. "Park Panel Mulls Beer Issue." *Chico Enterprise-Record.* August 26, 1975.

Boyd, Tom. 1942, January. "What Happened to Golf in 1918?" *GOLFDOM.* https://archive.lib.msu.edu/tic/golfd/article/1942jan13a.pdf

Boze, M. Jeanne. 1991. *The Nature of Bidwell Park.* Paradise, CA: The Village Printer.

Boze, M. Jeanne. 2005. *Bidwell Park: The Beginnings.* Paradise, CA: B. C. Publications.

Brace, Byron. 1988. "A Park Ranger and Danger." *Chico Enterprise-Record.* September 18, 1988.

Brown, Alex. 2020. "Vice Mayor Explains Unsheltered Homeless Policy." *Chico Enterprise-Record.* April 12, 2020.

Butler, Ed. 1976. "Bidwell Golfers Press for Course Corrections." *Chico Enterprise-Record.* October 1, 1976.

Butler, Ed. 1977. "Chico's Famed Hooker Oak Falls." *Chico Enterprise-Record.* May 2, 1977.

Butte Environmental Council. 2019. "2019 Final Cleanup Results." *Facebook.* https://www.facebook.com/ButteEnvironmentalCouncil/photos/a.384350168088/10156947696878089/?type=3&theater

Bylk, Andre. 2019. "Along for the Ride with Chico's Park Rangers." *Chico Enterprise-Record.* April 29, 2019.

Cagle, Susie. 2019. "Fire Is Medicine: Burning California's Forests to Save Them." *The Guardian.* November 21, 2019. https://www.theguardian.com/us-news/2019/nov/21/wildfire-prescribed-burns-california-native-americans

California State University, Chico. 2023. "Chico Facts." https://www.csuchico.edu/about/chico-facts.shtml#top

Cantu, Victor. 2010. "Fewer Cats Abandoned in Bidwell Park." *The Orion.* March 3, 2010.

Cassidy, Jason. 2005. "A Century in the Making: On the Eve of its 100th Birthday, We Spend a Day in Bidwell Park." *Chico News and Review.* July 7, 2005.

Cassidy, Jason. 2012. "Preserving Our Nature." *Chico News and Review.* June 21, 2012.

Chico Enterprise-Record. 1972. "Editorial: Main Problem of Park is Lack of Respect for Rules and Regulations." April 19, 1972.

Chico Enterprise-Record. 1973. "Nail Off-Road Drivers Damaging Park, Chicoan Urges." November 27, 1973.

Chico Enterprise-Record. 1974a. "City Wrestles with Park Problem." February 12, 1974.

Chico Enterprise-Record. 1974b. "Bidwell Park Report." March 27, 1974.

Chico Enterprise-Record. 1974c. "Local Officials Must Not Forget that Parks Belong to the People!" November 28, 1974.

Chico Enterprise-Record. 1977a. "Suggestions for Oak Flood Panel." May 21, 1977.

Chico Enterprise-Record. 1977b. "Tree Was No Stranger to Tragedy." May 21, 1977.

Chico Enterprise-Record. 1977c. "Why was the Fall So Deeply Felt?" May 21, 1977.

Chico Enterprise-Record. 1979. "Hooker Oak Surprise: It's 'Young,' and Two." June 7, 1979.

Chico Enterprise-Record. 1989. "What's the future of Bidwell Park?" July 12, 1989.

Chico Enterprise-Record. 1990. "Hooker Oak Removed to Be Cut Into Lumber." March 11, 1980.

Chico Enterprise-Record. 2005a. "From Annie with Love." July 8, 2005.

Chico Enterprise-Record. 2005a. "Bidwell Park Centennial Program." July 9, 2005.

Chico Enterprise-Record. 2017. "Citizens Share Ideas for Oak's Fate." May 21, 2017.

Chico News and Review. 1987. "The Issues." January 22, 1987.

Chico News and Review. 1990. "City Hopes to Expand Bidwell Park." November 8, 1990.

Chico News and Review. 2005. "Calendar of Bidwell Park Centennial Events: Bidwell Park Centennial Program." July 9, 2005.

Chico News and Review. 2018. "Upper Park Users Speak Up." August 2, 2018.

Chico Record. 1908. "Mrs. Bidwell Tells Why She Won't Open Park." August 28, 1908.

City of Chico, Parks Division Volunteer Program. n.d. "PALS Training Manuel." https://chico.ca.us/sites/main/files/file-attachments/volunteer_training_manual__v7_18.pdf?1597787982

Clayton, John. 2019. *Natural Rivals: John Muir, Gifford Pinchot, and the Creation of America's Public Lands.* Winnipeg, Canada: Pegasus Press.

Cleland, Dr. Robert C. 1915. "John Bidwell's Arrival in California." *Annual Publication of the Historical Society of Southern California* 10 (Parts 1 and 2): 110-115. https://archive.org/details/annualpublicatio10hist/page/n115/mode/2up

Cohen, Danielle. 2023. "Why Kids Need to Spend Time in Nature." *Child Mind.* https://childmind.org/article/why-kids-need-to-spend-time-in-nature/

Coles, Jeremy. 2016. "How Nature Is Good For Our Health and Happiness." *BBC Earth.* April 20, 2016. http://www.bbc.com/earth/story/20160420-how-nature-is-good-for-our-health-and-happiness

Cooper, Meredith. 2017. "Arming the Park." *Chico News and Review.* August 31, 2017.

Cory, Dick. n.d. "History of Teichart Ponds 1960-2010." *Teichart Ponds Restoration Foundation.* https://teichertponds.org/history/

DeCourten, Frank L., and James William Guyton. 1978. *Introduction to the Geology of Bidwell Park.* Chico, CA: CSU Chico University Foundation.

Dempsey, Dr. Wesley. 2000. "Suggestions from Wes Dempsey Regarding Prescribed Burns in Upper Park." *Friends of Bidwell Park.* http://friendsofbidwellpark.org/issues/vegetation/suggestions-from-wes-dempsey-regarding-prescribed-burns-in-upper-park-nov-21-2000/

Dempsey, Dr. Wesley. 2004. "Chico's Lost Arboretum." *Friends of Bidwell Park.* http://friendsofbidwellpark.org/park-info/environment-wildlife/chicos-lost-arboretum/

Dierdoff, Robert. 1974. "E-R Rapped for Editorial Views." *Chico Enterprise-Record.* December 6, 1974.

Disc Golf Association. n.d. "How To Play Disc Golf." https://discgolf.com/disc-golf-education-development/how-to-play-disc-golf/

Dougherty, Melissa. 2019. "Mark of Austerity: Tree-Felling Incident Underscores Chronic Underfunding of the Park." *Chico News and Review.* March 28, 2019.

Dow, Thomas Kirkland. 1884. *A Tour of America.* Melbourne, AU: The Australasian Office.

Downs, Brandon. 2023. "Chico's Measure H Collection to Begin in April: City Drafts Proposed Project." *Action News Now.* March 29, 2023. https://www.actionnewsnow.com/news/local/chico-s-measure-h-collection-to-begin-in-april-city-drafts-proposed-project/article_17d66db0-b6c6-11ed-9355-3fc262edbb10.html

Drennan, Ed. 1970. "The Filming of Robin Hood." *Butte County Historical Society Diggin's* 4(1).

Dr. Seuss. 1971. *The Lorax.* New York, NY: Random House.

Edmunds, Molly. 2023. "What Are Fish Ladders?" https://www.mapquest.com/travel/outdoor-activities/fishing/fish-conservation/fish-populations/fish-ladder.htm

Efseaff, Daniel. 1983. "Consideration of a Resolution That Would Allow Alcohol Sales at Bidwell Park Municipal Golf Course." Chico City Council Agenda Report. December 17, 2013.

Efseaff, Daniel. 2013. "Introductory Reading of an Ordinance and Adoption of a Resolution Amending Titles 12 and 12R (Parks and Playgrounds) of the Chico Municipal Code (Recommendations to City Council Regarding Policies on Traffic and Other Issues in Chico's Parks)." http://chicoca.granicus.com/MetaViewer.php?view_id=&clip_id=388&meta_id=32737

Ehrlich, Paul, David S. Dobkin, and Darryl Wheye, 1988. *The Birder's Handbook.* New York, NY: Simon and Schuster.

Ek, Richard. 1995. "The Bidwell Bungle." *Chico News and Review.* October 26, 1995.

Epley, Robin. 2010. "Worship Flocks to Bidwell's Easter Cross" *Chico Enterprise-Record.* April 5, 2010.

Epley, Robin. 2019a. "City Comments Explains Removal of 27 Valley Oak in Bidwell Park." *Chico Enterprise-Record.* March 25, 2019.

Epley, Robin. 2019b. "City of Chico Votes to Open Private Road to Private Vehicles—Sort of." *Chico Enterprise-Record.* December 4, 2019.

Ermini, Douglas. 1982. "The Production of *The Adventures of Robin Hood.*" Master's thesis. California State University, Chico.

Farrell, Ed. 1991. "Golfers or Woodpeckers? Petition Drive Launched to Save Oak in Way of Course Expansion." *Chico Enterprise-Record.* April 7, 1991.

Friends of Bidwell Park. n.d.-a. "Bidwell Park & Playground Commission." https://friendsofbidwellpark.org/park-info/city-management/bidwell-park-playground-Commission/

Friends of Bidwell Park. n.d.-b. "Potential Invasive Plant Species in Bidwell Park." https://friendsofbidwellpark.org/potentially-invasive-plant-species-in-bidwell-park/

Friends of Bidwell Park. n.d-c. "Timeline: A List of Proposed and Actual Developments in Bidwell Park." https://friendsofbidwellpark.org/park-info/history/

Gage, Helen, and Margaret Patty. 1958. "Need for Appearance of Freeway Challenged." *Chico Enterprise-Record*. March 28, 1958.

Gascoyne, Tom. 2002. "Lead and Glue Contaminate Bidwell Park." *Chico News and Review*. December 5, 2002.

Gascoyne, Tom. 2005 "Death in the Deer Pens." *Chico News and Review*. December 22, 2005.

Gascoyne, Tom. 2006. "The Man Who Milled the Hooker Oak Has Died." *Chico News and Review*. December 22, 2006.

Gascoyne, Tom. 2012. "Disc-Comforting." *Chico News and Review*. June 28, 2012.

Gebb, Ashley. 2023, January 18. "Big Chico Creek Ecological Reserve Partners with CalTrout, Mechoopda for Native Fish Passage Restoration Project in Bidwell Park." *Chico State Today*. https://today.csuchico.edu/bccer-partners-native-fish-passage/

Gerstein, Ory, and Dry, Olson S. 1985. "Alcoholism in America: Taking Action to Avoid Abuse." Washington, DC: National Academy Press. https://www.ncbi.nlm.nih.gov/books/NBK217463/

Gilliam, Carla. 1977. "What Do You Do With a Big Dead Tree That Everyone Loves?" *Chico Enterprise-Record*. May 11, 1977.

Gillis, Michael J. 1995, Spring. "John Muir and the Bidwells: The Forgotten Friendship." *California Territorial Quarterly*, no. 21, 4-5, 18-23, 26, 31.

Gillis, Michael, and Michael Magliari. 2004. *John Bidwell and California: The Life and Writings of a Pioneer 1841-1900*. Spokane, WA: Arthur H. Clark.

Gray, Elaine. 1992. "Council to Settle Golf Course Controversy: After 10 Years of Talks, Parks Panel Can't Resolve Alignment Dispute, Splits 3-3 on Plan." *Chico Enterprise-Record*. February 11, 1992.

Golf Course Trades. 2015. "Empire Golf to Manage Chico Course." January 1, 2015. https://www.golfcoursetrades.com/empire-golf-to-manage-chico-course/

Guardino, Josephine. 2005, Fall. "Bidwell Park in Peril." *Sierra Club, Yahi Group*. https://www.sierraclub.org/sites/www.sierraclub.org/files/sce-authors/u808/Fall2005.pdf

Hanson, Natalie. 2020. "Sheltering the Homeless Gets Funding: City Scrutiny Under Coronavirus Order." *Chico Enterprise-Record*. April 9, 2020.

Hanson, Natalie. 2021a. "Eviction Coming – Comanche Creek Campers Given 72 Hour Notices." *Chico Enterprise- Record*. April 9, 2021.

Hanson, Natalie. 2021b. "Protest Follows Police, City Staff from Bidwell Park." *Chico Enterprise-Record*. January 12, 2021.

Hanson, Natalie. 2022. "Bidwell Park Struggles with Increased Use, Dry Conditions: Californians Flock to Public Parks to Escape Lockdowns, Connect with Nature." *The Orion*. November 1, 2022.

Hardee, Howard. 2014. "Across the Booze Spectrum." *Chico News and Review*. January 7, 2014.

Hardee, Howard. 2015a. "Discology." *Chico News and Review*. May 28, 2015.

Hardee, Howard. 2015b. "Park Access Demanded." *Chico News and Review*. June 4, 2015.

Hardee, Howard. 2016. "Road Block: A Gate Prevents People from Driving Deep into Bidwell Park Should It Be Removed?" *Chico News and Review*. September 22, 2016.

Hardesty Associates. 1987. *Bidwell Park Draft Master Management Plan*. City of Chico, California.

Hartsell, Lynne. 1992. "Annie Bidwell, Elegant Pioneer." In *Ripples Along Chico Creek*, 161-172. Chico, CA: Heidelberg Graphics.

Historic Highway 99 Association of California. n.d. "What is US Highway 99? https://historic99.org/what-is-us-highway-99/

History.com editors. 2009. "Prohibition." https://www.history.com/topics/roaring-twenties/prohibition

Indar, Josh. 2005. "The Park that Never Was and Probably Shouldn't Have Been." *Chico News and Review*. May 26, 2005.

Jacobs, Margaret D. 1997, December 19. "Resistance to Rescue: The Indians of Bahapki and Mrs. Annie E. K. Bidwell." University of Nebraska, Lincoln, Faculty Publications, Department of History. 16. https://digitalcommons.unl.edu/cgi/viewcontent.cgi?article=1015&context=historyfacpub

Joye, Kathi. n.d. "The Magnificent Manzanita." *University of California, Agriculture and Natural Resources*. https://ucanr.edu/sites/Tuolumne_County_Master_Gardeners/files/157726.pdf

KRCR. 2019. September 22. "Bottles, Syringes and Mattresses Found During Annual Creek Cleanup." https://krcrtv.com/news/butte-county/bottles-syringes-and-mattresses-found-during-annual-creek-cleanup

Keilor, Garrison. 2019. "The Writer's Almanac." www.garrison,keillor.com/radio/twa-the-writers-almanac-for-june-29-2019

Kunman, Charles, Jr. 1958, July 23. *The Chico Freeway Location Controversy: A Case Study Prepared As Background for the Subcommittee on Public Works of the Assembly Interim Committee on Conservation, Planning and Public Works*. Sacramento, CA.

Larson, Phillip. 1974. "Park Protection Ideas Suggested." *Chico Enterprise-Record*. February 15, 1974.

Laslo, Karen. 2019. "23 Valley Oaks Removed from Bidwell Park" *Chico Sol*. March 10, 2019.

Layton, Leslie. 2022. "Settlement Ends Lawsuit against City of Chico Vice Mayor Makes 11th-Hour Bid to Postpone Settlement." *Chico Sol*. January 15, 2022.

Lederer, Roger, and Carol E. Burr. 2019. *The Trees of Bidwell Park*. Chico, CA: Stansbury Publishing.

Lederer, Roger, and Carol E. Burr. 2010. *The Birds of Bidwell Park*. Chico, CA: Stansbury Publishing.

Lederer, Roger. 1974. "Letter to the Editor: Park Destroyers Rapped by Reader." *Chico Enterprise-Record*. February 18, 1974.

Loss, Scott R., Tom Will, and Peter Mara. 2013. "The Impact of Free-Ranging Domestic Cats on Wildlife in the U.S." *Nature Communications* 4, Article 1396.

Louv, Richard. 2005. *Last Child in the Woods*. Chapel Hill, NC: Algonquin Books.

Lukes, Lara. 2019a. "The Blue Oak." *The Real Dirt Blog*. February 22, 2019. https://ucanr.edu/blogs/blogcore/postdetail.cfm?postnum=29462

Lukes, Lara. 2019b. "The Gray Pine." *The Real Dirt Blog*. March 8, 2019. https://ucanr.edu/blogs/blogcore/postdetail.cfm?postnum=29577

Lukes, Lara. 2019c. "The Buckeye." *The Real Dirt Blog*. March 22, 2019. https://ucanr.edu/blogs/blogcore/postdetail.cfm?postnum=29729

Lukes, Lara. 2020. "Discovering Verbana Fields in Chico." *The Real Dirt Blog*. June 19, 2020. https://ucanr.edu/blogs/blogcore/postdetail.cfm?postnum=42770

Lydon, Philip A. 1977, January. "A Brief History of Bidwell Park." *Friends of Bidwell Park*. http://friendsofbidwellpark.org/park-info/history/a-brief-history-of-bidwell-park/

Lydon, Philip A. 1997. "Geology of Bidwell Park: An Outline Summary." *Friends of Bidwell Park*. http://friendsofbidwellpark.org/park-info/geology/geology-of-bidwell-park-an-outline-summary/

Madsen, Kathy. 1977. "Hooker Oak: the Biggest, Oldest Valley Oak in North America, Right?" *The Orion*. May 18, 1977.

Mash, Guillermo. 2021. "Good Fire: A Close-Up Look At A Prescribed Burn in Bidwell Park" (video). *Chico News and Review*. May 24, 2021. https://chico.newsreview.com/2021/05/24/good-fire/

Maslin, Paul. 1997. "Horseshoe Lake, Bidwell Park, Chico, CA." http://www.sgreen.us/pmaslin/rsrch/Horseshoe.Lake/Horseshoe.html

Masten, Dani. 2022. "Settlement Agreement for Chico's Homelessness Lawsuit Signed by Judge." *Action News Now.* June 14, 2022.

McGee, Dennis M. 1983. "The History of Bidwell Park." Master's thesis. California State University Chico.

McGoogh, Michael, and Davidson, Amelia. 2021. "Update: CALFIRE, Local Crews Contain 400 Acre Fire in Chico's Bidwell Park." *Sacramento Bee.* June 19, 2021.

Megregor, Jena. 2020. "Corona Virus Shutdowns Are Making Golf Courses an Oasis for Stir-Crazy Americans Eager to Get Out and Tee It Up." *Washington Post.* May 20, 2020.

Micu, Alexander. 2019, August 20. "Urban Trees Make People as Happy as Clams (At Least on Twitter)." *ZME Science.* https://www.zmescience.com/science/urban-parks-make-people-as-happy-as-christmas-at-least-on-twitter/

Miller, Susan. 2018. "Colossal California Wildfire Finally Contained; Grim search for Bodies Continues." *USA Today.* November 25, 2018.

Milliken, Ted. 1974a. "Park Destruction Photographs." *Chico Enterprise-Record.* February 12, 1974.

Milliken, Ted. 1974b. "Vehicle Damage: May Prompt Upper Park Closure. *Chico Enterprise-Record.* February 15, 1974.

Moon, Debra. 2003. *Chico: Life and Times of a City of Fortune.* Charleston, SC: Arcadia.

Moon, Debra. 2005. "History of the Hooker Oak." *Chico Enterprise-Record.* July 9, 2005.

Mowry, Scott. 1976. "Golfers Offer Suggestions During Tour of Course." *Chico Enterprise-Record.* December 14, 1976.

Murray, Milan. 1992. "Chips 'n' Putts." *Chico Enterprise-Record.* March 8, 1992.

Murray, Milan. 1999a. "Bidwell Expanded in 1957." *Chico Enterprise-Record.* March 23, 1999.

Murray, Milan. 1999b. "Writer Recalls 50 Years of Golf at Bidwell Course." *Chico Enterprise-Record.* March 16, 1999.

NOAA Fisheries. n.d. "Chinook Salmon." https://www.fisheries.noaa.gov/species/chinook-salmon

Olenyn, Jerry. 2021, January 13. "6.3 Tons of Trash Removed in Tuesday's Bidwell Park Eviction." *KRCR.* https://krcrtv.com/news/local/65-tons-of-trash-and-debris-removed-in-tuesdays-bidwell-park-eviction

Payne, Jamie. 1974. "Cyclist Wonders Where He Can Ride." *Chico Enterprise-Record.* February 19, 1974.

Pierce, Grayson. n.d. "City Attorney's Letter Answers Questions Regarding Annie Bidwell's Will." *Friends of Bidwell Park*. http://friendsofbidwellpark.org/park-info/history/chico-city-attorneys-letter-answers-questions-regarding-annie-bidwells-will

Planet Drum Foundation. n.d. "About Planet Drum Foundation." https://planetdrum.org.

PMC. 2010. "Geology and Soils." Section 4.8 in *Chico 2030 General Plan Update, Draft Environmental Impact Report, September 2010*. https://chico.ca.us/sites/main/files/file-attachments/chicodeir_combined_noappendices.pdf?1577755314

Pyle, Amy. 1991. "CSU Faculty Senate Urges Campuses to Ban ROTC." *Los Angeles Times*. March 5, 1991.

Restore Hetch Hetchy. n.d. "Out Plan." https://hetchhetchy.org/our-plan/

Sacramento River Watershed Program. 2024. "Butte Creek Watershed." https://sacriver.org/explore-watersheds/eastside-subregion/butte-creek-watershed/

Scharaga, Ashiah. 2017a. "Sworn Park Rangers Key to Safer Parks, City Staff Says." *Chico Enterprise-Record*. September 3, 2017.

Scharaga, Ashiah. 2017b. "What's in Store for Chico's Sworn, Armed Park Rangers?" *Chico Enterprise-Record*. September 13, 2017.

Scharaga, Ashiah. 2018a. "Point of Preservation." *Chico News and Review*. March 29, 2018.

Scharaga. Ashiah. 2018b. "Four–Legged Weed Eaters. *Chico News and Review*. April 8, 2018.

Schiffman, Irving. 1974. "E-R Is Assailed for Park Views." *Chico Enterprise-Record*. December 16, 1974.

Schoenhauer, Allen. 1992. *A Natural History of California*. Berkeley, CA: University of California Press.

Siegler, Kirk. 2018. "In the Aftermath of the Camp Fire, a Slow, Simmering Crisis in Nearby Chico." *National Public Radio*. January 14, 2018.

Smith, Ken. 2020. "Roughing it During the Pandemic. *Chico News and Review*. July 15, 2020.

Sommer, Lauren. 2020. "To Manage Wildfire, California Looks to What Tribes Have Known All Along." *National Public Radio*. August 24, 2020.

Speer, Robert. 2001. "A Man in Love." *Chico News and Review*. August 16, 2001.

Speer, Robert. 1995. "The Other Side of the Canyon. What's Really at Stake in the Fight Over Expanding Bidwell Park." *Chico News and Review*. March 24, 1995.

Strickland, Amy. 2020. "When Cats Are Free to Roam, Wildlife Suffers." *CNN*. March 17, 2020.

Talbitzer, Bill. 1958. "Meriam Switched Sides in Freeway Controversy." *Oroville Mercury.* March 29, 1958.

Taylor, Bill. 1958. "Freeway Discord Background Aired." *Oroville Mercury.* March 28, 1958.

Teasdale, Rachel. 2009, March. "The Lovejoy Basalt: A (Fairly-) Large Igneous Province in Northern California." *Large Igneous Provinces Commission.* http://www.largeigneousprovinces.org/09mar

The Economist. 2015. "Why Golf Is in Decline in America." April 3, 2015. https://www.economist.com/the-economist-explains/2015/04/02/why-golf-is-in-decline-in-america

The Orion. 1977. "High Winds, Poor Roots Fell Hooker Oak." May 4, 1977.

Thoms, George. 1989. "Belated Thanks to a Park Ranger." *Chico Enterprise-Record.* September 3, 1989.

Thompson, Colin. 2007. "Canyon Passages Repairing A Set of Fish Ladders in Upper Bidwell Park Could Increase Salmon Runs Substantially." *Chico News and Review.* April 12, 2007.

Toussaint, Danielle. 1987a. "Bidwell Park's Destiny." *Chico News and Review.* January 29, 1987.

Toussaint, Danielle. 1987b. "Bidwell Park's Money Troubles." *Chico News and Review.* January 29, 1987.

Toussaint, Danielle. 1987c. "Thinking Like a Tree and Waiting for Woodpeckers*." Chico News and Review.* January 22, 1987.

Toussaint, Danielle. 1987d. "Turf or Trails? Golfers Eye Horseshoe Lake." *Chico News and Review.* January 22, 1987.

Trimbel, Peter. 1962a. "Battle over Freeway Divides a Town." *San Francisco Examiner.* March 19, 1962.

Trimbel, Peter. 1962b. "Is Chico Setting A State Pattern?" *San Francisco Examiner.* March 20, 1962.

Tuchinski, Evan. 2019. "Oak Grove Chainsaw Massacre." *Chico News and Review.* March 14, 2019.

Urseny, Laura. 1993. "Panel Brands New Park Road As Obtrusive, City Like." *Chico Enterprise-Record.* August 1, 1993.

Urseny, Laura. 2002. "Hooker Oak All But Gone, But Far from Forgotten." *Chico Enterprise-Record.* May 1, 2002.

Urseny, Laura. 2005a. "Mechoopda See Park as Their Home." *Chico Enterprise-Record*. July 9, 2005.

Urseny, Laura. 2005b. "Slice of Layer Cake Helps Explain Park Geology." *Chico Enterprise-Record*. July 9, 2005.

Urseny, Laura. 2006. "Man Who Milled the Fallen Hooker Oak Has Died." *Chico Enterprise/Record*. March 31, 2006.

Urseny, Laura. 2006. "Panel Wants to Revisit Tie Vote about Cars in Bidwell Park." *Chico Enterprise-Record*. January 11, 2006.

Urseny, Laura. 2008. "Bidwell Park's Ranger's Cherished Views Now Include Looking Toward Retirement." *Chico Enterprise-Record*. December 26, 2008.

Urseny, Laura. 2010a. "Hooker Oak Wood Returned to City of Chico." *Marin Independent Journal*. July 28, 2010.

Urseny, Laura. 2010b. "Bidwell Park Tackles Star Thistle with Pointed Plan." *Chico Enterprise-Record* August 14, 2010.

Urseny, Laura. 2012. "Deer Back in Bidwell Park Pen." *Chico Enterprise-Record*. April 21, 2012.

Urseny, Laura. 2013a. "Hooker Oak Remains Removed from Bidwell Park in Chico." *Chico Enterprise- Record*. March 22, 2013.

Urseny, Laura. 2013b. "More Emphasis Put on Understanding Bidwell Park Rules." *Chico Enterprise-Record*. March 31, 2013.

Urseny, Laura. 2017. "Park Panel to Recommend Rangers Be Armed." *Chico Enterprise-Record*. June 27, 2017.

Urseny, Laura. 2018a. "Proposal to Change Chico Disco Golf Agreement Aired." *Chico Enterprise-Record*. January 30, 2018.

Urseny, Laura. 2018b. "City Asking About Car Access in Upper Park Road." *Chico Enterprise-Record*. February 19, 2018.

Urseny, Laura. 2018c. "Chico Disc Golfers Upholding Their End of Agreement, City Says." *Chico Enterprise-Record*. June 8, 2018.

Urseny, Laura. 2018d. "Panel Supports Only Emergency Access to Upper Bidwell Park." *Chico Enterprise-Record*. August 26, 2018.

Urseny, Laura. 2018e. "Commission Makes No Decision on Upper Bidwell Park Road Access." *Chico Enterprise-Record*. August 27, 2018.

Urseny, Laura. 2019a. "Chico Plans on Reopening Peregrine Point Disc Golf Course in May." *Chico Enterprise-Record*. April 30, 2019.

Urseny, Laura. 2019b. "Changes Prompted by Bidwell Park Tree Cutting Incident." *Chico Enterprise-Record.* May 1, 2019.

Urseny, Laura. 2019c. "Commission Fed Up With Bidwell Park Crime Problems." *Chico Enterprise-Record.* July 30, 2019.

Urseny. Laura. 2019d. "Goats Back to Munching in Bidwell Park." *Chico Enterprise-Record.* August 28, 2019.

Urseny, Laura. 2019e. "Park Panel Against Full Upper Bidwell Park Access. *Chico Enterprise-Record.* October 29, 2019.

von Kaemel, Camille. 2019a. "Section 8 Voucher Holders Can't Find Housing." *Chico Enterprise-Record.* August 2, 2019.

von Kaemel, Camille. 2019b. "We are Helping the Community Steal the Fire Back: Tribe Driven Stewardship of Butte County Forests Gains Traction." *Chico Enterprise-Record.* December 7, 2019.

Waddell, Dave. 2017a. "Scaled Back Plans to Arm Park Rangers." *Chico Sol.* May 31, 2017.

Waddell, Dave. 2017b. "City Council: Arm the Park Rangers." *Chico Sol.* August 6. 2017.

Warren et al. v. City of Chico; City of Chico Police Department. 2021, April 8. https://www.govinfo.gov/app/details/USCOURTS-caed-2_21-cv-00640

Watts, Haley. 2018. "Upper Bidwell Slowly Reopens after Stoney Fire." *Action News Now.* August 14, 2018.

Weber, Michael. 2022. "Upper Park Sediment Reduction Complete." *Chico News and Review.* November 22, 2022

Weir, Kim. 2012. "Fighting Fire with Fire." *Chico News and Review.* June 6, 2012.

White, Adia, and Devol, Ken. 2022. "City of Chico Prepares to Clear Comanche Creek Encampment; Some Say They Don't Know Where They'll Go." *North State Public Radio.* July 2, 2022.

World Population Review. 2023. "Chico, California Population 2023." https://worldpopulationreview.com/us-cities/chico-ca-population

Woodward, John E. 1958. "The Location of the Chico Freeway: A Study in Community Dynamics." Master's thesis. California State University, Chico.

Yamane, David, Paul Yamane, and Sebastian L. Ivory. 2020. Targeted Advertising: Documenting the Emergence of Gun Culture 2.0. *Guns* Magazine, 1955-2019. *Palgrave Communications* 6(61): 1-9. https://doi.org/10.1057/s41599-020-0437-0

Highway 99 over South Park Drive.

INDEX

bold italic - photograph
f - footnote